BUILDING INCLUSIVE SCHOOLS

BUILDING INCLUSIVE SCHOOLS

Tools and Strategies for Success

ANN T. HALVORSEN

California State University, Hayward

THOMAS NEARY

Sacramento County Office of Education

ALLYN AND BACON

Boston ■ London ■ Toronto ■ Sydney ■ Tokyo ■ Singapore

Senior Editor: *Virginia Lanigan*
Series Editorial Assistant: *Jennifer Connors*
Marketing Manager: *Stephen Smith*
Manufacturing Buyer: *Suzanne Lareau*

Copyright © 2001 by Allyn & Bacon
A Pearson Education Company
Needham Heights, MA 02494

Internet: www.abacon.com

Library of Congress Cataloging-in-Publication Data

Halvorsen, Ann Tiedemann.
    Building inclusive schools : tools and strategies for success / Ann T. Halvorsen, Thomas Neary.
      p. cm.
    Includes bibliographical references and index.
    ISBN 0-205-27552-4 (alk. paper)
    1. Inclusive education—United States. I. Neary, Thomas. II. Title.
LC1201.H24 2001
371.9'046—dc21
                                                                           00-026669

Printed in the United States of America

This book is dedicated to our families with gratitude and love—

Jeannie, Jim, Conor, Devin, and Susan

as well as to all the trail-blazing and pioneering students, parents, and educators in today's inclusive schools, with special appreciation for

Anna, Tim, and Bonnie

CONTENTS

The English novelist John Galsworthy said, "Beginnings are always messy." Inclusive education is still new, an unwieldy innovation to some, merely a blip on the education radar screen to others. For families of students with disabilities, for the students themselves, for their committed educators, and the diverse communities of learners in inclusive schools, it is a way of life. It can be messy. It can also mark the beginning of a real integration of the systems of general and special education for the first time since the field of special education emerged as a separate discipline and, eventually, a separate place. We are no longer the invisible folks in the parallel universe of special centers or down the hall in that mysterious room with the paper-covered window in the door. We are your students, friends, children, and colleagues.

As you will learn by reading this book, inclusive education is not a fad to be replaced by yet another "new idea" nor a mere swing of the pendulum which will swing back ultimately to special schools. Inclusive education embodies the spirit and the intent of the Individuals with Disabilities Education Act (IDEA), which is the culmination of more than three decades of research, practice, advocacy, and civil rights litigation to ensure that the diverse population of students served by special education enjoys the same access to a free, appropriate public education as their general education peers across the nation.

As the title indicates, *Building Inclusive Schools: Tools and Strategies for Success* is designed to assist you in the development and implementation of classrooms and schools that work for all kids. Chapter 1 defines the elusive "I" word, inclusive education, a term that "operationalizes" IDEA's requirements in the least restrictive environment: the general education classroom, with supplementary supports, aids, and services appropriate to the individual's needs. In the first chapter we provide and discuss fifteen quality indicators of inclusive education, with the specific rationale and key characteristics of each, gleaned from the literature and from a decade of work with urban, rural, and suburban schools and districts. Chapter 1 thus provides an overview of the following seven chapters.

Chapter 2 focuses on effective instructional strategies for diverse classrooms, acknowledging the reality that all teachers encounter daily: that is, every class is composed of individuals from varying backgrounds, with varying educational and life experiences that inform their present capabilities. Therefore, effective teachers employ a variety of methods informed by an ever-growing understanding of how the brain works, how we learn, how we "construct" knowledge. Chapter 2 provides an overview of strategies that work and translates these into lessons within elementary, middle, and high school classrooms. In this chapter you will also meet four important focus students—Amanda, Joey, Melissa, and Raymond—whose educational experiences will illustrate the concepts and applications in this book. In Chapter 2 we visit each of their schools and are introduced to their teachers and classmates.

Chapter 3, "Planning for Individual Student Needs in the Inclusive Classroom," takes the reader through detailed processes for each focus student, from initial parent interviews, observations and assessments that inform the individualized education program (IEP), to the ongoing teamwork of all the key players in the students' lives as they engage in critical functional assessment, curricular development, and adaptation activities. Chapter 4 further extends the process with its focus on systematic instruction. Here we give the reader both the rationale for and the methodology of direct instruction within the context of the general education core curriculum. The chapter provides a basic understanding of the components of systematic instruction, supported by focus student examples. There are, of course, many texts devoted to the topic of systematic instruction. Our purpose here is to demonstrate the transfer of this body of knowledge to the inclusive classroom and to counter critics who claim that systematic instruction and inclusion are incompatible.

Chapter 5, "Peer Relationships and Support," begins with a framework for a positive school and classroom climate, articulating how this informs and sets the stage for sustained peer relationships among students with and without disabilities. Specific strategies are presented in context for Amanda, Joey, Melissa, and Raymond, with the emphasis on facilitation of natural supports and on individualization of the structured as well as the informal approaches used.

Chapter 6, "Adult Collaboration," explores the important set of skills that educators and parents need to develop and strengthen, as well as the ways that these skills are employed in proactive team planning and collaborative instruction, two essentials for today's inclusive schools. Again, the reader will see the application of those practices with the focus students.

Evaluation is the topic of Chapter 7. You will learn about program and system accountability as well as evaluation of student-level outcomes. Examples of specific methods and tools for program review are provided, including cost analysis of inclusive education. Student-level outcomes are discussed in terms of statewide assessments with accommodations and alternative measures as well as ongoing assessment strategies that are both functional and performance-based. These examples are illustrated with the focus students.

Chapter 8, "Inclusion in the Context of School Prestructuring," closes the book with beginnings. And, as we said, they are messy. We acknowledge that inclusive schools do not exist in many districts, and inclusive classrooms may be few and far between. This chapter provides resources and tools to develop action plans from the grass roots to the districtwide level. The chapter familiarizes the reader with the literature on change processes and with suggested personnel development activities to support change. It is only through acknowledging the legitimacy of others' concerns and supporting those who are changing that we will succeed in making sustained, systemic change that results in inclusive education.

Each chapter outlines specific objectives for the reader and closes with questions and activities to facilitate further understanding. The appendices contain a district inclusion plan, resource information, sample tools, and blank forms for applying the individualized strategies of Chapters 3 and 4.

Building Inclusive Schools is about and for school people. We hope that it will be used and useful both at the K–12 and university levels. It is a book for prospective and practicing teachers, for administrators, for parents, and for school and district teams. As such, it was written with aid of the wonderful individuals, schools, and districts with whom it's been our pleasure to work over many years. Acknowledging everyone is tricky, because, like an award winner at the Oscars, we are bound to leave someone out. So let us simply say that we especially acknowledge and appreciate the students, their families, and the educational teams from inclusive schools in the California districts of Davis, San Francisco, Oakland, Berkeley, Napa, San Ramon, Whittier, San Juan, and in the counties of Colusa and Sonoma. We are grateful for your commitment, enthusiasm, and hard work, and this book is better because of you.

We would also like to thank the reviewers of this book: Dr. Inge J. Carmola, Hamilton, Fulton, Montgomery BOCES; Linda G. Duncan, South LaPorte County Special Education Cooperative; Linda McCrea, Grand Valley State University; Margaret J. Sheehan, Behavioral Intervention Program, Stratton School.

We must also express our deep appreciation to Lori Adams for her excellent work in the preparation of the manuscript, and also to Jim Halvorsen, for stepping in to assist as deadlines loomed large, and for doing that so well. We could not have done this without you two! Finally, we want to express our sincere appreciation to the editorial staff at Allyn and Bacon for their support and guidance through the development of *Building Inclusive Schools*.

BUILDING INCLUSIVE SCHOOLS

CHAPTER ONE

WHAT IS INCLUSION?

Upon completion of this chapter, you will be able to

1. State a rationale for a clear definition of *inclusive education*
2. Identify fifteen quality indicators of inclusive education
3. Describe several strategies for initiating and supporting best practices in inclusive education

There is a rapidly growing movement to include students with disabilities in regular classrooms and schools. This increasing interest in inclusive education has resulted in a corresponding increase in controversy and conflict as parents and school staff attempt to change service-delivery approaches to address the needs of all students. Debates among educators and advocacy groups regarding the efficacy of and legal basis for inclusion as well as about student readiness for inclusive placement and the cost of support for inclusion are clouded by a multitude of varying definitions of inclusive education. Some define it as simply attending the same school site as typical peers; others speak of students being "included for first period"; others contend it means that students have exactly the same schedule and activities as nondisabled students for 100 percent of the school day. Definitions of classroom support for included students range from "sink-or-swim" to one-to-one staff-intensive approaches. A commonly accepted definition of inclusion will facilitate dialogue about critical issues such as curriculum and support and continue research and evaluation efforts regarding best practices for as well as outcomes of inclusive education.

Inclusive education, according to its most basic definition, means that students with disabilities are supported in chronologically age-appropriate general education classes in their home schools and receive the specialized instruction delineated by their individualized education programs (IEPs) within the context of the core curriculum and general class activities. Inclusive education is unlike mainstreaming in that students are members of the general education class and do not belong to any other separate specialized environment based on characteristics of their disability. The *full* in the often-used *full-inclusion* term refers to the question of *membership* in the general education classroom community. Mainstreaming, in contrast, confers a sort of "dual citizenship" on students who move between general and special education settings and are traditionally excluded from general education academic classes if they are unable to achieve near or on grade level without significant support.

In this chapter we identify indicators of inclusive education based both on the growing literature of inclusion (cf. McGregor & Vogelsburg, 1998), and on our work with teachers, students, parents, support personnel, and administrators over the past decade. Their voices have defined the true nature of inclusive education for us.

Fifteen specific indicators of inclusive supported education are discussed in this chapter within five broad categories—differences from mainstreaming, service delivery, planning and curriculum development, best practices, and training and personnel development. Each of these topics also contributes to the framework for the subsequent chapters.

> They told me if I wanted my son fully included, he would have to show he could be in regular class independently. I know he's going to have trouble with all the work in that class, but I want him to be around people his own age who talk and play games and act like kids. Right now he's in his regular class, but he doesn't have anyone helping him. The teacher is trying, but I can see she's frustrated. Isn't he supposed to have some kind of special education help?

> I really believe in inclusion and I'm trying to make it work as an itinerant teacher, but I have to cover eight schools with ten students. I'm not getting to see them much or their classroom teachers, much less actually work with them, and I have to rely on my instructional assistants. I'm afraid that if we have any serious behavior problems, the response will be to move the student back to special class.

There are a lot of things done in the name of inclusive education, and these two quotations illustrate situations that occur far too often across the country. Because inclusion is so often misunderstood, it is mistrusted and confused with the practice of putting students with special needs into general education classrooms with no support, with mainstreaming students who are "ready" for part of the day, or creating situations in which special education teachers can only be consultants because of the number of students and schools they serve. These versions of inclusive education are destined to fail because the necessary supports and planning are not formalized or even addressed.

Our history of services for students with severe disabilities reflects separation and segregation from students without disabilities. As Turnbull and Turnbull (1998) noted, "no requirement of the right to education movement...was likely to generate such controversy as the requirement that students with disabilities be educated in the least restrictive environment (LRE)" (p. 193), LRE being one of the six major principles of the Individuals with Disabilities Education Act (IDEA) both in its original form as PL 94-142 and in its 1997 reauthorization. This principle provides the legal basis for inclusive education. Although the words *inclusive education* or *inclusion* do not appear in IDEA, we can think of this term as one that operationalizes general education class placement or is the least restrictive alternative among a continuum of locations where education may be provided to students with disabilities.

When PL 94-142 was first enacted in 1975, most students with moderate to severe disabilities, if they were educated at all, were taught in separate buildings on separate special education campuses. Few districts offered the least restrictive aspect of the continuum to any of these students. Many still argue that a separate class or center *is* the least restrictive environment for students with certain "categorical" labels. This position flies in the face of state and federal laws that provide for each educational decision to be made on an individual basis and for no child to be removed from the general education class unless that class can be shown to be ineffective despite the provision of appropriate supports and services.

When Congress reviewed IDEA in the 1990s and reauthorized the Act in 1997, data or "findings of fact" were collected and examined to inform the law. As Turnbull and Turnbull (1998) note, the 1997 findings of fact extend well beyond those of 1975 in underlining the LRE presumption that students should be educated in general education classes and schools (p. 196). The findings of fact included these provisions:

Special education no longer should be a place to which students are sent, but instead, should be a service for the students, one requiring coordination of educational and other sources. [20 U.S.C. § 1401(c)(5)(C)]

Special education related services and other (supplementary) aids and services should be provided to students in the general education classroom, whenever appropriate. [20 U.S.C. § 1401(c)(5)(D)]

In recent years, through the advocacy of parents and educators and the successes of students in general education and community settings, increasing numbers of students with IEPs are now members of general education classes. This change is not easy, and the primary challenge is to change attitudes. Many educators and parents inside and outside special education find it difficult to understand why including students is beneficial and how students' individual needs will be met. It is incumbent upon those of us who support this shift to inclusive education to demonstrate to families and staff that not only can students of diverse abilities learn together but that specific student needs will be met. In doing so we will ensure that the powerful instructional strategies developed over time in special education are utilized in inclusive general education classes. This merger of powerful special education practices with the best practices in general education defines inclusive education.

Table 1.1 presents guidelines for inclusive education that have been developed through the authors' work with schools and districts throughout the nation. An overview to these guidelines is provided here with reference to subsequent chapters in which the practices are delineated in more detail.

INCLUSION: IT'S NOT MAINSTREAMING

Staying in the Local School

Students with disabilities should be members of chronologically age-appropriate general education classrooms in their local schools of attendance, in magnet schools, or schools of choice when these options exist for students without disabilities. The single most identifiable characteristic of inclusive education is membership. Students who happen to have disabilities are seen first as kids who are a natural part of the school and the age-appropriate general education classroom they attend. This is quite a different viewpoint from that of the more typical practice of mainstreaming in which these students are members of a special classroom and periodically visit the general education classroom for instruction. The distinction is critical and presented in a compelling manner in Schnorr's 1990 study of first graders' perspectives on a part-time mainstream student. Students speaking about "belonging" referred to the mainstreamed student as not being in their class—"Sometimes he's in this class and the other time he goes down to his room, his class in room 10" (p. 235). Similarly, general education teachers commonly see mainstreamed students as belonging to another class and, too often, being the responsibility of another teacher. The transitions, in terms of coming in and out of the general education classrooms, are taxing for students with special needs. In a U.S. Court of Appeals case, *Sacramento City USD v. Holland* (1994), the district proposed a plan in which the student would change classrooms six times a day, in early primary grades!

"Home schools" are not always the neighborhood school down the street. When a district has magnet or alternative schools that offer a focus such as the arts or the sciences, those options must be available to students with disabilities. Magnet schools may provide instruction in more active, thematic approaches, and for many students with disabilities, these practices may offer the best approach.

When students are members of age-appropriate general education classrooms in their normal schools of attendance, we avoid placing too many students with IEPs at a

TABLE 1.1   Inclusive Education Guidelines

INCLUSIVE EDUCATION AND SUPPORTED EDUCATION

The following characteristics are indicators of effective inclusive schooling. These guidelines are useful in planning for inclusion and also as a means for maintaining the integrity of the term, *inclusive* or *supported education.*

Inclusion: It's Not Mainstreaming

1. Students are members of chronologically age-appropriate general education classrooms in their normal schools of attendance or in magnet schools or in schools of choice when these options exist for students without disabilities.

2. Students move with peers to subsequent grades in school as indicated by their IEPs.

3. No special class exists except as a place for enrichment activities for all students.

4. Disability type or severity of disability does not preclude involvement in inclusive education.

Service Delivery

5. The staff-to-students ratio for an itinerant special education teacher is equivalent to the special class ratio, and aide support is at least at the level it would be in a special class.

6. There is always a certificated employee (special education teacher, resource specialist, or other employee) assigned to supervise and assist any classified staff (e.g., paraprofessional) working with specific students in general education classrooms.

7. Special education students who are included are considered a part of the total class count. In other words, even if a student is not counted for general education average daily attendance (ADA), she or he is not an "extra" student in addition to the contractual class size.

8. Supported or inclusive education efforts are coordinated with school restructuring at the district and site level, and a clear commitment to an inclusive option is demonstrated by the board of education and the superintendent.

Planning and Curriculum Development

9. The special education and general education teachers collaborate to ensure:
   a. The student's natural participation as a regular member of the class
   b. The systematic instruction of the student's IEP objectives
   c. The adaptation of core curriculum and materials to facilitate student participation and learning
   d. The development and implementation of positive behavioral interventions to support students with challenging behaviors

10. Supplemental instructional services (e.g., communication, mobility, adapted P.E.) are provided to students in classrooms and community settings through a transdisciplinary team approach.

11. Regularly scheduled collaborative planning meetings are held with general education staff, special education staff, parents, and related-service staff as indicated in order to support initial and ongoing program development and monitoring.

12. Plans exist for transition of students to their next classes and schools of attendance in inclusive situations.

Best Practices

13. Effective instructional strategies (e.g., cooperative learning, activity-based instruction, teaching to multiple intelligences) are supported and encouraged in the general education classroom. Classrooms promote student responsibility for learning through strategies such as student-led conferences and student involvement in IEPs and planning meetings.

Training and Development

14. General ability awareness is provided to staff, students, and parents at the school site through formal or informal means on an individualized basis. This is most effective when ability awareness is incorporated within the general education curriculum.

15. Ongoing training and personnel development are provided for all involved.

particular school and instead mirror the natural proportion of students with disabilities in our communities.

Continuity in Curriculum and Relationships

Students should move with peers to subsequent grades in school. The best environments for learning are those in which students are motivated; learning is active, and information is presented in a manner that recognizes the diversity of each student. The core curriculum achievement outcomes expected at each grade level may not be possible for all students, particularly those whose learning difficulties result from cognitive, motor, sensory, or communication disabilities. Many of these students will not maintain pace with their peers without disabilities, particularly in academic areas. To use the achievement of district grade-level outcomes set for students without disabilities would often require that students continue working at particular grade-level material and concepts for many years. In an inclusive school, students with severe cognitive disabilities are not held back if they do not meet grade-level standards. Rather, they progress according to their IEP and its objectives. Their progress is measured through both their IEP and through statewide measures or alternatives as discussed in Chapter 7. Both research and practice in educational programs for students with severe disabilities have indicated that involvement in chronologically age-appropriate environments and activities with typical same-age peers is critical (Falvey et al., 1997; McGregor & Vogelsberg, 1998; Sailor et al., 1989; Sailor, Gee, & Karasoff, 1993; Simon, Karasoff, & Smith, 1992).

If inclusion is to be effective, the student's IEP must be addressed within the *context* of the curriculum through a matricing process that is discussed later in this book. In this way, the student's IEP is used to guide adaptations as well as direct instruction that will be supported in the general education class. Students benefit from the role models their peers provide. These role models teach them how to behave in situations but also allow for an increasing number of shared, real-life experiences with others of the same age. For example, when students who are reading *Romeo and Juliet* in literature class discuss the story at lunch or make references to it, the student with special needs will understand the context of the conversation and know that the play is about teenage romance and relationships. If a special-class student joined her peers only for lunch, she would have no such common experience or shared understanding. These experiences are critical steps in the development of those skills that lead to full participation in the community as a valued member, and, without them, students fall farther and farther behind their peers. Strategies to facilitate peer relationships are provided in Chapter 5.

Friendships and social connections typically have their basis in shared history (Staub, 1998). Students who have had the same experiences have something to converse about. Their involvement in the same activities allows for a common bond. As students move from grade to grade or from school to school, friends who move with them make the transition more comfortable. For students with disabilities, who may have a number of challenges already, having a supportive social network is extremely important to their success. This support network brings background and insight to the people in the next setting and helps them get to know this person so that there are fewer misunderstandings and more success. In other words, these relationships are natural supports to the included student (cf. Nisbet, 1992).

Using Integrated Learning Environments

No special classroom should exist except as a place for enrichment activities for all students. Membership's importance cannot be overestimated. Successful inclusive education is difficult if a student is already seen as a member of a special education class. In many school situations, students who receive special education services are seen as and referred to as "special education students," and when students qualify for special education services, they are "sent to special education" as if it were a place. The problem is not that students might need individualized instruction in a quieter or more structured setting, it is the belief that they need to go somewhere else to receive it. In addition, it is in the belief and practice that *only* those students who qualify for special education need this type of instruction. We need to remind ourselves that even though the federal government has limited the funding of students who can receive special education services to 12 percent of all students, this doesn't mean that only 12 percent of the students in a given school need or would benefit from more support. When special educators are an ongoing presence in our general education classrooms, more support can be provided for all students (Sailor, 1991).

A second problem with the special classroom is that if it is available, it will be used. If a student is having difficulty with the curriculum or is behaving inappropriately in class, the teacher will most likely send the student to the special class. In almost every case, this is not the best solution to the problem. Rather than addressing the reasons why the student might be failing in terms of how the lesson is presented, the material itself, or specific requirements of the lesson and modifying these areas, teachers often reach for the first strategy that comes to mind: send him to the special class until he is "ready." The strategies in special classrooms are not appreciably different from the good teaching strategies in general education. A case might be made that the strategies can be more focused in a smaller setting, but this is an issue of the way in which support is provided rather than where it occurs.

Involving All Students with Disabilities in Inclusive Classes

Disability type or severity of disability should not preclude involvement in inclusive classrooms. Many times, school districts that are working to include students with disabilities assume that it makes sense to start with students who are "most capable" or those who are "most like" the typical general education student. Educators seek to ease fears about inclusion by starting with those students who we think will make the smoothest transition and will not be "noticed as much." In our view, this is a mistake, because it delays the issue, and avoids the real basis for inclusive schools—a belief in the capacity for *all* students to learn and contribute.

The former approach caused many problems. In the 1980s, as special schools began to move students back to general education school sites, many of them started with the students with the most skills. This did not lessen the fears or concerns in most cases and, in fact, made moving each subsequent group of students (who happened to have fewer skills) more difficult. Each transition meant starting over. The most successful programs have taken a zero-rejection approach (Baumgart et al., 1982). If a school believes in inclusive education, it believes in including all students, not just those who are considered "ready." This is another critical difference between mainstreaming and inclusive education. Mainstreaming has typically required students to perform in the general education class with little or no additional support. Inclusive classes provide the student with the support necessary to participate and to learn.

The categorical approach fostered by special education has also created a number of problems. There are classes for students with autism, for those with physical disabilities, vision and hearing challenges, cognitive disabilities, social–emotional problems, which by their homogeneous nature serve to support the view of individual students as part of a group that requires a certain approach in learning. The strategies found to be of value in supporting learning for a particular student can be useful to many students (Falvey et al., 1997; Jorgensen, 1998). Rather than place students according to their label or the severity of their disability, inclusive schools serve all students regardless of type or severity of disability by ensuring them the expertise and support they need. For example, in two rural districts, all elementary students with disabilities are supported in their general education classes by special education teachers and part-time paraprofessionals. The support teacher's caseload is noncategorical, and the special education staff presence in these classes has led to decreased referrals in one school and to team teaching, which resulted in added resources for general education students in both schools (D. Owens, personal communication, 1997). While some states' funding formulas for special education have been disincentives to such innovation in the past, many states have been reforming their funding systems for placement neutrality as required by IDEA 1997, and non- or cross-categorical approaches are one facet of several of these (Parrish, 1994).

SERVICE DELIVERY

Ensuring the Proper Support Staff

The staff-to-student ratio for an itinerant special education teacher should be equivalent to the special class ratio, and aide support is at least at the level it would be in a special class. One of the common concerns regarding inclusive education is that there will be insufficient support for students with special needs in the general education classroom. General education teachers will be required to spend an inordinate amount of time with students who have special needs. This perception has led to negative reactions from teachers' bargaining units such as American Federation of Teachers, which called for a moratorium on inclusion until we "know how to do it right." (Shanker, 1993a, 1993b).

It is important to consider the typical level of support currently provided in special classrooms. In many areas, a special class has one credentialled special education teacher and one instructional assistant for an average of ten students with moderate to severe disabilities. School districts often increase the support to two instructional assistants per special class when the class involves students with severe disabilities. Of course, the IEP may require additional support for individual students. When students are mainstreamed, the special education teacher must carefully manage a small pool of support resources across mainstream classes while continuing to operate the special classroom. Within the special classroom, it is also important to acknowledge that all students do not work on the same level or even on the same objectives. Staff typically work either with individuals or with small groups in the classroom. This is important in terms of the belief that when students are sent to the special classroom, they receive more intensive services. Every student with special needs does not have one-to-one instruction, and that level of support may not be available or desirable when they are included.

A benefit of inclusive education is that staff do not need to maintain a special class while supporting students in their general education classrooms. The limited support available can be focused on actual in-class support. The staff must ensure that the limited support is used to the best advantage. One strategy is for the special educator to meet with all general education cooperating teachers or all teachers at each grade level to determine how the available support will be allocated. Specific times when staff assistance is required are identified, and the whole group works collaboratively to set the support schedule. This approach avoids the situation common in many schools in which the special education teacher is expected to allocate support, usually to no one's satisfaction. In an era when competition for resources is high, the use of instructional assistants must be carefully considered. Involving those general educators and administrators directly impacted in the allocation of these resources creates an environment more conducive to understanding the demands on both general and special education.

It is extremely important to acknowledge that inclusive education does not mean placing students in general education classrooms without support. It is also important to note that it does not mean that every student is attended by a "personal aide," rather that the same level of support provided these students in the special education classroom should be provided in inclusive settings.

Ensuring Qualified Supervision

There should always be a certificated employee (special education teacher, resource specialist or other employee) assigned to supervise and assist any classified staff (e.g., paraprofessional) working with specific students in general education classrooms. Many school districts taking a piecemeal approach to inclusion are either placing students in general education classrooms without support or hiring an instructional assistant to work with the student in the classroom under the supervision of the classroom teacher. Students who qualify for special education services, particularly those with severe disabilities, require staff trained to meet their instructional needs. Very definite skills are required of educators serving students with special needs, and it is a grave mistake to ignore this. Special educators are trained in working with families, selecting goals and objectives, understanding the legal requirements of IEPs as well as the implications of particular disabilities, and supporting students who are learning specific academic, communication, motor, social, and cognitive skills.

Successful inclusive programs always provide a qualified, credentialled special education teacher to supervise the paraprofessional staff in cooperation with the general education classroom teacher. This special education or inclusion support teacher is responsible for overseeing IEP implementation and paraprofessional staff training, ensuring that instructional programs are implemented correctly. Effective schools and school districts are reorganizing services and taking a noncategorical service approach. Teachers credentialled in the area of learning disabilities may also be responsible for serving students with severe disabilities. When special education teachers begin operating outside of the area for which they have been specifically trained (e.g., in a noncategorical approach), administrators must ensure that they receive the specific ongoing training they require to serve these students. What is important is that students deserve qualified teachers, and inclusive education should provide them. Some districts have supported cross-categorical training by making it possible for teachers to complete additional credential work, releasing teachers from their duties to provide hands-on training to another teacher or selecting inclusion mentor teachers with expertise in particular areas and releasing them for a designated number of days per year, so that they can coach and support their peers. A noncategorical approach can ensure that students are served in their home schools by avoiding the clustering of students with a particular label, and special education teachers may be able to provide support and instruction in *one* school. This approach is discussed throughout this book and, particularly, in Chapters 2, 3, and 8.

Special Education Students on the General Education Class Roster

Special education students who are fully included should be listed as a member of the class. In other words, even when students are not counted for general education average daily attendance (ADA), they should not be considered "extra" students. Historically in many states, students mainstreamed from a special class were not counted as members of the general education class because they were already counted as a part of the special class. Today many states with recent special education funding reform are required by IDEA to be placement neutral rather than encourage separate settings. For general education teachers, this is important because mainstreaming means making accommodations in terms of space, materials, planning, and attention. General education teachers, who may be already overwhelmed by the numbers of students in their classrooms, are not thrilled about receiving another student beyond their contractual class size. In contrast, inclusive education, by definition, makes students with special education needs full members of the general education classroom and counts them as part of the class, thus ensuring that students with special needs do not unduly impact the class.

When schools count students as members of general education classrooms and at the same time generate special education support through "special class placement," inclusion appears to have a negative fiscal impact on the district. Depending on average class size, including students with special needs in the district can require additional classroom teachers. It is important that districts also analyze their expenses and savings in *other* areas, such as the lower transportation costs that may result from inclusion. In addition, as students are included, special education classrooms for ten students become available to general education classes of thirty students, thus saving space and lowering maintenance costs by several thousand dollars annually (Halvorsen et al., 1996).

Coordinating with Restructuring and Committing to an Inclusive Option

Supported or inclusive education efforts should be coordinated with school restructuring at the district and site level, and a clear commitment to an inclusive option should be demonstrated by the board of education and the superintendent.

With increasing pressure to examine their practices in light of what many perceive to be very disappointing outcomes, schools are beginning to restructure the way students learn and educators teach (Jorgensen, 1997; Roach, 1994; Sailor, 1991). These restructuring efforts hold great promise for re-examining our vision for education, the expectations for students, and the way we organize our learning environments in light of current variables.

In 1991, a Californian legislative initiative offered planning incentives for schools that were restructuring education. However, very few of the proposals for these restructuring planning grants mentioned special education, and it is difficult to understand how a school could restructure without special education being addressed. Not only are 10 percent to 12 percent of the students in a district receiving special education services, but many of these students are involved in both general and special education programs, and the coordination of the staff and students is an ongoing challenge. To be successful, any restructuring at the school or district level must include all students. The resources provided in many situations are not economically used and may even be wasted. When schools coordinate resources based upon what students need, they can use them to better advantage. Chapter 8 outlines strategies to facilitate effective restructuring and to work through a change process.

Unless those in positions of influence and authority support inclusive education verbally and in their actions, there will continue to be ambivalence about implementing the necessary changes in our schools. At every level of the district, inclusive education impacts people and practices. The necessary changes are difficult and require support. Resistance and outright conflict will require strong administrative leadership (Roach, 1992; 1994). This support need not be dictatorial or authoritarian. In successful districts, superintendents have charged their administrators with forming representative cross-constituency inclusion task forces to develop proposed policies for administrative and board review, to formulate training plans, and to recommend procedures to support effective inclusion. These districts have provided released time to support initial and ongoing training needs as well.

PLANNING AND CURRICULUM DEVELOPMENT

Sharing the Responsibility

The special education and general education teachers should collaborate to ensure (a) students' natural participation as regular members of the class, (b) the systematic instruction of students' IEP objectives, and (c) the adaptation of core curriculum and materials to facilitate student participation and learning. Inclusive classrooms are the shared responsibility of both general and special educators. In the past, students with intensive special needs have been the responsibility of special education staff in separate programs. Even when students were mainstreamed, their involvement in the general education classroom was defined by the expectations of the special education teacher. Decisions about appropriate goals and objectives and the need to adapt the curriculum were made by the special educator.

In contrast, inclusive education connotes the membership of not only students with special needs but the special education staff, too. The role shift is particularly evident in terms of how special and general educators operate. When students are valued members of the school and real members of the age-appropriate classrooms, decisions and responsibilities for their achievement are made by both general and special educators. This collaboration (Rainforth & York-Barr, 1997) offers the best opportunity for success, not only in terms of students' participation but of their achievement.

There are three major collaboration considerations for general education teachers and special education support staff. The primary benefit of inclusive education lies in the fact that all students have access to the variety of activities, routines, celebrations, responsibilities, choices, opportunities, and information. Sharing this history is critical to more complete participation in the community at large, now and in the future. The first concern of cooperating general and special educators is to ensure that each student is naturally involved in all these opportunities and activities. Every activity available in the general education program offers opportunities for skill development in cognitive, motor, and social areas. As cooperating educators inventory these opportunities, the critical point is not simply whether a particular student can be included. We must ask three questions. What degree of support is necessary for the student to participate and achieve? What are our expectations? What assistance can be provided to ensure success? Chapters 2 and 3 address effective classroom strategies and individualized student planning processes.

The second consideration is ensuring that students receive the specialized instruction they need to learn within the general education activities and curriculum. Over the years, powerful instructional strategies have assisted students with significant learning disabilities. These strategies are not obsolete in inclusive settings, and although some may need to be modified for use in heterogeneous settings, they must be available. Instructional strategies focused on analyzing activities and routines, assessing and teaching to specific learning styles, and prompting and correcting are relevant in any educational setting. Chapter 4 describes their incorporation in detail. Through collaborative planning, parents and general and special educators can share relevant information on formal and informal assessments and determine which systematic instructional strategies to use, how they will be delivered within lessons and activities, who will use them, and how they will be evaluated (Neary et al., 1992).

Finally, collaborative planning is a vehicle for adapting curriculum. The variety of activities and the depth of curriculum in most classrooms require planners to take the time to prepare materials and strategies for students with intensive special needs so that they may obtain the greatest benefit. Many adaptations are easily accomplished and can be generated by the general education teacher as a normal part of responding to the diversity of abilities within the general population. Others will require thought and special preparation. A number of published curriculum development approaches share common elements of an ecological approach (Giangreco, Cloninger, & Iverson, 1993; Gee, Alwell, Graham & Goetz, 1994; Neary et al., 1992). Each stresses the necessity of developing a *student planning team* involving students, parents, the students' close friends, and general and special education teachers to gain insight into students' strengths and needs as well the current and future environments and activities. There are a number of methods to gain this insight, including the Family Interview (California Dept. of Education, 1992), MAPS (Forest & Lusthaus, 1989), and Personal Futures Planning (Mount & Zwernick, 1988). Priorities generated through this approach form the basis for examining the school and classroom routines and activities for potential opportunities and to develop a plan for support and participation. Chapter 3 provides extensive detail on these processes. A *collaborative planning team,* which involves the general and special educator and parent as a core team, is responsible for identifying educational priorities and the activities they will be addressed within. Many collaborative teams use a matricing process to organize ideas about how educational priorities will be met throughout the day. The daily schedule for the class or a schedule of course options (secondary) is placed along one axis, and the other educational needs are placed along the second axis. The team brainstorms ideas for meeting student needs through this process, establishing an initial *student participation plan.* A number of ways to adapt curriculum have been suggested (Ford, Davern, & Schnorr, 1992; Giangreco, Clonginger & Iverson, 1993; Neary et al., 1992; & Jorgensen, 1998), including providing physical assistance or assistive devices, adapting materials, incorporating multi-level curricula, working on alternate goals within the core curriculum, changing instructional groupings and teaching formats, and providing varying levels of support. In selecting adaptations, collaborative teams select curriculum outcomes and strategies that are as close as possible to typical student outcomes and that allow for student success.

It is critical for teams to continue to refine student participation and staff support strategies. Developing personal futures plans and educational priorities can get the student started in the general education program, however, the program will probably need continual refinement and adjustment. *Transdisciplinary functional or ecological assessment processes* (cf. Snell, 1993) offer the best opportunity to identify critical skill needs in classroom, school, and community activities and routines so that students' participation improves qualitatively. Functional assessments outline the natural steps or requirements of an activity or routine, identify the current level of student performance, and identify potential adaptations and targets for teaching. They also help identify the level and types of supports necessary for success.

Functional analysis or assessment strategies are also critical elements in the design of *positive behavioral supports,* which are discussed in greater detail in Chapter 4. Mere movement of students with behavioral challenges to more restrictive environments rarely results in positive behavior change, and these students are at the most at risk for segregation in our public and private schools. However, a significant body of research documents positive behavior change in inclusive settings using the group of effective strategies described as positive behavior intervention or support. These strategies are team generated and involve all key people in the student's life, both in the plan's design and in its implementation.

Using a Transdisciplinary Approach to Provide Supplemental Services

Supplemental instructional services (e.g., communication, mobility, adapted P.E.) should be provided to students in classrooms and community settings through a transdisciplinary team approach. Because of their communicative, physical, sensory or social–emotional needs, many students with severe disabilities involve a number of specialists in providing services. Each discipline has its own approach, and each needs time with the student to assess and provide direct services. Often, these multidisciplinary services occur in isolation. There is a wealth of literature on the benefit of providing integrated therapy to students with special needs (Rainforth & York-Barr, 1997).

This transdisciplinary approach is promising because, by definition, it means a coordination of services, effective and efficient use of staff, and demonstration of communicative, motor, cognitive, and social skills in relevant contexts. A collaborative approach allows service providers to conduct joint assessments and share information regarding their assessments, impressions, suggestions about goals, and objectives and instructional approaches. Further, it begins a process of skill sharing among service providers. They can determine assessment and support schedules to assure the most efficient and effective use of their time. For example, speech and language services can be delivered within classroom lessons, with the therapist supporting the student during Language Arts. Physical therapy services can be delivered during classroom transitions, when positioning the student at tasks, or in P.E. activities. When related service providers work in this fashion—modeling collaboration on a regular basis in the general education setting—general and special educators can take advantage of their specific information and expertise in order to develop their own skills in other disciplines.

Supporting Programs with Regularly Scheduled Planning Meetings

Regularly scheduled collaborative planning meetings should be held with general education staff, special education staff, parents, and related service staff as indicated in order to support initial and ongoing program development and monitoring. Meeting the needs of students with special needs in inclusive settings requires frequent and focused discussions regarding students' progress and participation. The activities of the school and general education classroom are dynamic, requiring planning and preparation of materials to ensure students will achieve the full benefit. Often, teachers in mainstreaming situations find it difficult to meet except at lunch or on the run between classes. Including students, particularly students with significant challenges, requires a more carefully thought-out approach, and formalizing these planning periods is critical. Regular, structured planning meetings that are effective and efficient allow special education staff enough preparation time to best access the curriculum and other opportunities at the site and in the classroom. They allow general educators the opportunity to voice their ideas and any concerns they have about a student's progress and participation and allow parents to participate in the learning situation and keep in touch with their child's progress.

At the elementary level, meetings involve the student's general education teacher, the special education support teacher, parents, and when necessary, related services staff or instructional assistants. Meetings are generally held at least monthly and may be more frequent until staff and parents are comfortable with the program. At the secondary level, the special education support teacher commonly meets with general education staff during preparation time. If cooperating general education teachers have common preparation time, the number of separate meetings is reduced. At least initially, the team of cooperating general educators, the special education support teacher, and parents should get together to discuss expectations, learning approaches, and concerns.

Scheduling planning meetings is often a problem. Many sites have these meetings before school. This keeps the team on track because they must finish before students arrive for the day. It is amazing how quickly decisions are made in this time crunch. Other sites plan after school, which may allow for more leisure but often means tired team members. Common teacher preparation time allows more flexibility in meeting during the school day. Some sites hire a substitute one day of the month to free cooperating teachers for a period to meet with the special education inclusion teacher. Other sites use "banked" time. By agreement among staff and families, instructional days are lengthened, and shortened days are established periodically for preparation time. Schools that provide quality inclusive education make this planning time a priority. The collaborative processes of these school communities are addressed further in Chapter 6.

Planning Transitions

Plans should exist for transition of students to next classes and schools in inclusive situations. As students prepare to move to their next grade or school, it is critical that planning team meetings begin to address this change and ensure that those individuals who will be working with the student (for example the next general education teacher) are part of the planning. Many school sites have established a formal process for transition planning by scheduling a series of meetings in the spring that allow sufficient time for a smooth transition.

Transition meetings involve the core planning meeting team—the current general education teacher, the special education support teacher, the parent(s) and the next general education teacher(s). In some situations, they involve the student's friends. They focus on informing the next teacher(s) or other important staff about the student's needs and progress. They allow parents to meet the next teacher and share their hopes and dreams for their child. They allow team members to share the stories of success for the year and identify those approaches that they believe will continue the success. They also help establish a support system for the new teachers involved. Like the collaborative planning team meetings, transition planning meetings should be organized, efficient, and action oriented. Transition planning meetings identify specific activities for team members to take, for example, arranging a visit to a new school or class, working out mobility or accessibility issues, meeting other students, and examining curriculum for adaptation strategies. Taking the time for open communication among all involved is a wise investment of our resources and critical to supporting students in inclusive situations.

BEST PRACTICES

Encouraging Effective Strategies

Effective instructional strategies (e.g., cooperative learning, activity-based instruction, teaching to multiple intelligences) should be supported and encouraged in the general education classroom. Classrooms promote student responsibility for learning through strategies such as student-led conferences and student involvement in IEPs and planning meetings. Many special educators who have been working to integrate or mainstream students with severe disabilities from the basis of a special class often have a limited number of opportunities. As Biklen et al. pointed out in *Achieving the Complete School: Strategies for Effective Mainstreaming* (1985), one of the most common strategies for mainstreaming is the *teacher deal*. This is described as follows: "…administrators and the educational system do not provide support for mainstreaming or, at least in any significant way, participate in it. They may recognize it, even speak positively about it, but its life depends upon the individual teachers who make it happen" (p. 28). The special education teachers in this situation approach general education teachers they feel might be amenable to integration or mainstreaming and attempt to get their students into their classes. General education teachers can say yes or no. Integration then depends upon this agreement, not on what the student may need. In inclusive education, the team attempts to match student needs, classroom environment, and teaching style.

There is a large body of literature on the advantages of active, hands-on learning for students with severe disabilities (cf. Horner, Dunlap, & Koegel, 1988). Learning has been shown to be more rapid, and skills are more likely to be generalized and initiated when learning situations are relevant, functional, and active (Hunter, 1982; Wang, 1992). Teachers, if they have the choice, will usually opt for the general education classrooms that provide this type of learning environment as those most likely to support success.

General educators have also recognized the benefits of cooperative structures in supporting learning (e.g., Johnson & Johnson, 1992; Slavin, 1991). Classroom populations have become increasing diverse in terms of the abilities of students who do not qualify for special education. Teachers have also recognized that the skills students need to participate and succeed in the world today go far beyond reading, writing, and arithmetic. In an increasingly complex, diverse, and immediate world, cooperative and collaborative skills are critical. Cooperative learning offers enormous benefits for students with disabilities. It allows for students to work at their own level on a variety of skills with the support of the other group members. Research continues to support the effectiveness of cooperative learning in terms of both acquisition and mastery for students with and without disabilities (Slavin, 1991) and for both groups of students in inclusive situations (Hunt, Staub, Alwell, & Goetz, 1995).

Finally, many schools have found success in supporting student skill development through increasing their involvement in decision-making about their education and evaluating their own progress (Ford, Davern, & Schnorr, 1992; Jorgensen, 1997). Students with special needs also participate in "person-centered planning" to determine their own goals and objectives (Forest & Lusthaus, 1989). They work with staff to select examples of their own work and plan student-led conferences to share progress with families.

TRAINING AND DEVELOPMENT

Providing Ability Awareness

General ability awareness should be provided to staff, students, and parents at the school site through formal or informal means on an individualized basis. This process is most effective when ability awareness is incorporated within general education curriculum. In many situations, students in general education have not had any experience with students with disabilities, particularly those with significant cognitive, motor, social, or sensory challenges. Their teachers and parents may also have very limited personal experience of disability, because they were not educated in inclusive settings themselves. When a school is changing its approach to include students who were previously excluded, students, teachers, administrators, and others may need a better understanding of the impact of disability and strategies to support those who have disabilities.

There are many ways to provide ability awareness at a school site. Most ability-awareness workshops include experiential stations, small-group opportunities for participants to see what it might be like to experience a sensory loss, cognitive difficulty, motor problem, or communication barrier for a brief time. These experiences do not represent the true experience, because they are transitory and out of context; however, they do stimulate conversation about the impact of a disability. The simulation experience is one very important part of these activities. Another important component is the opportunity for participants to discuss how disabilities might affect many of our life activities, including school work. Equally important, ability-awareness simulations and discussions educate participants as to the ways that people adapt, accommodate, and compensate.

While large-scale experiential and informational approaches have been implemented in many areas, e.g., "Disability Awareness Fairs" or "Disability Awareness Week," many schools are incorporating information about disability *within* the curriculum in a more natural, relevant manner. For example, discussions about attitudes toward and treatment of people with differences can be part of our social sciences or history curriculum. We can discuss many of the physiological bases for disability within our science or health curricula. Examples from literature provide an enormous opportunity to discuss the flexibility and adaptability of people as well as role models of people who overcome challenges daily. Much of the exciting electronic and mechanical equipment developed for students with communication and motor challenges can also be part of our computer sciences, home economics, or science curricula. Rather than developing add-on disability awareness days or assemblies, educators have found ways to weave relevant and current information and experiences within much of the core curriculum. Some school districts have incorporated discussions of diversity in ability as part of their multicultural education curriculum (Davis Joint Unified School District, 1992).

It should be noted that the most beneficial ability awareness approach is to make sure that our schools, teachers, parents and students model their belief in the value of each person in the community. Talking about treating each other with respect regardless of our abilities means little if we are not living the experience each day. Similarly, encouraging peers to interact with and be friends with students with disabilities means little if adults do not welcome, interact with, and seek out these students themselves.

Providing Adequate Training and Staff Development

Adequate training and staff development should be provided for all involved. Many school districts have initiated inclusive education for individual students or groups of students without adequately addressing the training and staff development needs. These initial efforts have succeeded or failed according to the skills of those advocating for or implementing inclusion. Often the special education teacher takes on the responsibility for providing information and resources to others who are cooperating. These initial efforts are commendable but rely on a very few people to maintain the inclusive practices, and each year they must be repeated with new staff.

An increasing number of school districts and school sites are taking a more formal approach to training and staff development by pulling together site- and district-level planning teams to assess the current situation in terms of factors that support and hinder inclusive education. A critical part of this effort is the design of an inservice plan for staff, students, and parents to ensure that those involved have the necessary skills to meet the needs of all students. The best way to create a relevant and effective personnel development plan for inclusive education is is to develop the plan through a school-site team involving the site administrator, general and special educators, paraprofessionals, and parents. These key individuals can identify not only the most important content but also the best way to structure the inservice training. Site teams often arrange to visit other inclusive programs and may invite teams from these schools to meet with site staff to share experiences and strategies. Effective training should include awareness-level presentations, skill-practice workshops, follow-up sessions on application, teacher-to-teacher dialogue, and peer coaching (cf. MacGregor, Halvorsen, et al., 1998). Strategies for personnel development are contained in Chapter 8.

Inclusive education is not an add-on program. It is not for one student whose parents advocate it or for students who are "ready" for inclusion. With the increasing interest in inclusive education and the corresponding increase in controversy about this initiative, we must have standards defining inclusion. In Chapter 7, we discuss ways of evaluating inclusive programs and student progress. When we operate from a common understanding of what supports success, we can more easily establish these inclusive environments and assist those schools to work through the challenges of implementation.

SUMMARY

Chapter 1 describes fifteen quality indicators of inclusive education. Without a clear definition, many educational service models which have been described as *inclusive* or *fully inclusive* may actually be poorly organized and have implemented educational placements that are destined to fail. Placement of a student in a general education classroom with or without an instructional assistant but without attention to general education curriculum, special education support, training, planning, and curriculum adaptation is a disservice to the student and to educators and parents.

Inclusive education does not discriminate by disability type or severity. The underlying basis for this educational approach is that all students can be successful in inclusive educational service models if attention is paid to key quality indicators. As more local educational agencies begin to implement inclusive education and as research on the outcomes of this service model becomes more available, educators, families, researchers, and advocates must all use a common definition. Best practices in inclusive education may be categorized into five areas: (a) full participation as a member of an age-appropriate general education class, (b) support and service delivery, (c) planning and curriculum development, (d) best practices in general education, and (e) training. As we examine the success of particular students who have been included, these quality indicators provide a basis for evaluating the implementation of this service model.

CHECKING FOR UNDERSTANDING

Through the strong advocacy of her parents, Diane has recently joined the fourth-grade classroom at Concord Elementary School. Until this year, Diane had attended a special class for students with severe disabilities at another school site. Her family felt that her abilities were not improving there, and, because she traveled out of her own neighborhood, she wasn't making friends that she could spend time with after school and on weekends. They were very excited to have her attend the school in their neighborhood and hoped the staff there would be, too.

Diane's change in placement occurred in late August, and, because Diane is the first student with disabilities Concord has included, staff did the best they could in preparing her fourth-grade teacher and hiring an instructional assistant to support her. The district program specialist is the inclusion specialist for Diane and consults with her teacher and instructional assistant as needed. Materials were sent over from her previous class, so she could work at her level. She also has the option of going to the resource room if the class is involved in something that would be difficult for her.

After the first month, Diane's fourth-grade teacher requested a meeting to discuss her progress. She expressed her fears that Diane realizes that she's different and that she sees she's not doing the same work as the other students. Her instructional assistant is working very hard with her, but she's not very motivated, it seems. Diane doesn't seem to have any friends, and the other students, although helpful, don't really know how to behave when they are with Diane. Her principal has asked for some assistance to help make this situation work. You have been asked to consult with this school site.

1. What information do you need to have to support this team?

2. How would you gather that information?

3. What key indicators of inclusive education may need to be addressed?

4. What recommendations might you consider regarding her special education support?

5. What steps can be taken to assist other students in their interactions with Diane?

CHAPTER TWO

EFFECTIVE INSTRUCTION
FOR ALL STUDENTS

Upon completion of this chapter, you will be able to

1. Describe effective practices for instruction within diverse classrooms, including

   ■ Cooperative, heterogeneous learning structures

   ■ Peer collaboration and support systems

   ■ Multiple intelligences across the curriculum

   ■ Multilevel instruction

   ■ Outcomes orientation and authentic assessment

   ■ Technology integration and problem-based learning

2. Articulate how effective practices are operationalized within elementary, middle, and high school settings

3. Describe the participation and learning of students with mild to severe disabilities during effective classroom instruction in general education settings

In 1992, Servatius, Fellows, and Kelly reflected that our contemporary understanding of how individuals learn is rooted in the work of early twentieth-century philosophers such as John Dewey, who, in turn, based much of his work on ancient Greek philosophy. Dewey believed that learners acquire knowledge by connecting their own life experiences and applying that experience to new situations. In his view of education, learning requires activity by the learner, a stark contrast to the traditional knowledge-factory notion in which students were seen as empty vessels or blank slates to be filled up with facts. Current brain research as well as investigations of knowledge and skill acquisition in general and special education have moved the field to a constructivist interpretation of learning (e.g., Wiggins, 1991), according to which students build on their previous knowledge to "make" new knowledge, and thus, learning is driven in part by its context as well as by students' own family and community experiences.

Given the premise that we learn through a combination of active participation and "scaffolding" on prior learning, Servatius underscored the necessity that schools work to "counteract the tendency of the 'knowledge-rich' to become richer while the 'knowledge-poor' fall further and further behind" (1992, p. 38). We go some distance toward addressing this critical issue when we design heterogeneous classrooms and schools, in which students will learn by working collaboratively with their peers who come with a wide variety of backgrounds, talents, and experiences. As Slavin (1991) noted in his review of cooperative learning research, this strategy is superior in terms of retention and maintenance of learning.

Jorgensen and Calculator (1994) summarized several characteristics of educational reform from the current literature and described these as necessary components of our goal of meeting the needs of students from at-risk situations as well as those who bring a richer variety of experiences to the learning process. These reform characteristics have been identified across "restructuring," "effective," and "essential" schools rubrics (Sizer, 1992) and involve a critical review of expected student outcomes; the curriculum and instruction necessary to reach these outcomes; and the underlying school structures needed to support these efforts (cf. Sailor, 1991; Skrtic, 1987; Thomas, Correa, & Morsink, 1995). These eight characteristics (with some adaptations) are as follows:

1. Curriculum driven by a small set of desired student outcomes
2. Teacher empowerment in decision-making processes of the school
3. Site-based management
4. Active involvement of students in the learning process
5. Increased collaboration among staff
6. Coaching as the dominant pedagogy for students *and* faculty
7. Use of authentic, nontraditional evaluation processes
8. Personalization or individualization of instructional approaches based on students' learning needs and styles

This chapter will focus on the instructional aspects of these components with particular emphasis on strategies for diverse classrooms, which will be further illustrated in the classroom and the school-level case examples that follow. Table 2.1 lists instructional strategies. Later chapters will focus on the structural changes needed to support these efforts.

HETEROGENEOUS GROUPINGS AND COOPERATIVE LEARNING

The efficacy of cooperative group learning approaches for positive student outcomes has been supported by extensive research (e.g., Glatthorn, 1987; Hunt et al., 1994; Slavin, 1991). Heterogeneity is one of the five prime components of cooperative learning, and refers to structuring student groups which will be diverse in terms of characteristics such as ability, interests, ethnicity, and gender. Johnson and Johnson (1987, 1989), Villa et al. (1992), and many others have described the elements of cooperative learning and their application within inclusive classrooms. Face-to-face interaction within small heterogeneous

TABLE 2.1 Effective Instructional Practices for Diverse Classrooms

- Heterogeneous classrooms and groupings
- Cooperative learning structures
- Peer collaboration and support systems
- Curriculum designed to address and develop multiple intelligences
- Multilevel instruction
- Outcomes-oriented instruction
- Integration of technology across the curriculum
- Activity and problem-based learning
- Providing models for complex tasks; opportunities for low-risk practice, minimizing error repetition
- Authentic assessment

groups; positive interdependence through common goals, products, labor, materials, or roles; direct instruction of social interpersonal skills; individual accountability for achievement of academic and social objectives; and a process for examining the effectiveness of group functioning are necessary to realize the benefits of this approach. Table 2.2 presents the components of effective cooperative learning structures. The 1994 study by Hunt et al. illustrated the effectiveness of cooperative learning in inclusive classrooms. The authors conducted their study in three second-grade classrooms in two California school districts. Each class contained a student with multiple severe disabilities. The participants in the study were the child with disabilities, members of his or her cooperative group, and members of a second cooperative group that did not include a child with disabilities.

Included students were supported in their classrooms by special education teachers and paraprofessionals who utilized systematic instructional techniques as well as informal facilitation strategies (Hunt et al., 1994, p. 291) to assist them in learning and social endeavors. In addition to the individualized levels of in-class support, consultation was provided as well to the general education teacher, along with any necessary curricular and materials adaptation.

TABLE 2.2 A Quick Guide to Essentials of Cooperative Learning

1. *Heterogeneous Groups*

   The teacher constructs heterogeneous groups along several dimensions including ability, gender, ethnicity, interests, and task orientations. Groups can be from two to six in size, and four is a good size for younger students as well as for students who are new to the structure.

2. *Face-to-Face Interaction*

   Cooperative learning requires proximity for effective communication. Students should be "knee to knee and eye to eye" to ensure effective verbal exchanges.

3. *Team Building*

   The amount, type, and timing of team building depend on factors such as the students' age and the learning task. It is especially important to engage in team-building activities before complex cooperative learning activities are scheduled, particularly when there is a wide range of student achievement in the class.

4. *Positive Interdependence* (We sink or swim together.)

   Cooperative learning activities are based on positive interdependence; goals are structured for the students, and teachers need to be concerned about the performance of ALL group members. Projects should be designed so that students *need* to interact in activities such as: plays, science experiments, interviews, data collection, and story writing.

5. *Individual Accountability*

   Every student is given feedback on his or her progress through quizzes, tests, and individual performance-based assessments (e.g., build a pulley, make a parallel circuit). The group is given feedback on how each member is progressing, so help can be given accordingly. Groups may receive additional rewards such as "no homework tonight" for group achievements such as groups in which each member has raised their score.

6. *Direct Teaching of Social Skills* (collaborative skills)

   Students are taught and practice those specific behaviors that will help the group complete the task and *like* each other when the task is over. These skills include asking for assistance, helping others, and taking responsibility for group members. Teachers will need to role play and model these behaviors.

7. *Group Process* (small group and total class)

   The teacher structures procedures for the group to discuss how effectively they are working together and using their social skills and how they could use them even more effectively. This is the key for groups that are not working collaboratively together as well as rewarding those who are. Intergroup collaboration should also be encouraged by structuring opportunities for groups to check in with other groups, to give and receive assistance and encouragement.

Cooperative group instruction focused on an eight-to-ten-week daily math unit. Students were randomly assigned into groups of four. Additional adult support included periodic parent volunteers, university practicum students, and special education staff. At the unit's completion, all students were assigned to new groupings for Math or Art. This provided an opportunity to examine students' skill generalization across people and activities.

A multiple baseline research design was used to analyze skill acquisition by the three targeted students, and a pretest/posttest control group design was used to evaluate the math and money skill achievement of general education students. The control group was randomly selected in each case.

The typical peers in the cooperative learning groups provided cues, prompts, and consequences to promote the learning of the member with disabilities. Prior to the intervention, project staff met with each group and described the skills that students were learning, asking peers to provide cues that would, for example, signal the student to, for example, communicate or pass materials. During the intervention phase, peers were assisted to provide cues, assistance, and positive feedback when appropriate. Brief review meetings took place before each math session, and staff reminders during sessions were gradually reduced to zero.

After the unit's completion and the students' reassignment, project staff met with the new groups but did not provide information on prompting or the reinforcement procedures used in the previous group. Peers were made aware of the ways the student had learned to participate.

The three students with disabilities were able to demonstrate the targeted skills within the first cooperative groups and to generalize them to newly formed groups later. Tests of typical peers' achievements indicated that the groups with students with disabilities performed as well as members of the control group, which had not included a child with disabilities. Both the target and control groups significantly increased their knowledge in the specific academic areas, so there was no negative impact on students who worked with another child. Equally important is the fact that students with severe multiple disabilities were able to learn to independently perform communication and motor skills within the context of academic activities. As Hunt et al. noted, educators who support and promote inclusive education are challenged "to contribute to the design of educational contexts and processes" that allow students to have meaningful and successful participation in the academic activities of the school day (p. 299). A second illustration involving included students in cooperative groups is provided later in this chapter in the discussion of Monroe High School.

Servatius (1995) has commented that we never hear the phrase, "Don't look at your neighbor's paper," once we leave school for the diverse, interdependent world of work and life as adults. Cooperative structures prepare students for the world outside of school while ensuring that students acquire and master both academic and interpersonal skills. Many other structures also foster peers providing assistance to peers. Several others are described in the following sections.

PEER COLLABORATION AND SUPPORT SYSTEMS

Students' support of other students is now recognized as one of the most valuable methods to facilitate *all* students' learning (cf. Villa & Thousand, 1992). Cooperative learning approaches set the stage for a climate of positive peer collaboration and for strategies such as peer tutoring, peer networks, and peer planning teams.

Peer Tutoring

Villa and Thousand (1992) have reviewed the extensive benefits to students of tutoring relationships, which include positive results for both the tutor and "tutee." For same-age and cross-age tutors, research and practice have long demonstrated the fact that a person masters material and skills most effectively when teaching these to others. In addition, the tutor's self-esteem is enhanced by the experience as is his peers' self-esteem through the acquisition of new skills. Hunt et al.'s 1994 study of basic skills instruction by peers to included students within cooperative math groups is an excellent illustration of this.

Teachers have developed informal as well as systematic strategies to recruit and support tutors across the curriculum and across ages and student ability (e.g., Murray-Seegert, 1989; Sailor et al., 1989). In our experience, these programs are most effective when tutoring relationships evolve as a part of the school or classroom's culture, and such strategies are not viewed solely as a vehicle for supporting students with disabilities. In fact, in many schools, students with mild to moderate disabilities are supported in their role as cross-age tutors with younger students or with students for whom English is a second language.

Table 2.3 presents a sample lesson format that illustrates how peer tutors support a student's instruction throughout their ninth-grade science period.

TABLE 2.3   Participation Plan

Classroom: Mr. Whitman and Ms. Dickinson
Date: 2nd Semester

REGULAR CLASSROOM PARTICIPATION PLAN—GENERAL ROUTINES

1. Activity Instructions for Assistant and Peers

    Raymond will listen to directions, participate in discussion, transition with his small groups, and complete assignments. He should follow the general lesson format as much as possible.

2. Student Considerations

    If R. does not notice who is talking, make sure to point the person out to him. Whenever appropriate, he can raise his hand and answer questions in discussion. If he makes noises, be sure to very seriously remind him that there are no noises at school—it is absolutely uncool. It is always best if the input comes from Mr. Whitman or Ms. Dickinson because they are the teachers. Before he arrives, take time to talk about his objectives and what he will be working on during the period. *Remind him to ask for a break if he needs a break.* At the end of the period, take time to talk about how the period went and make sure to end on the positive (e.g., Instructional Assistant: "I really liked how you raised your hand to answer a question in class today." Peer: "That was a cool answer, Ray.").

3. Goals and Objectives

    - Talk about feelings
    - Maintain behavior appropriate for a ninth grader
    - Complete modified assignment
    - Arrive at class on time
    - Use full sentences
    - Ask classmates or Mr. Whitman or Ms. Dickinson for help
    - Initiate and acknowledge interactions: social, task related, ask for and provide information to others
    - Work independently *and* cooperatively
    - Make choices

4. Support Needed and Student Directions

    Ray will need assistance to complete some of the lessons, particularly those that involve writing. In small groups, be sure to let Ray know that he has a job in the group and give him a choice of jobs and explain what his job will involve. Use your judgment about how much assistance he will need. (Directions to assistant: It is time for R. to work more on his own and with his classmates. Whenever possible, fade back and give him a chance to solve problems on his own. Make yourself unavailable and see if he can figure out what to do. Now that the kids know how to provide information to R., bring them in and fade yourself out to facilitate peer-to-peer interactions. As much as possible, give him opportunities to be independent and to use his peers and teachers as a resource. Try to be a resource to Mr. Whitman and the rest of the class. This will help R. to see that you are not always there just for him.)

Adapted lesson plan from N. Graham, 1992, Workshop presentation. Napa, CA: PEERS Project, Statewide Institute on Inclusive Education for Collaborative School Teams. Adapted with permission.

Peer Networks

This category comprises a wide range of activities variously labeled as support circles, circles of friends, circle meetings, pal groups, etc. Peer networks are designed to provide the necessary level of support for a student within and beyond the formal school day and to encourage or facilitate friendship development. The natural support that typical peers provide within the instructional context is a critical component of effective learning communities and extends well beyond the social benefits to all students involved (cf. Hunt et al., 1994). For example, in one middle school in which we have worked, peer tutors engage in team-building and training exercises to enable them to provide this instructional support to a classmate for one period each day. Tutors do this as an elective course within the Unified Arts component of their curriculum in the seventh and eighth grades (Heidi Bjorgan, personal communication, May 21, 1999). The frequency of peer meetings and the format of these networks vary according to ages and individuals, however, most networks meet weekly or at least twice a month, usually after school or at lunch. Students select their circle members, with assistance if needed from the group's facilitator, who may be the special or general education teacher, an instructional assistant, speech therapist, parent, or another person who knows the student well.

A case in point: Maureen, who is nonverbal, selected classmates for her fourth-grade circle by pointing to their pictures. Maureen uses a Dynavox to enhance communication during interactions with her peers and others. Her support teacher assisted her in inviting these students and told the group that the first meeting would be a brainstorming session about ways that Maureen could participate to a greater degree in activities with her classmates. In the first circle meeting after school, the special education support teacher opened with an ice-breaker activity and then discussed with all eight students what kinds of activities they would like to pursue in their meetings. They watched a videotape of a student and her circle at another school, at which students had developed a photography club. Maureen and her circle decided to pursue an interest they all shared, starting some kind of business together. They discussed several possibilities that two girls had read about in *American Girl* magazine. One, making friendship bracelets, held some appeal for all. The meeting closed with plans for the teacher to obtain the materials prior to the next meeting.

As the circle meetings progressed, students' shared interests led to much conversation throughout their crafts activities, and Maureen was an active part of it all as these students planned how, when, and where they would "market" their new commodities, and whether they would save, reinvest, or spend any proceeds. This extracurricular event paved the way for students' inclusion of Maureen in many activities outside of school as well as in increased natural supports for her during academic and other school periods.

Peer Planning Teams

Increasingly, students' friends are attending and actively participating in instructional planning meetings as well as IEPs. Over and over again, we have found that students' peers have some of the best notions about what they need to learn as well as how to teach it. Some educators in Wheaton, Illinois, have dubbed these student groups "pit crews," using a car racing analogy (*Choices,* 1991). These groups come together when, for example, a new instructional unit is about to begin. Students are asked for their suggestions about ways to ensure, for example, that Bill will participate and learn to his maximum ability. For example, when planning a new unit about animal habitats, students suggested that Bill, who draws well, make illustrations of each habitat studied for his cooperative group's books on habitats. His classmates would then assist him in labeling these pages. Bill would identify and cut out the appropriate words from a list that a peer had printed on the computer.

Students are our greatest resource in supporting effective classrooms. We will discuss these and other strategies for a positive classroom climate further in Chapter 5.

CURRICULUM AND MULTIPLE INTELLIGENCES

Multiple Intelligence Theory

Howard Gardner's first book, *Frames of Mind* (1983), which laid out the theory of multiple intelligences, was quite controversial fifteen years ago. Gardner's original target audience was psychologists (Gardner examined the nature and assessment of intelligence) rather than educators at large. But in the intervening years and with the publication of his and other educators' research on application of the theory to classroom practice, the study of the pluralization of intelligence has led to a significant shift in how many schools see and teach students.

Gardner redefined intelligence as "the ability to solve a problem or to fashion a product in a way that is considered useful in one or more cultural settings" (1983, cited in Gardner, 1995) and has stated his hypothesis that each of the eight intelligences defined to date works with the others to develop useful "products." Gardner tells us that the more individuals strengthen their various intelligences and become aware of their stronger areas, the more skills and choices they will have. Table 2.4 lists each of the eight intelligences and briefly defines them.

Boggeman, Hoerr, and Wallach (1996) argued that because multiple intelligence (MI) theory is *not* a curriculum and was not conceived for use in schools, it has even more potential for educators. Specifically, they point out that because there is not a cookbook approach, each school's implementation will reflect the context of the school and classroom and thus meet one of the key requirements to effective education noted here—personalized, individualized education for *all* students.

Table 2.5, adapted from the work of the faculties at New City Elementary School in St. Louis (Boggeman, Hoerr, & Wallach, 1996) and Whittier High School in California (Falvey et al., 1997), lists materials and strategies that might be employed for instruction for each of the intelligences.

Why is this new framework for pluralizing intelligence important to us in ensuring effective classrooms for our diverse student populations? Julie Stephens, a teacher whose own traditional background had informed her practice, reflected on her transformation to a "dyed in the wool MI teacher" (1996, p. 233). New City School of St. Louis is an independent school that has been a pioneer in revamping its curriculum and instruction to reflect multiple intelligence theory. As Stephens noted, the traditional classroom is "teacher centered," but the MI classroom is kid centered. The activities drive the classroom. Ms. Stephens has become a facilitator of learning—a coach, who ensures that access to all the information and materials necessary for learning are there, so that students can *make* their own knowledge and collaborate with others in the process. As Emily Grady, a New City parent described it, "…the intangible skill of 'learning how to learn' is better supported

TABLE 2.4   Gardner's Multiple Intelligences

Linguistic	Facility with use and meaning of language, with oral and oral or written communication
Logical/mathematical	Ability to handle rational sequences, recognize patterns and order
Spatial	Ability to use perception of the world to recreate or transform aspects of it
Body/kinesthetic	Ability to use body and handle objects skillfully
Musical	Sensitivity to and ability to use pitch, melody, rhythm, and tone
Interpersonal	Ability to access one's emotional life in order to help understand self and others
Intrapersonal	Ability to understand people and relationships
Naturalist	Ability to recognize flora and fauna, to make other consequential distinctions in the natural world, and to use this ability productively in hunting, farming, and biological science

TABLE 2.5   Materials and Strategies That Teach to Multiple Intelligences

LOGICAL/MATHEMATICAL	BODILY/KINESTHETIC
logical problem-solving exercises	hands-on thinking, manipulatives
classifications and categorizations	classroom theater
creating codes	competitive and cooperative games
logic puzzles and games	crafts
calculations and quantifications	cooking, gardening, other activities
scientific thinking	physical awareness exercises
logical–sequential presentation of subject matter	using body language and hand signals to communicate
heuristics	
Socratic questioning	
SPATIAL	**INTERPERSONAL**
charts, graphs, diagrams, and maps	conflict mediation
visualization	peer or cross-age teaching
videos, slides, and movies	board games
photography	cooperative groups
visual puzzles and mazes	academic clubs
construction	brainstorming sessions
painting, collage, ceramics, etc.	peer sharing, conferencing
art appreciation	
idea sketching	
color cues	
visual awareness and visual literacy activities	
creation of graphic symbols	
MUSICAL	**INTRAPERSONAL**
musical concepts, singing, humming, whistling	independent study
playing instruments	self-paced project or instruction
playing recorded music	reflection periods
group singing	interest centers
rhythms, raps, chants	personal journals
linking tunes with concepts	goal-setting sessions
mood music	self-esteem activities
	private work spaces
NATURALIST	**LINGUISTIC**
classify wildlife	lectures
identify and distinguish between species through observation	small and large group discussions
observe animals in natural habitats	reading of all types
notice relationships in nature	word games
student docents for class garden or zoo	storytelling
	debates
	journals
	the writing process

Adapted from "Developing a Community of Learners at Whittier High School," by M. Falvey et al., 1997, in D. Sage (Ed.), *Inclusion in Secondary Schools* (pp. 45–47). Port Chester, NY: National Professional Resources; and from *Succeeding with Multiple Intelligences: Teaching Through the Personal Intelligences,* by S. Boggeman, T. Hoerr, and C. Wallach, 1996, St. Louis, MO: The New City School.

and probably more consistently taught and assessed, thanks to the MI theory and the language of learning it gives us" (1996, p. 217).

The following lesson plan outline illustrates how middle school students might approach their analysis of Robert Frost's poem, "The Road Not Taken," from the vantage point of several different intelligences (Halvorsen, 1997).

Multiple Intelligences Lesson Plan

Instructions
1. Read the poem.
2. Discuss with your group how you might teach its meaning, structure, etc., using the particular intelligence you have been assigned to focus on (spatial, musical, bodily/kinesthetic, interpersonal, intrapersonal, linguistic, logical/mathematical, or naturalist).
3. Create your instructional plan.
4. Teach the rest of the class.

Examples of Student Lessons
1. Linguistic: The group put on a radio show: One person played an interviewer, asking the traveler why he chose this road and what he experienced as well as what he thought he had missed.
2. Musical: The group set the words to music of different types, and each member selected a verse to sing. One verse was in rap, one to a classical melody, one jazz, and one a popular rock song.
3. Spatial: This group designed a three-dimensional diorama to illustrate the traveler and his choice. To the diorama they added representative materials at the end of each fork in the road that the traveler might have chosen indicating what the results would be (e.g., family, house, at one; money, material objects, at the other).
4. Interpersonal: This group devised a board game complete with cards about life decisions that directed the traveler to certain paths. There were two possible paths or ways to win the game.

MULTILEVEL INSTRUCTION

Giangreco, Cloninger, and Iverson (1993) noted that a multilevel approach, in which students are working on different goals and objectives within the same curricular area and the same lesson or activity, is not new to education but is rather an application of Bloom's Taxonomy of Educational Objectives (1956). Eby (1996) worked further with Bloom to identify relevant products associated with each level of learning (p. 298). Her analysis illustrated how each of the strategies discussed above can be woven together through multilevel instruction. For example, students working at the initial knowledge level with Frost's poem might memorize the poem (linguistic intelligence) or a song based upon it (musical intelligence), or a song might assist them in memorizing it. Students working at the synthesis level in Bloom's Taxonomy might create a group painting or diorama of the scene depicted by the poem (interpersonal, spatial intelligence).

All teachers engage in multilevel instruction; the key factor is that multilevel instruction must be purposeful, with specific outcomes expected for each level of knowledge acquisition and mastery.

OUTCOMES ORIENTATION AND AUTHENTIC ASSESSMENT

It's no longer enough for educators to claim, "we taught it, we provided the service; they should have learned." Accountability is key—how *all* students are performing; what essential skills they have mastered at each level of their education is what counts. And an integral part of that process is student and family knowledge of those expectations. Grant Wiggins said it well in 1991: "…stop covering the basket and let them *make* a basket" (cited in Servatius, 1995). The outcomes—what students should be able to demonstrate—should not be a secret. When students understand the objective and the direction of the lesson or unit, they can build on what they know about a subject through their experiences and background as they "construct" their learning.

Schools, districts, and state education agencies are spending increasing amounts of time and energy defining the outcomes they expect from all of their students at specific benchmark points. In turn, they are investigating ways to effectively connect instruction with measurement strategies that enable students to demonstrate their learning, for example, across multiple intelligences (Falvey et al., 1997). High school senior exhibitions such as those completed by students attending "essential schools" (Sizer, 1992), may take the form, for example, of computer-assisted designs, videotapes, musical compositions, photographic displays, plays, debates, mobiles, murals, children's books, sculptures, or draft legislation, to name a few choices (Falvey et al., 1997, p. 68). Portfolio assessment from kindergarten through graduate school is another highly effective tool for students to demonstrate progress, to show that knowledge has actually been constructed through a highly structured approach. This strategy, now used as a state-sanctioned alternative assessment to standardized tests throughout Kentucky (Kleinert et al., 1997), is discussed in Chapter 7.

In Mr. Vasquez's multiage class, students at Vineyard Elementary School (see the description later in this chapter) compose their individual portfolios from school and homework completed over the past quarter. They are directed to select examples of work that illustrate some things they learned well since the last period, some things they are working on, and some that interest them for other reasons. At school and at home, they write about each piece selected before the scheduled parent-student teacher conference, and Mr. Vasquez works with them to identify goals and areas about which they would like to report. The amount of writing is individualized, and students can construct a variety of formats to display their work.

At the conference, the portfolio guides discussion. Third graders are able to lead the conference within the structure Mr. Vasquez has laid out—reviewing the portfolio with parents, highlighting accomplishments, and setting goals. Student, teacher, and parents each set one goal, and Mr. Vasquez writes up a meeting summary.

These "authentic" alternatives to pen and pencil assessments foster both instructional and student creativity and imagination. Their use demands that our schools and communities agree on expectations or standards and the criteria for meeting these up front, so that we can identify multilevel, "multioutput" performance alternatives that are acceptable within the assessment rubric. These authentic strategies involve students in a process that "…joins what is taught, how it is taught, and how it is evaluated" (Kreisman, Knoll, & Melchior, 1995, p. 114).

TECHNOLOGY INTEGRATION

A colleague has compared the ubiquitous computer lab in most schools to the traditional special education classroom: General education teachers often aren't quite sure what goes on in there, don't really want to send their students there and have them "miss valuable instructional time," have noticed that there's paper on the room door's window (so you can't look in), and figure that the person in charge of that program is the best person to know about that stuff (Pressman, 1997, personal communication). They may also be worried that someone will soon expect them to know about it, and it's an area in which they may have next-to-no experience. Many general education teachers see technology as an add-on, especially when they have minimal to no technological equipment in the classroom itself and may only have seen "drill and kill" type exhibitions or heard about the horrors of adult content on the Internet. Pressman and Blackstone (1996) have also written successful teacher-led technology projects to assist the "techno-peasants, techno-phobics, and techno-skeptics" among us to integrate technology, to embed its use within our instruction, and make it work for and with us and our students.

And so we need to close those separate labs and bring the technology *into* each classroom to ensure its availability for every subject area. Some examples of technology use *within* curriculum and instruction are described in the examples below.

Problem-Based Learning

In an Ecology unit, sixth-grade students are studying pollution. Different small groups are looking at the water, air, and ground quality. Students utilize the Internet to contact the water department, meteorological services, and environmental groups for information, which they utilize in status reports, projections of future trends, and community service pursuits. Groups use a computer-assisted design (CAD) program to construct maps of atmospheric levels, ground layers, and water location.

Mathematics

Students in the second grade are learning to collect and graph data. They begin by conducting group surveys about student preferences on a variety of areas (e.g., favorite ice cream, time of day, animal, sport) and then input their data to a graphic program that creates the x and y axis and the visual display. They then write a paragraph analyzing the data and report on it to the class.

Literature

An eleventh-grade group reading *The Great Gatsby* conducts an on-line search to locate reviews of Fitzgerald's work during his lifetime. They use this information to compose a script for a radio show and take the roles of Fitzgerald, his peers, and an interviewer. They perform the radio show for the class.

Individualized Supports

Students with disabilities will use technology in concert with their classmates through group activities described here and later in this chapter. Many will also use individualized technology to assist them with the input (e.g., braille, enlarged print, pictures) or output (e.g., word prediction software, braille, speech synthesizer) of information. Some students will use technology that augments or assists their critical receptive and expressive language skills.

Technological supports range from low-tech adaptations such as a small photo album organized as a student's *conversation book* (Hunt, Alwell, & Goetz, 1992), to high-tech items such as computer-generated large print, braille translators, customized keyboards, and synthesized speech.

Beukelman and Mirenda (1992) have articulated detailed considerations for a decision-making process when *augmentative* or *alternative communication systems* are being developed and selected for students. Their participation model of assessment, planning, and intervention emphasizes the principle that any individual's communication needs can be addressed, regardless of the extent or nature of the disability, and it involves intensive inventory of an individual's activities, the patterns and effectiveness of participation with peers, as well as an identification of "opportunity" (e.g., segregated environment) and "access" (e.g., mobility issues) barriers to communication. As plans for intervention are developed for the present and future, instruction in the use of the system is the critical component: instruction of specific skills, in natural contexts, and with both peers and facilitating adults. The reader is referred to this excellent research-based resource for evaluating the decision-making, intervention, and specific merits of an extensive array of options and possibilities as well as implementation examples for each.

Amanda, one of four students whom you will meet in this book, is a middle school student with multiple disabilities including physical, communicative, and possible cognitive difficulties. She is nonverbal and uses a wheelchair because of her uncontrolled seizures. Amanda uses both a communication book with key pictures as well as a Macaw electronic device. The Macaw enables one to program recorded speech across overlays that can have varying numbers of touch keys, as few as two or three and as many as thirty-two.

Keys can be programmed with specific symbols, pictures, or words. Amanda's peers assist in the programming and recording on her Macaw. She is using it in her elective Spanish class to ask questions in Spanish and to greet friends in Spanish.

The Macaw is just one example of augmentative or alternative communication devices. The reader is encouraged to investigate this area further in the references at the end of this book.

Technology that promotes student access to the curriculum is constantly evolving as well for students who have a wide range of needs. Latham (1997) reviews the ongoing debate as to whether technology should seek to circumvent or to remediate disability and provides as an example a student with a reading disability who might use a computer with a speech synthesizer that is programmed to read the book aloud to him. This would circumvent his reading disability, assuming that his auditory processing is good, and allow him to obtain the necessary content from the passage. He might use earphones to ensure that this does not disrupt the class. However, others would prefer that this same student use software that would focus on phonological awareness and word-identification skills. We propose that the two choices are not mutually exclusive; rather, both may be used at different times of the day.

For example, during a "silent sustained reading" period such as occurs daily in many schools, this student (Raymond) might listen to the chapter or story on a tape recorded by a peer using a speech synthesizer if the software is available. At another time, while his classmates are engaged in an independent work activity, he might use the EDMARK or other reading instruction program with teacher or paraprofessional assistance.

Melissa, a middle school student with learning disabilities who finds writing tasks challenging, might use word-prediction software to assist her in writing a paragraph about basic first-aid procedures she has learned in her elective class, Child Development and Safety.

Joey, an included student with autism, uses computer overlays (developed by his special education teacher in collaboration with his general education teacher) with an overlay maker program such as those designed by Intellitools. The overlay maker is designed on a computer screen to fit on the computer keyboard. A template with text and graphics has been constructed for Joey to use in his primary classroom unit on neighborhoods.

Ryba, Selby, and Nolan (1995) noted that for students with disabilities technology can be an effective (1) empowering tool, giving students increased control over their learning; (2) social development tool, creating learner-centered environments and assisting with cooperative learning tasks; (3) tool to enhance both learning opportunities and intellectual growth. These goals are certainly congruent with technology integration for *all* students. Ryba, Selby, and Nolan (1995) emphasized the facility with which personalized programs can be developed, using as an example a student with Down syndrome whose individualized word recognition program included a multimedia format. The student viewed a picture of each object, clicked on the picture to hear the word, or used the arrow key to display the target word and hear it spoken. Words that were targeted for instruction in her IEP and had specific relevance to her life and grade-level curriculum were programmed. Multimedia programs such as the one in this example allow teachers and students to integrate sound, text, graphics, and scanned images and can thus be powerful learning tools.

TOOLS FOR EVERYDAY INSTRUCTION

Effective teachers have a vast array of specific strategies in their "toolkits" for a variety of situations. Three especially relevant strategies for diverse classrooms are minimizing error repetition, providing opportunities for low-risk practice, and providing models for complex tasks. These three are also highly related to each other.

Madeline Hunter has noted that "practice makes permanent," thus emphasizing the importance of ensuring that students *don't* practice incorrect responses! In special education lingo, this used to be called "errorless learning," a process of assisting the student to make correct responses through a variety of cueing and prompt hierarchy strategies and creating antecedent conditions that would facilitate the student's ability to obtain or provide the correct response. Today, teachers are utilizing a combination of new and "old" techniques to determine whether students are learning the materials being taught and to implement new teaching strategies when they see that a few, some, or most of the students aren't "there" yet. For example, chalk and individual slates are provided so that students can hold up their answers, (e.g., Is it *a, b,* or *c?*) for a quick scan of the room. Paper "think pads" provide another version of the same checking process, and choral responses still another. A fourth strategy can be "numbered heads together," in which students have assigned group numbers and are requested to get together to solve the problem. The teacher randomly selects a numbered group to call on for the answer.

These and any number of similar creative techniques rapidly provide teachers with essential information about student learning so that course corrections can also follow as quickly as needed.

These techniques are closely tied to "low-risk" practice opportunities. When we examine the structure of a given classroom, we see that many students rarely raise their hands to respond and may avoid eye contact with teachers rather than risk being called on. A low-risk technique such as "think, pair, share" allows students to think individually about a question, pair with a partner, and share their response, thus increasing the volume of responses by increasing student confidence in their answers and by correcting them in a lower risk situation. Having student "appointments" with other students is a similar structure for this purpose. For example, students can make a series of "appointments" with classmates at the start of the day. Then later, the teacher directs students to think about the rationale for the decision to drop the bombs on Hiroshima and Nagasaki, to write down three reasons it was made, and to go to their "9:00 appointment" to discuss these reasons together.

Providing models for complex instruction is the third in this trio of techniques. When, for example, students are learning long division, a model that delineates each step facilitates instruction. Leaving the model in place when students go to individual or group work is critical. This enables the teacher to "praise, prompt, and leave" (Servatius, 1995), thus increasing the number of students he or she is able to assist. Specifically, if a student is able to successfully complete Steps 1–3, the teacher can provide individual instruction for Step 4, direct the student to complete Steps 1–4 on all ten problems, move to another student, and return later. Models also assist with homework completion as well as helping students who were absent for the initial instruction period.

We have provided a brief review of effective teaching practices that support inclusive environments. In the remaining pages of the chapter, we'd like to introduce you to several classrooms, teachers, and schools in which these practices come alive.

CLASSROOM STRATEGIES: ELEMENTARY SCHOOL

The School

Vineyard School is a small elementary school of 200 students with strong ties to its families, who are all from the immediate neighborhood, an agricultural area just outside of a town well known for its wineries and tourists. The school population is largely Latino (88 percent) and composed of "working poor" people who are seasonally employed. The school's calendar is adjusted for a longer-than-usual winter break, during which many families return to their native countries for holiday celebrations. The school has received state department of education awards for its family involvement and its inclusive approach and commitment. Students with IEPs are all in the general education classes they would be attending if they did not have a disability, and special education staff work in the classroom. Recently, the school designed a learning center to address the unmet needs of students at risk for failure as well as some additional needs of labeled students. Faculty members have worked out a schedule to staff the learning center during specific periods with *both* general and special education support personnel.

The Classroom and Students

Mr. Vasquez is a first–third grade teacher of a heterogeneous multiage class at Vineyard Elementary School. He teaches twenty-four students, eight from each grade level, using activity-based "*developmentally appropriate practices*" (cf. Linder, 1993) combined with a focus on students' *multiple intelligences* (Gardner, 1983; Armstrong, 1994). He also participates weekly as a facilitator in Vineyard's learning center, which helps to support the diverse learning needs of the school's K–5 population including students identified as being at risk for school failure, students with disabilities, and any students in need of assistance who come into the center on a weekly basis, scheduled by faculty. Students can self-refer or be referred by their teacher, and the schedule is designed every two weeks by the school's student study team. Faculty volunteer to staff the center for an hour every two weeks. During this time their own classes are either scheduled for special activities such as Physical Education or are taught by the school's special educator, who takes over the instruction of specific subjects, thus affording her the opportunity to work with included students in the context of their classrooms and to work with all students in the class.

Mr. Vasquez's first–third grade class is an exciting learning environment. The basic schedule is as follows:

BASIC SCHEDULE

8:30	Arrival and class business
	Journal writing with partners
9:00	Transition to mixed-age academic groups
9:05–9:45	Sharks: Language Arts
	Bats: Math
	Whales: Science or Social Studies
9:45	Second academic group period—rotate—transition to
9:50–10:30	Second academic groups
10:30–10:45	First recess
10:50–11:30	Third academic groups
11:30	Class meeting
11:45–12:30	Lunch
12:35–12:50	Silent sustained reading
12:50–1:50	Plan, do, & review
	12:50–1:05 Plan
	1:05–1:40 Do
	1:40–1:50 Review
1:50–2:45	Library—Mondays
	Phys. Ed.—Tuesdays
	Special Projects—Wednesdays
	Homework Planning or shareathon—Thursdays
	Drama or Multicultural Art—Fridays
2:50	Dismissal

Let's spend a day with Mr. Vasquez's class. When we look in on them at 8:45, students are seated throughout the room—some on cushions in the rug area, some at tables in the floor area, some inside a small tent at one corner of the room, others on window seats that border one side of the classroom by the room's "library." Joey, a second grader included for the second year with Mr. Vasquez, is working with Larry on their journals. Joey was diagnosed as having autism when he was assessed by the developmental disabilities clinic at a local university. The clinic recommended an intensive home-based behavioral intervention program when he was three; his parents selected a local typical private preschool with the support of a special educator and part-time paraprofessional for direct instruction and curricular adaptation.

Joey, a charming, attractive African American boy, has a particular interest in geography and often studies and will draw maps for extended periods of time. His teachers and parents have recognized his talent in this area and capitalized on it. Joey has several friends at school who communicate with him primarily through sign language and his communication picture books. He is beginning to speak more and to demonstrate reading skills as well as writing ability. He enjoys model airplanes and is a member of a Boy Scout troop. Joey occasionally shows his frustration with certain tasks and with changes in routine by talking loudly and throwing materials. He has a support circle of friends facilitated by his classroom and his special education support teacher who are currently working on a new plan to address these areas.

Larry asks Joey questions as Mr. Vasquez has taught him to find out what Joey wants to write about today. Joey shows Larry pictures from his communication book or signs one or two words to him. Larry then assists Joey by writing those words for Joey to copy. Joey completes his work by illustrating his writing. Larry also tells Joey what he is writing about, and they often draw illustrations together. Larry is part of Joey's *circle of friends,* a group that meets with him and the inclusion support teacher, Ms. Ruben, or with Mr. Vasquez every two weeks at lunch. The circle consists of six students in the first–third grades who talk about what's working for Joey in his day, new skills he is acquiring and how to build on these, ideas for adaptations, and close each session with a game, story, or other student-selected activity. (See Chapter 5 for more detailed discussion.)

As students break into groups, we follow Larry and the Bats into Language Arts. This group is brainstorming ideas for stories that they will write in pairs and illustrate in part with pictures they will take using disposable cameras purchased for the activity. Mr. Vasquez introduced the activity with the story *Dogzilla* by David Pilkey (1993). He read and demonstrated the parts of a story on a large storyboard, and now elicits ideas from the group about what might come next or how they would change the story if it were theirs. Students then have a choice of drawing their story idea, writing it, or telling it to a partner who acts as scribe. Story ideas are then hung from work lines that stretch above the rug area. Tomorrow the students will begin listing the photographs they need and start taking pictures around the campus with a parent volunteer. Natalie, a student with limited English, works with Suzanne as her partner. The ESL itinerant teacher, Ms. Lopez, is scheduled to join the group halfway through this period, when Mr. Vasquez moves to the Bats Math group. Ms. Lopez supports both students in the activity by assisting Natalie with the English words for her ideas and by facilitating Suzanne's interaction with her. Suzanne, a first grader, dictates ideas to Ms. Lopez, which ensures that her beginning writing skills don't limit her storytelling.

Mr. Vasquez joins the Bats who are in the middle of a Mathlands activity. The directions for the activity were posted at the table station, and a third grader was assigned to read them aloud to the group at the start of the period. The students' objective for this activity has been to create groups from the objects in a box on the table and to state or write the rules for the grouping. This sorting activity assists students with categorizing according to a variety of attributes and is useful to new learners as well as more sophisticated students. As we join them, one grouping they have made includes a paperclip box, unifix cubes, a small pad of paper, and a comb. The rule the students have generated is "things that are rectangular."

Now Mr. Vasquez has the students work with partners to select new items and form additional groups. After these attributes are identified, the pairs work to illustrate their groupings and rules either with a picture, graph, or Venn diagrams, which they will complete the next day. Joey's spatial abilities are capitalized on here: He and his partner construct a drawing of the objects that shows how many different groups each object can belong to.

The third group is engaged in their Social Studies unit about neighborhoods and communities with a paraprofessional who provides part-time support to Joey and other students with learning disabilities (under the special educator and classroom teacher's direction). Two students are working together on the Internet to pull up telephone company pages that provide neighborhood maps of streets, services, transportation, and so forth. The remaining six students are working in trios. One trio of beginning readers is using a template to fill in the blanks about their community; the other is working on individualized descriptive passages following a brainstorming activity yesterday. As an end product, each student will construct a binding for their book, and these will be part of the class library for silent sustained reading (SSR), shareathon, and other activities.

Groups rotate through their busy morning and come together in a class meeting just before lunch. The questions of the day are, "What worked best for you today?" and "How could something work better in our groups?" Students' ideas are charted, and the group assists Mr. Vasquez in identifying one change (e.g., more objects in the math box) for the next day.

After lunch, students read silently at any location in the room, and one partner reading station is set up just outside the door. Students sign up for partner reading and are paired so that one student can read to or receive assistance from another.

The plan, do, and review period combines individual choice for free time with writing, planning, and evaluation. Students have a daily binder, in which they must write what they want to do, where they want to do it, and with whom. Some follow a template sheet or graphic organizer that outlines possibilities; others write freehand. After Mr. Vasquez signs off on their plan (or requests revisions prior to approval), students are free to engage in art, play, reading, or outdoor activities for thirty-five minutes. During review, they are responsible for writing about how the activities went: Did they enjoy it? What did they build or make? This period facilitates social interaction, creative play, and concept expansion: It is completely individualized but can be used to encourage community at the same time.

Finally, the day ends with the subject for that particular day of the week. Students use the library for book checkout, on-line research, research for specific reports, and reading alone or with others. Multicultural Art is a PTA-sponsored effort staffed by parent volunteers. Drama uses local actors who volunteer with specific classes for several weeks, working on movement, expression, impromptu skits, and the like. Shareathon involves one group of students (e.g., Bats), who rotate weekly to provide stations for their classmates. Stations can be about a student's specific interest (e.g., whales) and involve the student teaching something to her peers or involving them in an activity (seeing a brief video, drawing, and labeling whales). Students always rejoin the teacher in the carpeted area for any announcements and dismissal.

Mr. Vasquez's teaching strategies and classroom environment illustrate well Gardner's principle of multiple intelligences, that schools should relate their activities to something that's valued in the world (Checkley, 1997), to looking at the performance that we value, whether it's linguistic, logical, aesthetic, or social, and to allowing students to show their understanding in a variety of ways (Wiggins & McTighe, 1998). This structure and foundation provide for meaningful instruction of a group of learners who are diverse in their ages, current abilities, backgrounds, and social skills while addressing critical core curricular areas. Additional adaptations for specific students are often less necessary or superfluous. When adaptations are necessary for acquisition of specific skills, they are easily infused into such an environment.

CLASSROOM STRATEGIES: MIDDLE SCHOOL

The School

Emerson Middle School is located in a suburban neighborhood close to a medium-sized city. The school is part of a rapidly growing school district that was previously rural in nature. The school is three years old and currently serves students in seventh and eighth grades. Emerson has organized the learning environment into four "houses" to allow for a closer relationship between teachers and students. Each house contains approximately 200 students. This structure facilitates collaboration among teaching staff through the creation of teaching teams, whose members not only plan in a more comprehensive and integrated manner but support each other as teaching becomes more challenging. Teachers team teach in some of the classes.

Scheduling at Emerson allows for extended periods of uninterrupted instructional time in the core curriculum areas. Staff have implemented block scheduling to allow for a more integrated approach to Math and Science and Language Arts and Social Sciences. Teachers in these disciplines have coordinated lessons to provide more meaningful learning opportunities that allow students to better understand the relevance of the information presented. The year is broken into three twelve-week trimesters during which students are required to take six mini-courses and three electives in addition to their core studies. Mini-courses are designed to provide students with enrichment and special skills instruction. Drama, Art and Math, Cell Biology, Home Science, Criminology, and Introduction to Singing are some of the mini-courses offered. The schedule for the seventh grade is organized in this manner.

TRIMESTER 1	TRIMESTER 2	TRIMESTER 3
P.E.	P.E.	P.E.
Elective	Elective	Elective
Science	Math	Math
		Science
Mini-course (2)	Mini-course (2)	Mini-course (2)
Lunch	Lunch	Lunch
Language Arts/Social Science	Language Arts/Social Science	Language Arts/Social Science

The staff at Emerson have stressed the importance of a learning environment that facilitates learning, and the house structure and block scheduling attest to that. In terms of the instructional environment, Emerson staff not only team teach but provide an active learning approach, including easy access for both students and staff to a variety of learning resources. A media center, library, independent work areas, studios for developing multimedia products, and other resources are provided and regularly used by individuals and more usually, by small groups. One instructional grouping approach in most classrooms is cooperative learning. Emerson staff recognize the importance of cooperation and collaboration as critical life skills and have actively worked to develop these skills. Many of the learning opportunities are exploratory; students are expected to do research and apply information in completing projects. Exhibitions of learning and portfolios are part of the evaluation process. Some of the staff are experimenting with having students participate in developing grading rubrics for class assignments. Teacher planning time is valued and prioritized to allow for continual communication among house staff. Through this team planning approach, curriculum is coordinated and integrated so that, for example, math concepts are continually incorporated and utilized in science. It is not uncommon to see students at Emerson working outside the classroom—measuring dimensions, experimenting with real-life materials, and conducting surveys among staff and students.

Finally, the attitude conveyed at Emerson is one of respect, responsibility, and contribution. Each student is required to complete community service hours either on or off the campus. Hours are approved by advisors. Some worthwhile services that have been offered by Emerson students over the past three years include food drives, disaster relief efforts, and tutoring for younger students.

Emerson, like many schools, is becoming increasingly diverse in terms of culture and ability. The school has implemented a number of strategies to support students and their families including Math, Science, and Literature nights during which staff work with families on how to study these subjects at home in an enjoyable and effective manner. There is also a homework club available after school for one hour for any student. Teaching staff are available during this time, and students who wish to sign up as peer tutors are also available.

In setting up the structure of the school, the site administrator and staff decided to take an alternative approach to special education services, providing them not only to those students who qualify for special education, but also to those who are at risk for school failure. A learning center, located centrally on the site, is staffed all day by both general and special education staff. Students who believe they need extra assistance may refer themselves to the learning center; their parents may request this assistance, or the student study team may recommend this resource. Students who qualify for special education services may also use the learning center as specified by the IEP team. There is also a tutorial period within the school day, during which students may receive advance instructional help for assignments they will receive the following week. This "heads-up" approach has greatly increased the value of in-class work and reduced the need for pull-out services.

Let's look at how two students are involved in this program at Emerson. Melissa is an outgoing student who enjoys going to school and being around others. She is a leader and appears to have a good grasp on important concepts but has had some difficulty in attending to instruction, completing assignments, and performing on examinations. Amanda is a student with multiple disabilities including physical, communicative, and possible cognitive difficulties. She also enjoys being at school, particularly being around other students. She uses a wheelchair due to uncontrolled seizures and has a picture communication system with both a communication book and a Macaw system. How are these students needs being met through this middle school program?

The first learning block is P.E. Melissa is very capable in this area and participates with no adaptations or support. She has no trouble staying with the game as long as there is no long lecture about the activity prior to getting physically involved. The class is currently in a volleyball unit and is divided into groups of fourteen, with seven on each side. One day a week, Amanda uses this time to work with an adapted P.E. specialist on building strength in her upper body through activities such as raising her hands to hit a large balloon. The aim of the game is to keep the balloon in the air. Other students are invited to participate with her. On other days, Amanda may work with an instructional assistant to independently move her chair through an obstacle course set up in the gym. Amanda uses her communication board to choose activities from a choice of two and indicate when she needs to stop and rest.

The elective Melissa has selected is Child Development and Child Safety. This course is designed for students who are interested in baby-sitting and child care. Students learn about things children are typically able to do at certain ages, expectations about their behavior, safety tips, basic first aid, and CPR for infants and small children. Today Melissa is learning first-aid steps for stopping bleeding and choking. She is working with a partner as are all the students. Her teacher asks Melissa to demonstrate actions she would take in emergencies in addition to giving her brief written quizzes each day. Because the class is mostly activity based, lectures are brief and always followed by practice and discussion—two areas in which Melissa excels.

Meanwhile, Amanda has selected beginning Spanish as her elective. This is quite a challenge, but Amanda's parents want her to be involved in a variety of experiences. Each day, students are responsible for new vocabulary words and for functional conversational phrases. Amanda's friends have programmed greetings and questions in Spanish on her Macaw. Upon entering the room each day, Amanda is responsible for approaching at least two students to greet them in Spanish and ask one question by touching the corresponding picture on her Macaw. Students are responsible for returning the greeting and for answering the question. Greetings and questions are changed each week. Amanda's special education support staff and her parents have created a picturebook of people, places, and things, and when she is asked to point to the item named in Spanish, she points to the picture. When she is working with a peer, she points to the picture, and that peer is responsible for naming the item in Spanish.

During the Math period, Melissa, who seems to be able to figure out many word-type problems in her head but has not been successful with textbooks and worksheets, works in a small cooperative research workgroup that is predicting the cost of first-class mail in the year 2010. Melissa contributes by brainstorming with the members of the group about the information they need to make this prediction. Her ideas, as well as the ideas of other students, are documented by the group's recorder. After the group prioritizes the list, Melissa chooses one of the tasks and with a partner goes to the library to do research on the history of the postal service. She will make notes with her partner to bring back to the team.

Amanda is also involved in this Math activity. Her IEP objectives focus on choice-making, initiating communication with a picture system, naming items, gaining mobility in her wheelchair, and carrying items on her wheelchair tray. As part of her cooperative group, Amanda moves herself to her group, chooses a student partner, uses her communication board to ask that student to be her partner, carries resource materials back to the team on her tray, and hands them to peers. She also looks through resource books with her partner or with an instructional assistant and points to pictures requested by her peer or the assistant.

Melissa has enrolled in a mini-course called Introduction to Drama. This course provides students the opportunity to present and perform in front of large and small groups and to learn voice control, movement, and stage direction. Melissa enjoys being the center of attention and excels when the material is familiar to her. To prepare for her presentations, Melissa has a tutorial period, during which tutors help her practice her lines and prepare for upcoming presentations. Amanda has also chosen Introduction to Drama. Her participation involves taking direction from the instructor and moving within performances and practices. She uses her Macaw in performances at the appropriate time with assistance from a peer. Movement within her chair is also an important skill for Amanda. As part of drama, she is working on moving her body in the wheelchair as part of dance routines. This is a favorite class for Amanda because there is often music involved.

For Amanda, lunch is an important time for communication, choice, movement, and social skills. Getting to the cafeteria, selecting a friend or friends to sit with, choosing what to eat, communicating to the cafeteria staff, and being part of a lunch conversation are addressed during this time. Instead of an instructional assistant or special education teacher, peers who are part of Amanda's circle of friends take on a support role, ensuring that she gets there, obtains her food, and eats. They are knowledgeable in the way that she uses her communication book and try to involve her in their conversations.

Following lunch and a brief recess, Melissa and Amanda return for the Language Arts or Social Science block. The class is studying the Middle Ages in Europe, specifically, the social, economic, and political life. A variety of activities occur during this trimester that involve research, discussion, and exhibitions. Currently, the class is building a replica of a medieval community based upon classroom reading and research. Materials are provided by several sources: the media center, the classroom teacher, and students. Melissa has had assistance in the tutorial period and has also used the learning center to gather information. Her assignment, as part of the cooperative group, was to research medieval dress. The support staff at the learning center and tutorial period have helped her gather materials showing common garb of the Middle Ages. She has had the opportunity to reproduce the pictures by drawing them. Illustrated books from the library are also checked out and brought to class.

Amanda is again involved in gathering materials for her group. She works with an instructional assistant and peers to identify potential pictures that will give ideas to team members. She identifies the items in the replica by pointing to them and helps to paint the scenery with the assistance of a support person. Amanda's peers have recorded a portion of their presentation on her Macaw, and she initiates this presentation by touching a picture.

The ideas suggested in this example are not complex or demanding. They do, however, demand a view of the potential of the classroom environment as being able to meet the educational needs and current skills of a great variety of learners. The key is the belief that it is not the student who must fit the learning environment but rather the learning environment that must be designed to accommodate the learning of all students.

CLASSROOM STRATEGIES: HIGH SCHOOL

The School

Mr. Whitman and Ms. Dickinson are the ninth grade core teachers for the Humanities block (Language Arts and Social Studies) in the Buckeye team, one of three teams in the Frontier family at Monroe High School, a restructured high school. In addition to these two core teachers, the team is supported with collaborative instruction by Ms. Horace, who is the *special education support teacher* for all of the students with IEPs on the team. Monroe is a diverse high school, one of two in a fast-growing district that borders a large midwestern city. Classes of thirty-two to thirty-five students are scheduled mornings and afternoons in integrated Humanities and Math–Sciences blocks with additional elective coursework. The school's population is 19 percent African American, 12 percent Latino, 6 percent Asian, less than 3 percent Pacific Islander and Native American, and 60 percent Caucasian. There are 180 students in the Frontier family, 60 on each team. Fifteen of the Buckeye students have IEPs, and their disabilities range from mild to severe.

Monroe's restructuring effort was supported by district leadership in conjunction with parent–community input over a year's time, and the ninth grade entered into the effort first. Teacher–administrator work groups reviewed brain research as well as the work of the Coalition for Essential Schools (Sizer, 1992) to inform their transformation. They have also been guided by Gardner's work on multiple intelligences (1983, 1995) and by other educators' applications of the theory to instruction (cf. Armstrong, 1994). They developed their curriculum in conjunction with recently approved state and district frameworks.

The Classroom and Students

Today's Humanities lesson is the culmination of a unit focused on human rights during the twentieth century. Students have been exploring in depth the issues of human rights and violations of these rights during periods such as World War II and the Holocaust, the Vietnam War, China since the Cultural Revolution, and events in the United States during the civil rights era of the 1950s–1960s. Their assignment for this week (described in Table 2.6) is to develop and produce a public service announcement or commercial of thirty seconds to one minute in length. The announcement must be related to a current social problem in America (Eshilian, 1997). Students work in cooperative groups of four to five, with assistance from the two core teachers and Ms. Horace during the first ninety minutes, after which Ms. Horace moves to the Math–Science block, exchanging with a special education paraprofessional who now joins the Humanities group.

Student groups have multiple materials available to them, including (a) specific activity instructions that have been given orally are in hardcopy form at each table, and are projected up on the screen; (b) paper, pencils, pens, chart paper, and tape; (c) costumes, props from the classroom or brought from home; (d) music tapes; (e) primary and secondary research materials; and (f) access to one of four on-line computers for research, word processing, and graphics. The activity has been designed both to demonstrate student performance of the objectives or competencies expected by the culmination of the unit, and in so doing to maximize demonstration and use of multiple intelligences including logical, interpersonal, linguistic, musical, spatial, mathematical, kinesthetic, and naturalist.

Jose is the *student facilitator* for his group, which includes three girls and two boys, one of whom is Raymond, who receives special education support.

Raymond is fifteen years old. Until this fall, he had attended a special school in the same district. His parents requested that the school try supporting him through the special education program at the high school instead. Raymond has had a history of problem be-

TABLE 2.6   Final Product—Video

PUBLIC SERVICE ANNOUNCEMENT COMMERCIAL: "WE CAN MAKE A DIFFERENCE"

- Choose a social problem current in America today that is caused by stereotyping, prejudice, discrimination, or oppression of one group of Americans. (Logical, Interpersonal)
- Assign roles: actors, video production, writers, special effects persons, etc. (Intrapersonal, Interpersonal)
- Write a script using powerful words that would help the public to respond to your "cause" to stop the stereotyping, discrimination, or oppression. (Linguistic)
- Use visuals, sounds, props, and costumes that would help communicate your concerns and change people's behavior. (Musical, Spatial)
- The commercial should be from thirty seconds to one minute long. (Mathematical)
- Filming will take place during class on Thursday, March 27. We will watch the film on Friday, March 28 (minimum day) and show it again to Mr. Whitman on Monday, April 6, when we return from Spring Break. (Bodily/Kinesthetic)
- Fifty points total—including a group participation grade.

FINAL PRODUCT: "WE CAN MAKE A DIFFERENCE" GRADING RUBRIC

Brainstorm Page	5	_____
Project organization	5	_____
Script	5	_____
Creativity (use of visuals, sounds, etc.)	10	_____
Technical (timing, clarity, thirty sec–one min)	10	_____
Followed directions (social issue related to stereotyping, discrimination, oppression in America)	10	_____
Group contribution grade	20/4	_____
Total		_____

Adapted public service announcement commercial: "We Can Make a Difference," Whittier High School presentation, by L. Eshilian, 1997, Oakland, CA: California Confederation on Inclusive Education, Summer Institute for School Teams. Adapted with permission.

havior and has a reputation in the district of being very disruptive and aggressive. He has hurt staff members and has also destroyed materials and equipment in his school and home.

Raymond has a significant hearing loss and poor communication skills. He is fairly independent in terms of his self-care and daily living skills; however, his behavior can significantly affect the amount of independence he has. He has had very little academic instruction, but his parents believe he could learn many academic skills if he were exposed to them in a positive manner.

It appears that many of his problem behaviors occur when he can't get people to understand him and when he has to wait for something. He also does not like to be corrected and will often strike out in those situations. Historically, staff made an effort to avoid putting too many demands on him and tended to avoid confrontations.

Raymond is supported at the high school by services from a special education teacher and an instructional aide. At the present time, either an aide or Ms. Horace is with him most of the day. His present behavioral intervention plan involves having him request a break when he is upset and then go to the resource room or outside for a walk. Staff also provide easy, preferred tasks and activities between more demanding tasks to increase his ability to stay involved in class.

Jose starts the activity with a brainstorming session, asking the students for their ideas for the commercial. Maria records the ideas on chart paper. Raymond has a series of pictures in a small binder that depict a variety of current events related to the topic. Josephine, his student assistant, helps him look through the pictures and select ones of interest to him. The pictures illustrate situations such as poor housing conditions in urban projects, lines at soup kitchens and food banks, homeless people, and so forth. The group lists eight ideas for the social problem they might target. Jose prompts Raymond to put his selected picture (which depicts homeless people being asked to leave a park) up on the chart, and Maria records the idea next to it. The group selects eviction and homelessness as their focus and discusses their roles. Josephine and Jose decide to be actors and invite Raymond to join them. Maria and Suzanne will be the primary writers.

While the initial script is being developed, the three actors work on costumes, sounds, and props. Jose sketches costume ideas and suggests that Raymond add color to the drawings with markers. Then the three begin listening to audiotapes that they might use for background music. Raymond wants to operate and hold the tapeplayer, and he grabs it away from Josephine and puts it closer to his ear. Josephine remembers that Raymond doesn't hear well and goes to ask whether earphones are available. She comes back with two sets, but Raymond throws them on the floor. Ms. Horace comes over and suggests that Josephine demonstrate how to use them, which she does. Then, with Ms. Horace's help, Raymond is persuaded to try them. He listens with Josephine while Jose reviews the script draft, proposing various changes and additions. They decide to do a read-through and ask Maria and Suzanne to join them. Raymond gets up and leaves the table when Josephine asks him to take off the headphones. Mr. Whitman comes over to the group as Ms. Horace moves to assist another group. He asks Raymond if he needs a break and models the break request for him. Raymond nods yes, and Mr. Whitman gives him permission to leave. He suggests Raymond leave the earphones and recorder on the desk and go to one of two free-time areas of the class. Raymond heads for the book area and seats himself in a chair. Mr. Whitman stays with the group for about five more minutes as they read through the script draft and discuss where to have musical accompaniment as well as who will play which part. Mr. Whitman gives the players feedback on their script and discussion and suggests that they create a pictorial storyboard to show the announcement sequence. He then calls Raymond back to the group, letting him know that break time is over. Raymond returns slowly, encouraged by enthusiastic remarks from group members that they need him to play his part.

The students each get their props and costume items (hat, bag, backpack, microphone, tie, etc.) at this time, and put them on for the next reading. Maria has the idea that the storyboard could show everyone in costume. Raymond gets up and begins strolling around the room in costume and sits down with another group. Ms. Horace reminds him where he belongs. When he returns to the group, Jose asks him to help Josephine with the storyboard by numbering each separate panel and coloring the various scenes. Raymond follows through on this with interest.

Another *participation plan* for Raymond in his Humanities class can be found in Chapter 3.

SUMMARY

In this chapter we provide an overview of effective strategies for diverse classrooms, followed by school-level cases that demonstrate their implementation. Strategies reviewed emphasize active, engaged learning to maximize all students' participation, such as cooperative learning structures, teaching to multiple intelligences, utilizing natural peer supports, and designing multilevel instructional plans. Emphasis is placed as well on the integration of technology within curriculum and instruction and on outcomes-oriented instruction, in which all students are aware of the expectations for learning and are provided with frameworks that assist them in building on their current knowledge. Each of these strategies fits well with the constructionist orientation to learning: students are active "makers" of knowledge rather than passive recipients of information. In turn, performance-based assessment of these outcomes is described with a specific example provided for a cooperative group lesson. These case studies illustrate as well the specifics of including students with disabilities across instructional experiences. In Chapter 3 we will describe further the individual planning process, which forms the foundation for included students' programs.

CHECKING FOR UNDERSTANDING

1. Consider a lesson or unit that you are currently teaching or have taught in the past. How would you address the same material with activities that emphasize different intelligences from those in your original plan?

2. Describe possible performance-based "authentic" assessments for evaluating student learning in an area in which you have used traditional methods (e.g., pencil and paper) in the past. How could this strategy be utilized or adapted for an included student who has communication difficulties?

3. Describe how you would integrate technology into a unit or lesson if most of the school's computers are located in a separate room with limited access. Could you still achieve technology integration? How?

4. Give an example of a model for a complex task that you could integrate into instruction. Who would this benefit?

5. Think about how you would present a shift to cooperative, heterogeneous group learning structures to the parents of your students. What would you say? How would you address concerns regarding individual accountability and opportunities for especially skilled students to excel?

CHAPTER THREE

PLANNING FOR INDIVIDUAL STUDENT NEEDS IN THE INCLUSIVE CLASSROOM

Upon completion of this chapter, you will be able to

1. Describe an individual student planning process
2. Describe a process for inventorying school sites for instructional opportunities
3. Describe a process for collaborating with families to identify critical skill needs
4. Identify ways to meet specific IEP needs in the context of general education curriculum and school routine using a matrix
5. Assess the current level of performance in general education activities and routines
6. Develop a support plan for students based upon functional assessments
7. Describe a team planning process for meeting individual student needs

DOES THIS MEAN THE END OF SPECIAL EDUCATION?

In their 1979 article, "The Education of Severely and Profoundly Retarded Children: Are We Sacrificing the Child to the Concept?" (1979), Burton and Hirshoren asked whether those who advocate for and work to develop more integrated schools might be more interested in "their own edification" by "forcing normal educational experiences and expectations on them" than in the growth and development of students with disabilities. Their 1979 position paper stressed that these students could not benefit from a program that emphasized the traditional goals of education and that placement of these students even in self-contained classrooms in regular schools was inappropriate. Their concerns acknowledge the critical need to create a curriculum that is meaningful and attainable.

Many in the field of special education have examined the assumptions and approaches in developing curriculum over the years, leading to a more functional, family-based curriculum and at the same time, because of the experiences of students on integrated school sites, finding benefits in integration. The skills of special educators in supporting learning have grown. Many express the fear that inclusion means that students with learning disabilities will forfeit the expertise and focus of the specialized programming in pull-out or special class settings (Smelter, Rasch, & Yudewitz, 1994). Indeed, many believe that families of students with significant disabilities are willing to sacrifice the skill development in language, motor, cognitive, and self-care skills for social interaction and friends. It would be wise for us to take these concerns seriously. Many schools are including students in age-appropriate general education classrooms. Some are having more success than others, depending on how success is determined by those involved. The social benefits are reported extensively for both students with and without disabilities. Empirical evidence regarding skill development in other critical areas is growing and has been summarized recently in a review by Hunt and Goetz (1997).

Over the course of many years, we have developed a wide range of strategies and practices in education to support learning for those students who have not been successful with more traditional approaches. Our skill at identifying specific problems in learning through assessment and developing remedial approaches has continually improved. Research in the field of vision, hearing, and physical impairments has not only generated important advances in specialized equipment but has also established teaching and learning approaches that allow students to benefit from participation in the mainstream educational system.

The approaches our field has explored in educating persons with significant disabilities have also provided an opportunity for parents and educators to better understand learning and how to support it. Through the developmental approach, we learned that all students can learn. Through the more functional and remedial approaches, we learned the importance of relevance in learning and the importance of context. Community-based approaches taught us about motivation and the readiness of communities to accept and support persons with significant disabilities. The work of Marc Gold and others in task analysis and feedback to learners as well as others who focused on prompting and correcting strategies gave us a strong instructional technology.

Most of the instructional technology however, was developed in separate instructional settings. After all, that was where students were. As students began to participate more and more in integrated and inclusive school and community settings, many of these strategies appear to have dropped by the wayside. It may be that because of the sometimes intrusive nature of the strategies, some were difficult to incorporate in integrated settings. For more information, see Billingsley and Kelley (1994), regarding the acceptability of instructional practices in general education settings. Certainly, some of the behavioral interventions more common to segregated settings fit into this mold. However, many of the powerful instructional practices and interventions that could have been used have also been left behind. There may be a number of reasons for this, including their applicability in general education classrooms; however, in our view, this is a mistake and not necessary.

When we examine those strongly held, and in many cases, empirically validated approaches to supporting the learning of students with cognitive, communicative, vision, hearing, physical and social disabilities, there are many things to agree on. For example, it *is* important to understand the basis of the impairment and the implications for learning. There is a critical need for direct instruction and for the teaching of compensatory skills. Context is important in learning, and students need to have the opportunity to demonstrate skills in context. The family must help to define what is critical in the student's life and how skills will be used. Finally, continually evaluating our instructional and support strategies allows for needed changes so that students are more successful. We have come a long way in understanding that the power of instruction is what makes the difference, not the disability type or degree. Our challenge is to ensure that these approaches are available and incorporated in the inclusive classroom.

How does a teacher or, better yet, a teaching team go about building a truly individualized instructional program for a student with significant learning problems? How does such an IEP team incorporate all the most relevant information available, determine what other information is critical, and design a program that builds critical skills applicable today, allows for the student to continue to learn and associate with his peers, and ensures continued progress? How would *you* go about it?

If you were to ask a room filled with educators and families to forget current structures and practices and just step back for a moment to identify what makes the most sense in deciding what to teach and how to help a student learn, we believe you'd find pretty widespread agreement about certain things. We'd get all the information we could about the disability and what it means for the student. We'd find a way for getting other information regarding questions that were nagging us about this student. We'd talk to people who know the student best, family members, former teachers, friends, the student herself. We'd examine the potential of the environments in which the student is involved in terms of opportunities for learning. We'd try to ensure that we spent our time on the most important things. We'd work out a way for support to be provided when the student needed it and let natural support work when it can. We'd find ways for the student to be involved through adaptations and equipment if necessary. We'd continually evaluate how we're doing and always relate it to how well the student was doing in his or her entire life. We'd provide direct instruction in a manner that fits the student's style and provides the student with strategies to use when we aren't there. Stepping back and taking this commonsense approach are exactly what we can do and *must* do in meeting the promise of special education.

AN INDIVIDUAL STUDENT PLANNING PROCESS

Planning for individual students is a dynamic process that involves continually gathering and examining relevant information about how a student is currently participating in home, school, and community settings; her family's hopes, dreams, and expectations as well as her skills in basic communication, motor, social, and cognitive areas. Although federal and state laws require assessment prior to IEP development, in fact, assessment should also occur after the actual IEP meeting, continually providing feedback on the instructional strategies and supports in place.

The individual student planning process outlined in Figure 3.1 details a number of critical steps in the dynamic process. The actual IEP meeting can be held at any time during this process, provided that initial assessments have been completed.

Student Records

There are those who don't want to read records until they get to know a student so they won't be unduly influenced. Others want to know everything about a student so they will be prepared. Student records can provide a good deal of information about the specific

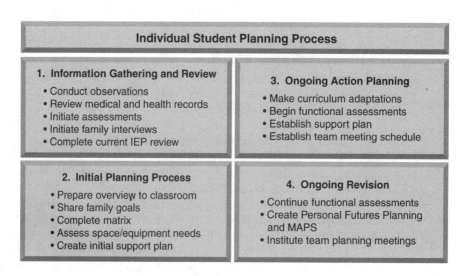

FIGURE 3.1   Individual Student Planning Process

challenges a student has in learning as well as the approaches others have used to facilitate that learning in past years. Relevant medical information may also be helpful in understanding the needs of the student. It is important that teams do not neglect it for pearls of wisdom.

The Parent Interview

One particularly effective method of gaining insight into the needs of a student and family is the parent interview. This ecological assessment process involves a visit to the student's home or other mutually agreed-upon location for a conversation about what is currently happening in his or her life and what the family hopes and expects to happen in the future. The process may take one to two hours and proceeds through four parts: the current daily schedule of the student; the basic communication, motor, social, and cognitive skills the student is demonstrating; identification of future activities and environments, and the parents' summarization of their highest priorities. Many parents and educators have found this process to not only provide a great deal of relevant and useful information but also to establish a sound working relationship between parent and educator. What is critical for educators to remember is that their role is to listen to and understand the perspective of the family.

An Inventory of the School
and Classroom Environments

One of the primary benefits of inclusive education is that students with significant disabilities can access and experience the multitude of (one hopes) interesting and motivating activities and opportunities available in the general education classroom. Not only the classroom teacher brings content and opportunity to the setting, the other twenty-five to thirty students also bring information, ideas, materials, and excitement to the classroom. The support and attention offered by others in the school—teachers, administrators, support staff, parents, students—provide an enormous opportunity for learning experiences. During the initial student planning process, these school and classroom environments must be examined or inventoried for opportunity. With all the interactions occurring throughout the school day between and among staff, parents, and students, investigate all the communication that is available. There are numerous opportunities to develop receptive and expressive communication, to practice the pragmatics of language, to be available to hear new ideas and styles of communicating.

At this early stage in student planning, a collaborative team is beginning to emerge. The special education support teacher and often the parents meet with the general education classroom teacher to gain an insight into the routines, culture, special activities, and approach to teaching and learning in the general education classroom. This is an opportunity to begin to "smooth the fit" between the student and the expectations of the general education classroom. One of the strategies at this point that has proven to be most helpful is the use of a *matrix process* to reference specific IEP objectives and other student needs with the routine of the classroom. IEP objectives are listed along one axis, and opportunities are listed along the other. The team brainstorms ideas for ways in which IEP objectives may be addressed at each opportunity (subjects, activities). Sharing the IEP objectives with the general education teacher is critical, and doing it in a way that allows for discussion of how those IEP objectives can be addressed throughout the school day across subject areas, activities, and instructional groupings allows for creativity. It also may serve to reduce any stress felt by team members. The matrix process is discussed in more detail later in this chapter.

During this initial planning team meeting to inventory the school and classroom, the insights generated through the parent interview can also be shared with the general education teacher. This can offer some direction to the classroom teacher regarding what families (and special educators) hope to accomplish during the school year and over the course of the next few years. Hearing what families hope and dream for their child brings the planning process down to the level of real life.

For many children, specialized equipment is critical to their success. In many of our already overcrowded classrooms, finding space for some of this equipment is a major problem. Wheelchairs and walkers can take up a good deal of space or require even more space when they begin to move around in the room. This is an important issue. Where will students be located so that mobility is not impeded? How will students using special equipment or other assistive technology gain access to classroom materials and sub-environments? This problem arose recently in planning for a student with vision and hearing impairments at junior high. If he was going to be moving from classroom to classroom, how could he always have access to his closed-circuit TV and computer?

Finally, the *school and classroom inventory* meeting process also allows the team to establish an initial support plan for the student. One of the first questions general education teachers have is, Who is going to support this student in the classroom? Support plans at this point are best guesses and will probably change over the course of the year. It is critical to identify when support is likely to be needed and when it is not. It is also important to discuss other means of supporting students without using paid support. Inclusive education does not mean that every student has an instructional assistant. Building the natural supports in a classroom is important. Student groupings, peer support systems, and the development of independent tasks that the student can accomplish are strategies that supplement paid support.

Developing an Action Plan for Success

Only so much can be accomplished before a student starts a new classroom program. It is critical to understand that the planning and assessment processes are continual. During the matrixing process, ideas for adaptations and modifications are shared and planned for, and this process allows the team to get started. However, continued work is necessary as the demands of the classroom change and increase and as the student learns and becomes more skillful.

Often, when students are participating in general education classrooms without any undue problems, teams may become complacent (after all, she's getting along nicely) and neglect the critical next step: beginning the process of on-going functional assessment. The functional assessment process is a means of examining the student's participation and progress in activities. It is based upon the task and activity analyses that have proven to be of great value over the years and incorporates the discrepancy analysis process to (a) identify the demands of the activity, (b) describe the student's abilities in the activity, (c) generate potential adaptations for steps in the activity that would facilitate active participation now, and (d) select targets for instruction. The *functional assessment* process allows the team, including related services staff, to examine student participation in context. It demands that we look at motor, communicative, cognitive, social, and activity performance skills in an integrated manner and plan as a transdisciplinary team.

Many educators, already stretched, wonder when functional assessments can be accomplished and may neglect them in favor of more direct instruction. However, it is critical for us to step back periodically to examine the effect of what we are doing. Is our instructional approach working? Are we providing less support for learners as they progress? Can we increase the demands of the activity? Would a different adaptation be more effective or efficient? It is wise to schedule periodic reassessments for this reason and to protect this time as being equally necessary as direct instruction.

As we learn more about how the student learns and performs in the general education setting, and as we are able to incorporate natural classroom supports (those available to all students—other students, volunteers, classroom staff), we can get a better idea about what additional support is necessary for the individual with special needs. At this point, we can revise our *support plan* to both provide critical levels of support necessary for learning and to avoid interfering in the natural supports we want to become more common in the student's program.

The last activity in this portion of the planning process is to establish a team meeting schedule. Many times, teams do not plan to meet unless there is a problem. Such an approach will probably guarantee that there will be a problem. Periodic and regularly scheduled planning meetings are a must. They allow for the team to anticipate issues that will need resolution; they provide a routine opportunity for feedback among staff; they encourage the sharing of information and skills, and they provide a chance to celebrate successes.

Measuring the Impact of the Instructional Program

If you don't know where you're going, it doesn't much matter which direction you take. Not only do effective planning teams constantly examine their strategies and evaluate student progress, they also reassess their vision for the future. The expectations expressed and the objectives established initially will change as the student changes and grows and as conditions change. New opportunities are always opening. Life is dynamic. At the same time, there may be changes for the worse in the student due to health issues. It is critical that teams have a process for continually setting a vision and a plan. Personal futures planning and the McGill Action Planning System (MAPS) (Falvey, Forest, Pierpont, & Rosenberg, 1994) are strategies some teams use to set the course and build support. They involve the people most important to the student, including friends and relatives, to ensure that our efforts strengthen rather than weaken natural community support.

THE INDIVIDUAL STUDENT PLANNING PROCESS IN ACTION

Gathering Information

Let's examine the planning process just described in terms of the four students with special needs that we have already discussed. Amanda and Melissa attend Emerson Middle School. Amanda has been a member of general education classrooms since preschool and has had a successful experience in the view of both parents and school staff. She has multiple motor, communication, and cognitive disabilities. This is her first year at the middle school, and because the academic demands are increasing, there is some concern among staff about how she will do at this level.

Melissa is a natural leader and does very well in group activities, performing and applying knowledge in practical situations. However, Melissa has had difficulty in dealing with written information, attending to instruction for long periods, and in performing on examinations.

Joey attends a multiage class at Vineyard Elementary School. He has been diagnosed as having autism and communicates primarily through sign language and communication books. Joey shows a particular interest in geography and will often study and draw maps for long periods of time. He is beginning to speak more and to demonstrate some reading skills as well as writing.

Raymond is a fifteen-year-old student at Monroe High School, a restructured school. He is fairly independent and is in an inclusive program for the first time this year. Raymond has a history of problem behavior and a reputation as being very disruptive and aggressive toward staff. He has a significant hearing loss and poor expressive communication skills.

How are the needs of these four students with very different educational abilities accommodated along with those of their peers at Emerson, Vineyard, and Monroe? You'll recall that Emerson has organized its seventh and eighth grades into four houses, allowing for a number of innovative educational approaches to be incorporated, including block scheduling, team teaching, active, experiential learning, and additional support for all students within an inclusive educational model. Vineyard has a multiage, heterogeneous class for first through third grade students. The school uses activity-based, developmentally appropriate practices combined with a focus on multiple intelligences. Monroe has restructured to incorporate three teaching teams, which include special education teachers as team teaching members for all students. The school utilizes block scheduling for Math, Science, and Humanities and is part of the Coalition of Essential Schools (Sizer, 1992). Multiple intelligences is also an integral part of this school (cf. Gardner, 1985).

For most students at Emerson, Vineyard, and Monroe, these collaborative, creative practices provide a fertile ground for learning and will be sufficient to meet their needs. These learning structures also offer a multitude of opportunities for our four students to demonstrate their interests and skills and to receive the type and amount of support necessary. However, it is critical to *also* use the specialized instructional practices and supports that have proven successful over the years for students with learning challenges.

Student Records

From the individual student planning process depicted in Figure 3.1, we can see that the first step in designing these specialized instructional practices and supports is to gather information from a number of sources. The performance of students around different people and environments will vary, and these variations are a source of useful information. Past and current IEPs and assessments will provide information about how learning was approached and what kind of progress occurred. They may answer a number of questions about how best to support a particular student's learning. What types of objectives have been set for this student and which of these were successfully achieved? Have objectives been set repeatedly with no positive results? Has the student had the opportunities that would support optimum learning? Have appropriate supports and services been provided? What do the assessments tell us? Is there relevant information about learning style? Are specific learning challenges identified and strategies suggested for remediation or accommodation?

From an examination of Amanda's records, we can see that her communication objectives did not seem to be changing in terms of outcomes (signs needs) and that there was no consistent communication system identified. Sign language, object systems, picture systems with photographs and line drawings, electronic communication devices with one word, one phrase, or with up to six words or phrases were noted on past IEPs. Assessments noted a strong interest in music, and yet none of the objectives or support services addressed music as an approach.

An examination of Melissa's IEPs noted services from the resource specialist for one period a day and objectives that targeted improvement in reading and writing skills. Information on the amount and type of services and even written objectives such as these are not particularly helpful in deciding how to support Melissa's learning. Her assessments, however, noted severe discrepancies in her short-term visual memory skills. They also pointed out her real strength in auditory skills. One question that emerges regards the instructional approach her teachers are using to build short-term visual memory. Are the educational staff using the auditory channel and providing ample opportunity for Melissa to demonstrate her knowledge and application of knowledge in ways that incorporate her auditory strengths?

Joey's records show that he has been involved in a private preschool with special education support since the age of three. His talents in drawing and geography are documented although his parents, who see this as a special talent to be capitalized on, and school psychologists who see his interest as perseverative, disagree on the value. Past IEPs show progress in communication, reading, and writing skills, which his parents and preschool teacher attribute to the models from his peers in preschool.

Raymond's history in school is clearly documented in his records and seems to focus primarily on his behavior, which appears to have resulted in his placement in special schools and classrooms. His access to integrated school and community environments and activities has been extremely limited, and it is difficult to tell if he could have made more academic progress in other settings. Raymond's hearing loss is significant, and there is no record of the use of frequency modulation (FM) systems or hearing aids.

Medical information may also be critical. Of course, when students have specialized health care needs, medical protocol must specify how these specialized health care services are provided. More typically, there are medical considerations to understand and make provisions for.

Amanda has a seizure disorder that requires antiseizure medication. Besides the obvious need to know how to cope with possible seizures at school, it will be important to know how seizures may affect her learning, behavior, motivation, interactions, and energy level. Many students experience irritability prior to or following a seizure. In addition, what potential or actual side effects does her medication have?

Melissa has no obvious medical problems at present; however, her records note that at one time her parents tried medication for hyperactivity but stopped because they felt Melissa had "lost her spark."

Joey's health has always been very good. He has very definite food preferences, at one point refusing to eat anything but chicken and macaroni. He has been a bit more flexible in the past two years.

Raymond's records show good health although he has had occasions of self-injurious behavior in the past, hitting his ears and scratching his hands. He is more likely to hit others now.

Observation

There is no substitute for observation. Meeting students before beginning to serve them can be enormously helpful, particularly if we meet the individual on their own ground. Seeing the abilities and challenges of students when they are with friends and others provides a much more interesting and useful picture of a person than what is on paper. Talking to people who know the student and have worked with him or her may set up expectations, unless we receive that information from the perspective of and opinion of individuals. Making time for observations and talking to people can be difficult. Schools that believe observation is important will make the time. In some schools we have worked with, principals or related services staff have covered for classroom teachers to allow them free time for observations and discussion. Observations may be scheduled for teacher prep periods or when students are at special events. Special education inclusion support staff may cover for classroom teachers as they observe.

One of the teachers from Amanda's house at Emerson visited her in her sixth-grade classroom before she left that campus. Her inclusion support teacher also supported her in elementary school and is familiar with her learning style and skills.

Staff at Emerson did not have the opportunity to observe Melissa; however, they reviewed her portfolio of work from elementary school.

Mr. Vasquez worked with Joey during the previous year, and this arrangement has given him an enormous advantage in understanding his learning style and communication skills. For many students and teachers, the first month is a time for getting to know one another. Mr. Vasquez and Joey can get right back to work. Raymond's new teaching team did not have the opportunity to meet him prior to the new school year. His family was not sure he would be allowed to attend Monroe until just before school started; however, the special education inclusion teacher had the chance to see Raymond during the school year. This observation and a talk with his former special education teacher were very helpful, particularly in helping her understand the situations that could lead to aggressive and disruptive behaviors.

Parent Interviews

Finally, we can't overlook the importance of hearing directly from those who have the most information and have the greatest stake in the success or failure of our educational and support services—the student and their family. Some time ago, when the son of one of the authors was about to start preschool, the preschool teacher set an appointment to meet at home to talk about this child. The teacher wanted to know who this child was from our point of view. What were his strengths? What did he like and what did he have trouble with? How did he learn things? This made his parents feel a whole lot better about the people he was going to be with for a lot of the day. The fact that his preschool teacher came to his home demonstrated that she wanted to know the real child. Parent interviews are not new ideas, but they are often overlooked in designing educational programs for students with special needs. Many educators view the IEP as the time for parent input. However, this time with parents can be the most important first step we can take.

There are a couple of keys to family interviews. First, the role of the educator is to gain the perspective of the family and the student, not to communicate our ideas or what we want them to do. As Stephen Covey advises us, "Seek first to understand, then to be understood" (1989). First, we listen. Her family sees Amanda as important to the community because of the gifts she brings. They are not naive about her multiple disabilities or about the challenges of finding ways to include her in all aspects of community life, but they are interested and motivated in working to find those ways. They speak about involvement in dance, music, drama, and community recreation. They want her to go to friends' homes as friends come to hers; they expect her to take on some home and school responsibilities, and they want her to always be expected to participate in the academic activities of her classmates. The interview process allows us to discuss these expectations and hopes and dreams and to begin to collaborate right from the start as we begin to define the outcomes that make sense to the people who are most important in the life of the student.

Conducting the Parent Interview.   Interviews with families should be held at their home unless parents prefer another location. They involve discussions of the following subjects:

1. The schedule of the student for the complete day, including what he or she is involved in and how well he or she is able to participate
2. Basic communication, motor, cognitive, and social information as well as any medical or health issues that are important
3. Hopes and dreams in terms of environments and activities for the next two to three years
4. A summary of priority areas from the family's perspective

The interview begins with the family describing all the typical routines of their child's day from the time the child wakes up until bedtime. The families can talk about the capabilities they see and the challenges the children face in real life. It allows us, as educators, to understand who this student really is and what is important to focus on. It allows us to see the strengths of the family (Wickler, Wasow, & Hatfield, 1983) and to build on those. You'll notice that Amanda's family spoke about how she helps get dressed and how they have her choose clothing for each day (Figure 3.2). They also want her to be able to have communication materials readily available at all times, and they want her to begin pushing her wheelchair on her own. The impact of her seizures and the medication she is taking to control them is evident.

The interview also provides a way for families to share information about how their child communicates, how they interact, the behaviors that are a problem, and how they handle them. This part of the interview offers a rich source of information and also allows us to acknowledge the abilities of a child and praise the way the family has supported their child's learning. Amanda enjoys a wide variety of things, including wrestling, music, bike rides, candles, and smoke. When she doesn't like an activity, she bites her hand, yawns, or sucks on her hand. We also get a sense of the other kids in her life and what she does with them outside of school. Her parents have described Amanda in terms of her strengths—she perseveres; she's easy to be around; she's curious, expressive, loving, surprising. It's so important to remember that we all need to see the good things in children and not simply view our students by their disabilities.

The third part of the interview process asks families to dream about things they want to see their child doing in the next two or three years across the home, school, community, recreation, and vocation domains. This envisioning process gives us an image to

FIGURE 3.2   Form for Family Interview

FAMILY INTERVIEW

Interview date 8/14/00

Student Amanda

Birthdate 3/24/86

Address _____

_____

Phone (Home) _____   Phone (Work) _____

Directions to place of interview Amanda's home—80 E. to Russell Blvd. Go left on 8th St.;

right on Alta Dr. (3917 Alta Dr.)

Parent or care provider's name Joe and Sharon

Other individuals to contact:

   Name Shawna, Megan, Rebecca, Steven—friends; Alice and Bill—grandparents

   Phone _____

   Relation _____

   Permission granted _____

   Best time and day for contact _____

   Phone _____

   Best time and day(s) available for planning meetings Wednesday, 2–5:00

Local environments: Park across the street; school three blocks away; convenience store

two blocks away

Medical considerations: Recent onset of atonic seizures; side effects of medications—

ataxia and lethargy

Equipment considerations: Uses wheelchair, gait training walker, stander—soon to be

acquired

Additional service providers (Regional Center, CCS, etc.): Alta California Regional Center;

Kaiser physical therapy (temp.); occupational therapy (Elks).

Adapted from *Teaching That Works: The Individualized Critical Skills Model,* by K. T. Holowach, 1989, Sacramento, CA: Resources in Special Education.

(continued)

FIGURE 3.2 CONTINUED

WEEKDAY SCHEDULE

Student <u>Amanda</u>

List information from the time the student gets up and goes to school until the time he or she arrives home from school and goes to bed.

Morning Routine

STUDENT PARTICIPATION		AREA TO TARGET	FAMILY	STUDENT
7:45	Getting up Tries to get up, needs lots of assistance from parents. Very unstable in the a.m. Parents get her to the bathroom quickly (dry all night!) Happy in the a.m. Medication may be affecting her waking up on her own. Must watch very closely due to the seizures.	Learn intervention method to inhibit onset of seizures.	X	
8:00	Getting dressed Amanda chooses from outfits held up. She looks and reaches for one. Mom talks about clothing and Amanda helps by putting her hands/arms up to help dress. Not able to help with pants—seems weaker with the medications, less muscle tone.	Increase Amanda's participation in putting clothing on.		X
8:30	(Nonschool day—summer) Flexibility/movement Joe works with Amanda on the rug—stretching, rolling, crawling. He feels the medications have affected her disposition—she tolerates things now, rather than enjoying them as before.	Teach school personnel how to do exercise routine.	X	
	Eating breakfast Parents help her walk—different amount of help each day. Sits in the stroller to eat—this is a concern due to the slant of the seat. Regular chairs don't have sides. Appetite in the a.m. is good. She takes medications independently and eats independently (left hand). Sometimes puts cup down in plate or on side. Uses picture communication board—selects from choices. Reaches for the board when it is not available. Beginning to show some frustration when she can't have her choice.	Make communication board readily available at all times.	X	
8:30	To school Pushed to school in wheelchair—friends walk with her. Enjoys this trip, friends talk with her.	Pushing own chair.	X	
9:00	(Nonschool day) Activities with Marietta Playing piano, using communication board—trying to isolate finger, working on scales. Hand over hand, sometimes from wrist. Amanda enjoys this. Exercises on floor (physical therapy), doesn't seem to enjoy this.	Consider having her change channels, turn up sound.	X	
		Work on facilitated communication.	X	

FIGURE 3.2   CONTINUED

Morning Routine

STUDENT PARTICIPATION	AREA TO TARGET	FAMILY	STUDENT
10:00 (Nonschool day—summer) Children's Day Park Three days a week. Amanda is dropped off at the recreation program. Amanda seems to enjoy this. Suggest talking to Kristin (staff person there).	Take pictures of choices at park. Learn to use communication board.	X	
Child Development Center Two days a week. Doing OK—sometimes too many kids there. Amanda gets no extra help; there may be some resentment about this. She sometimes comes home wet.	Talk to staff about Amanda's day.	X	

Afterschool Routine

STUDENT PARTICIPATION	AREA TO TARGET	FAMILY	STUDENT
1:00 (Nonschool day—summer) Coming home and lunch Amanda is a bit more groggy lately. She eats a light lunch. Sharon hands Amanda dishes and wheels her to the table where Amanda puts them down. She wants to sing during the lunch. Takes medications at lunch.			
1:30 (Nonschool day) To bathroom Amanda is often wet—she shows it on her face. Mom can tell her to hold it sometimes. Seizures are making it difficult. Parents help her wash her hands. Tries to grab the towel to dry hands. Afraid to let her near sink alone due to seizures. Not turning on faucet lately.	Indicating need to go to the bathroom.	X	
3:00 Nap Not able to get herself into bed lately. Wants mom to stay and sing—initiates this by starting to hum.	Getting into bed by herself.	X	
4:30 Waking up and play Someone needs to wake her up—she's generally happy and refreshed. Parents help her out of bed. Will eventually sit up and try to get out of bed. Brady (dog) comes in and nuzzles her. Goes to bathroom (usually dry).	Can we get a teenager to supervise kids instead of parents?	X	
	Friends come over to play—read to her, play house, store, restaurant, Barbie. Plays the customer. Uses communication board with friends. Kids report to Sharon what Amanda is doing. Sometimes swimming in the backyard or bike ride with the family. Amanda loves these things. Kids are great at finding ways for her to participate.	Use communication board to choose who she wants to play with.	X	

(continued)

FIGURE 3.2 CONTINUED

Afterschool Routine

STUDENT PARTICIPATION	AREA TO TARGET	FAMILY	STUDENT
6:00 Swimming lessons—summer Dropped off, program provides instructors. Friends go to watch. Not sure how she feels about it. 7:30 Dinner Very hungry; parents have her help, hold things, use communication board to choose. Family talks about her day with her.	Communication board for choices, conversation	X	

Evening Routine

STUDENT PARTICIPATION	AREA TO TARGET	FAMILY	STUDENT
8:00 Family time Amanda likes to play with her dog, listen to music, watch a video, go to the park across the street, or go out with her family. Sharon and Joe work on her use of the communication board and the computer. Friends are often over. She remains engaged with them and really enjoys their visits.	Play independently for longer stretches of time.	X	
9:00 To bed Helped to the bathroom, assisted to wash her face and hands and to brush her teeth. Lots of hand over hand support. Helps remove some of her clothing when parents start. Able to raise arms to put on pajamas. Helped into bed, likes a song. No problems sleeping.	How can we work on this now that her stability is so poor?	X	

Weekend Routine

STUDENT PARTICIPATION	AREA TO TARGET	FAMILY	STUDENT
Activities Goes shopping with her family, friends. Amanda in wheelchair. Parents and friends have her reach and hold items, make choices. Walks with someone at her side. Goes to family cabin at the lake. Out with other kids to park, events.	Find teenager to accompany Amanda and friends instead of only her parents.	X	
	Needs to visit other kids in their homes instead of only in her own home.	X	

FIGURE 3.2 CONTINUED

BEHAVIORAL AND BASIC SKILLS INFORMATION

Student <u>Amanda</u>

ACTIVITIES STUDENT LIKES TO DO OR DOES NOT LIKE TO DO

Likes: music, singing, TV, rides in car, bike rides, slapstick, animated rhymes, sings songs, piano scales, watching bubbles, candles, smoke.

Doesn't like: taking clothes off, going to the bathroom.

HOW DOES SHE OR HE LET YOU KNOW? *(IF PARENT IS PROVIDING INFORMATION)*

Smiles, kicking feet, vocalizing.

Bites her hand, disinterest (sucks on hand, yawns).

INTERACTION STUDENT ENJOYS OR DOES NOT ENJOY

Wrestling, affection, talking to her dramatically, highs and lows of voice.

Enjoys most interaction.

HOW DOES SHE OR HE LET YOU KNOW?

Same as above.

TELL ME ABOUT FRIENDSHIPS OR RELATIONSHIPS. WHAT ARE SOME OF THE THINGS YOUR CHILD DOES WITH FRIENDS?

Friends over all the time—they play with her and advocate for her in and out of school. They swim together, bike, go to the store and other places. This has been a real joy for her family. Kids are very creative and stand up for Amanda.

WHAT ARE YOUR DREAMS FOR YOUR SON OR DAUGHTER?

Greater independence; communication system that goes beyond "needs"; more ways to contribute; achievement; unique role in life; controlled seizures; happy; solid support group.

IS THERE ANY ADDITIONAL INFORMATION ABOUT YOUR SON OR DAUGHTER THAT WE HAVEN'T TALKED ABOUT?

Communication (receptive/expressive):
This is critical! We all need to use her system consistently. We should use it receptively, too. Facilitated communication should be used—trying it at home now.

Mobility:
Stay close to Amanda right now. When seizures are controlled, we'll get back to the walking.

Toileting:
Watch her face, ask her during the day if she needs to go. Singing is a real reward.

Foods/drinks she or he likes or dislikes:
Doesn't like sour juices or things too hot. She seems more finicky now. Doesn't like peanut butter and jelly; swallowing is more difficult now. Sometimes stops and holds food in her mouth; needs it taken out (since medication).

ARE THERE ANY BEHAVIORS OF CONCERN?

Appears more passive; less zest for life; less energy, excitement. Parents are certain this is due to medication side effects. Sometimes she hugs people she doesn't know. Mom doesn't like this. Drooling and putting things in her mouth are a problem.

(continued)

FIGURE 3.2 CONTINUED

BEHAVIORAL AND BASIC SKILLS INFORMATION

HOW DO YOU DEAL WITH PROBLEM BEHAVIORS?

Hugging: Mom intervenes, encourages her to take their hand. Drooling or hands in mouth: Tell her to take it out, "show me nice hands"; sometimes we don't stop her.

DESCRIBE THE BEST WAY FOR YOUR CHILD TO LEARN A NEW SKILL.

Hand over hand, repetition, trial after trial. Careful selection of target skills. We need to find a way for her to get the repetition and drill she needs in an inclusive setting. Parents would like to see this happen a couple of times a day. (15 minutes?)

DESCRIBE YOUR CHILD'S OPPORTUNITIES FOR DECISION OR CHOICE-MAKING.

Meals; choice of activities; choice of clothing; choice of people to see; places to go; tapes to listen to (friends have taped their singing and have a picture of them on the cassette case.)

LIST SOME OF YOUR CHILD'S STRENGTHS.

Perseveres; pleasant, easy to be around; draws people to her; charismatic; attractive; curious; healthy; likes to learn; expressive; loving; surprising.

HOW DOES YOUR CHILD PROBLEM SOLVE? MAKE DECISIONS?

She's accepting of most situations. She may try to get away and move to something else—mobility is a real problem now. It's hard for her parents not to do everything for her now. If she's upset, she'll scream, cry, or vocalize.

MEDICAL

Medications used Lamictal 100 mg.

When 2 × day (Breakfast, dinner)

Physician Dr. Morehead

Allergies None

Side effects of medication Reduced muscle tone; lethargy; less alert; nausea; more sleep.

Impact on learning Sometimes falls asleep in class; not as mobile.

Other

What thing that we haven't talked about yet are important to you or other family members?

FIGURE 3.2   CONTINUED

	STUDENT	PARENT
How do you feel about the school program?	Amanda smiles and shows enthusiasm when arriving at school.	Great. Her teachers are doing a wonderful job, and her friends are a real plus.
Types of support you would like?		Wish she didn't need so much physical support now. Administrative support. Knowing that her principal and whole staff understand supported education.
What are your preferences for: Extracurricular activities? Classes or subjects Activities Clubs Jobs	Likes music.	Need more older students planning for her. Could use more opportunities for Drama and Music. More physical games, after-school clubs. More responsibilities, class jobs.

	PARENT	
How would you like to be involved in the school?	Would do Music with children—once per week. Help out in class once per week. Sports events.	
What is the best way for us to communicate?	Notebook; write each day—anything notable to talk about. Keep track of progress, problems, seizures.	
What are some of the benefits you see as a result of the school program?	Friendships, network of support. Learning to communicate. Attention, listening, focusing on things.	

(continued)

FIGURE 3.2 CONTINUED

FAMILY PREFERENCE FOR ACTIVITIES AND ENVIRONMENTS

Student Amanda   Date 8/14/00

1. List the preferred activities (not basic skills) and environments for one, two, or three years from now in each of the following areas.
   Interviewer: Use your information from community inventory file and student's immediate neighborhood inventory to assist parents and care providers.
2. After completing the list, note if it is a student or family preference for each activity.

DOMESTIC	S F PREF.	RECREATION/LEISURE	S F PREF.	SCHOOL	S F PREF.	COMMUNITY	S F PREF.	VOCATIONAL	S F PREF.
Open drawers to pick own clothing.	F	Turn on TV; look at easy books independently.	F	P.E. activities out of chair.	F	Take community recreation classes; gymnastics, horseback riding.	F	Vacuum; do dishes.	F
Get something to eat by herself.	F/S	Play games on the computer.	F	Learn classroom routines.	F	Be part of something musical; weekly music or drama club.	F	Fold her own handkerchiefs.	F
Cook a simple meal. Waffles? Hot dogs?	F	Ride a large trike; do some kind of dance movement.	F	Engage in typical academic activities.	F	Go to a friend's home more often without parents.	F/S	Walk Brady, the dog.	F
Open gifts at her parties; cut her cake.	F	Play a short song on the piano.	F	Daily computer activities.	F	Be in Girl Scouts or church group.	F	Make her bed.	F
				Have kids involved in planning for her.		Attend local musicals with friends.	F		F/S

FIGURE 3.2 CONTINUED

INITIAL SUMMARY OF BASIC SKILLS AND CRITICAL ACTIVITIES

Student Amanda   Date 8/14/00

Category	Priority 1, 2, 3, 4	HIGH-PREFERENCE ACTIVITIES	USE COMMUNICATION BOOK	MAKE CHOICES	INDEPENDENT PLAY	INHIBIT SEIZURES	FACILITATE COMMUNICATION	GET BODY MOVING	INDICATE NEED FOR BATHROOM	REDUCE HANDS IN MOUTH	USE DISCRIMINATION IN GREETING BEHAVIOR	RECOGNIZE LETTERS AND WORDS	RECEPTIVELY LABEL OBJECTS
DOMESTIC	3	Open drawers and choose clothing	X	X				X					X
DOMESTIC	1	Get something to eat—independently		X				X		X			
DOMESTIC	2	Cook simple meal	X	X						X			X
DOMESTIC	4	Open gifts and cut cake	X					X			X		
REC./LEISURE	4	Turn on TV and look at books	X	X	X							X	X
REC./LEISURE	1	Computer games	X	X	X		X			X		X	X
REC./LEISURE	3	Large trike and participate in dance	X	X	X		X		X	X	X		
REC./LEISURE	2	Piano song	X		X					X			
SCHOOL	4	P.E. activities in chair		X				X		X			
SCHOOL	1	Learn class routines	X	X	X		X	X	X	X	X	X	X
SCHOOL	3	Daily computer activity	X	X	X		X			X		X	X
SCHOOL	2	Engage in academic activities	X	X			X	X		X		X	X
COMMUNITY	3	Community recreation	X	X				X		X	X		
COMMUNITY	2	Musical and drama	X	X	X		X	X	X	X	X		
COMMUNITY	1	Friends' homes without parents	X	X	X			X	X		X		
COMMUNITY	4	Girl Scouts and church group	X	X	X			X	X		X		
VOCATIONAL	3	Vacuum and do dishes	X					X		X			
VOCATIONAL	4	Fold own handkerchiefs	X					X		X			
VOCATIONAL	1	Make her bed	X					X		X			
VOCATIONAL	2	Walk Brady	X	X				X		X	X		

guide our efforts, a way to really evaluate whether what we're doing is having an impact of the quality of life of this individual. Amanda's family hopes for greater independence in her self-help skills, dressing, preparing food for herself, opening her own gifts. They want her to be involved in active movement on a large trike and in dance as well as with computers, television, and books. In school, they want her to engage in typical academics, learning classroom routines and doing physical activities out of her chair. They would like other students to be involved in planning for her. Their expectations and dreams for her in recreation concern involvement in the community with friends and in organized groups for kids her age. They want her to be involved in household chores. As you look at these dreams and expectations, you can see a rich, interesting, and engaging life—a life we can keep in mind as we organize our services and make our decisions about how to go about the educational process. Each of us participates to varying degrees in activities. We go from being intensely active to passive observers of the actions of others (spectator sports). Our challenge is to find ways to increase Amanda's participation and provide the supports to allow that participation.

Finally, the interview process ends with a summary of what was discussed. Rather than simply review everything that seemed important, it helps to organize the material in an informative way. The activities identified are listed on the vertical axis, and the basic communication, social, cognitive, and motor needs discussed are listed on the horizontal axis. The educator and the family discuss how basic skills can be addressed and taught within those activities in a natural and relevant way. For example, you'll notice that the basic skill of using a communication board is addressed in almost every activity for Amanda, so her family can see that direct instruction in communication will be provided throughout the day, not simply for a twenty-minute "communication" time. Similarly, choices will be stressed throughout the day in many activities. As this information is being summarized, both the family and educator should brainstorm ways for this to occur. One of the habits of highly effective people is to "begin with the end in mind" (Covey, 1989). Creating a vision with a family can be an exciting and rewarding venture. It energizes us.

The interview process as described here is comprehensive and examines skills in detail. It is obvious that this information is critical in planning for Amanda. The same process can provide extensive information for designing a relevant instructional program for Joey and Raymond, and will also assist in building a collaborative relationship between their parents and the educational staff.

The amount of detail needed in developing an instructional support plan for Melissa is not nearly as great, but the insights of Melissa's family are important, and the interview provided could be used as a guide. It might be more helpful to simply schedule a time to meet to discuss the family's (and Melissa's) perspective on her strengths and problems, and their hopes and dreams for Melissa. One important question for Melissa (and her family) is, "What can we do to help you be more successful at school?"

A second process, McGill Action Planning System (Falvey et al., 1994), is also an excellent way to establish a plan for a student by including the people most important in her life in a structured planning process. MAPS and personal futures planning will be discussed with other social supports and planning strategies in Chapter 5.

The Initial Planning Process

The information gained through review of records, initial observations, and the family interview gives us a good foundation for an educational program and support services. We can now see where we've come from and the special medical considerations we need to take into account and formulate a vision of the future. Now we need to begin defining the activities each of us will use to support learning.

One of the keys to successful inclusive education is collaboration among general and special educators and the family, preferably through the work of an individual student planning team. Each member of the team has an important role, defined through collaborative planning. Key members of a core individual student planning team are

1. The inclusive education support teacher (special education teacher)
2. The collaborating general education teacher (In elementary grades, this will be the classroom teacher, and in secondary school, this includes all the student's general education teachers.)
3. Parents
4. Any other key special education support staff

As students become involved with more general education teachers, scheduling meetings can be difficult. When scheduling all members of the team is not possible, the inclusive education support teacher may meet separately with each general education teacher, although this procedure is not as effective and certainly not as efficient. Common preparation periods or meetings before or after school are more common. In schools structured like Emerson, common planning time is built in to allow for collaboration on a regular basis for all.

Planning Team Scheduling Strategies

1. Using common grade level planning time
2. Scheduling planning team meetings during specials (P.E., Music, Art, assemblies, Drama)
3. Scheduling before school
4. Holding planning meetings on one day and hiring a roving substitute to cover for teachers on planning meeting day

The initial individual student planning team meeting is held after the family interview and the person-centered planning process and provides the opportunity for the following

1. Providing general information about the classroom(s)
2. Sharing family goals
3. Determining space and equipment needs
4. Generating ideas for the student's participation in class
5. Establishing an initial support plan

Individual student planning team meetings are structured for efficiency. One of the major complaints teachers have is that there are too many meetings, and they are often a waste of time. We need to respect teachers' (and families') time by refining our meeting skills. When inviting members of the team to the first meeting, the inclusive education support teacher should set a time limit and establish an agenda. The time limit and the agenda may be renegotiated; however, that is up to the team.

Amanda's team met during their regular house planning time, and Amanda's family was invited to be part of the meeting (Figure 3.3). Her house team began by sharing their program, including the way block scheduling worked, the mini-courses available, the types of projects they would structure during the year, and their own thoughts about how children learn. The teachers made a point of expressing their interest in having Amanda in their classrooms. When Amanda's teachers spoke of the program, they did so with enthusiasm and obvious pride and conveyed the belief to her parents that this would be a good learning environment for any student. The projects and approach to learning were exciting and seemed to offer a great deal of potential for learning.

Amanda's inclusive education support teacher and her family shared the ideas generated during the family interview, giving everyone on the team an idea of what would be meaningful for Amanda and her family and a vision for the future. The team was able to

FIGURE 3.3   Amanda's Team Meeting

TEAM MEETING FOR:

Student: <u>Amanda</u>

Date/time: <u>8/26/00 2:45 p.m.</u>

Location: <u>Room 8</u>

If you are unable to attend, please contact: <u>Cindy F.</u>

Team members:

<u>Barbara M. (mother)</u>

<u>Linda B. (inclusion support teacher)</u>

<u>Louise Z.; Cindy F. (general education house staff)</u>

<u>Tammy A. (instructional assistant); Jerri S. (speech)</u>

Communication backup:

<u>Louise and Cindy will advise Mr. Jones (Math and Science) about plans.</u>

<u>Linda will arrange to meet with Mr. Wright (P.E.)</u>

Agenda for this meeting:	Time limit:
1. Hopes, dreams, program outline	10 minutes
2. Peer interaction	10 minutes
3. Communication systems	15 minutes
4. Seating	5 minutes
Curricular adapting	20 minutes

Agenda for the next meeting:	Next meeting date/time: <u>9/22/00 7:30 a.m.</u>
1. Curriculum update	15 minutes
2. Friendships	15 minutes
3.	
4.	

Roles:

For this meeting	For next meeting
Facilitator <u>Cindy</u>	<u>Louise</u>
Recorder <u>Louise</u>	<u>Linda</u>
Timekeeper <u>Mrs. Monroe</u>	<u>Cindy</u>

FIGURE 3.3   CONTINUED

MEETING NOTES	TO DO:	PERSON(S) RESPONSIBLE	DATE TO BE COMPLETED
1. Amanda's mother shared her hopes for Amanda at junior high school. Skill development in communication, movement, and self-help are key. Also it is important that she enjoy school and have friendships. Amanda needs to have the chance to participate in the same activities most of her classmates participate in.	Keep family apprised of all school activities.	Linda Louise Cindy	Weekly
2. Staff provided an overview to the program at Emerson, noting the block scheduling, mini-courses, and activity orientation. Amanda's family wants to think about which mini-courses to select.	Select two mini-courses for first trimester.	Family	9/2/00
3. The team talked about ways to ensure peer interaction. Decided to meet with students in Amanda's house on how she communicates with the Macaw, signs, and pictures. Students from her circle in sixth grade may be interested in being in a circle at Emerson.	Demonstrate systems at all-house meeting. Invite friends to form circle.	Linda Amanda Friends Linda	9/30/00 9/30/00
4. The Macaw was demonstrated to all team members. Discussion about how to keep it current.	Program changes first thing in a.m. Change at home in p.m.	Linda Mom Louise	ongoing
5. Seating was discussed to ensure that Amanda would have sufficient room.	Seat in group near door.	Louise Cindy	immediate
6. The inclusion support teacher shared a process for adapting curriculum. Initial ideas were generated.	Begin functional assessments.	Linda	9/22/00

share some ideas for building a support system for Amanda among her peers and identified some impediments to that support system, such as overdependence on an instructional assistant. Amanda's Macaw communication system was discussed, and each team member got a chance to see how it operates. Because Amanda uses a wheelchair, team members arranged her seating assignments so that she could easily move into and around the classrooms. Her family expressed the hope that, with controlled seizures, Amanda might be able to use a walker again, and the team talked about where the wheelchair might be placed if that occurred this year.

Amanda's house has organized the school day into a number of blocks including P.E., elective (Beginning Spanish), Math, mini-course (Introduction to Drama), lunch, and Language Arts or Science. The courses naturally have specific expectations in terms of projects, homework, in-class activities, and evaluation. In this first meeting, the team determined how Amanda will participate, specifically how she will work on the critical skills she needs in the context of all classroom activity, projects, and homework and the support necessary to ensure success. A simple matrix can align critical IEP objectives with course work. Amanda's team listed all of her IEP objectives along the vertical axis of a matrix (Table 3.1) and her school subjects and activities along the horizontal axis. Team members began to brainstorm ideas about how she might best work on these critical skills and increase her involvement in the activities. Many of her IEP objectives are communication and choice objectives. During Math, for example, she will work on the following

1. Communicate "yes" that she is ready to begin or end
2. Choose a Math activity from a choice of 2
3. Indicate the need for a break
4. Identify numerals using her Macaw
5. Look at her teachers and peers when interacting
6. Work on Math sorting activities and number correspondence

During Beginning Spanish, the team identified these ways for her to participate

1. Respond to a Spanish greeting with a wave
2. Respond to "what do you want?" in Spanish using sign or the Macaw with an appropriate message
3. Greet peers in Spanish
4. Ask "question of the day" in Spanish to peers
5. Communicate using preprogrammed Spanish phrase on the Macaw during conversation
6. Maintain eye contact when peer or teacher is talking with her

Introduction to Drama gives Amanda the opportunity to work on moving her chair independently as well as using her communication system appropriately and in a timely manner. The team discussed involving Amanda's peers in finding ways to use her abilities in class activities and productions.

This initial discussion about Amanda's involvement in class and ways of addressing her IEP objectives gives team members a good basis for starting the school year knowing that Amanda has skills and that there are many ways she can continue to work on what is critical to her in the context of the activities in each class. Both teachers and parents know there is a plan.

For Melissa, the planning process can be less intensive; however, the same steps we outlined for Amanda are relevant. An initial student planning team meeting allows for the educators on the team to get to know Melissa from her family's perspective and also allows her family to gain a better understanding of the program at Emerson (see Figure 3.4). They can anticipate the types of homework, projects, and evaluations Melissa will have and can offer ideas about how she can be successful. For example, homework has always been difficult for Melissa, and she has just neglected it more and more as the work becomes more complex. Having someone to work with seems to make it easier, but her parents have not been successful in that role. The team discusses ways for her to get additional help through the learning center and through tutorial help. In terms of her specific disabilities in written language, Melissa's team identifies alternative ways for her to demonstrate knowledge for evaluations (Table 3.2). A portfolio approach is suggested, and team members discuss some of the major projects in their classes for the year, brainstorming how Melissa might show her understanding of the concepts.

For example, in her elective, Child Development and Child Safety, Melissa will demonstrate the actions she would take in simulated emergencies rather than rely solely on written exams. For short written exams, Melissa will be allowed to supplement her written answers with oral explanations. In Math, Melissa will continue to participate as a

TABLE 3.1 Amanda's Matrix

Student Amanda

Grade/Teacher 7th

School Emerson J.H.

Date 8/00

SCHOOL SUBJECTS AND ACTIVITIES

IEP GOALS	SCIENCE/TECHNOLOGY	READING/WRITING	ART	ENGLISH/HISTORY	HOME ECONOMICS
Recognize names of peers in class	Identifies who is speaking by pointing to picture Signs "Yes" to question "Is that (name)?"	Chooses partner for reading activity Indicates who is reading using pictures	Same as Science and Technology	Same as Science and Technology	Same as Science and Technology
Demonstrate ability to perform initial job skills in a real job	Passes out materials Gathers materials upon completion of activities	Hands out materials to peers Collects material from groups in class	Cleans up workplace	Same as Science and Technology	Uses spatula and other kitchen utensils Cleans kitchen area Gets out and puts away materials
Respond to adapted curriculum questions using augmentative communication system	Uses Macaw to respond to questions using programmed responses related to lesson	Responds to questions from teacher and peers regarding reading subject using programmed responses	Uses Macaw to describe artwork using programmed responses	Same as Science and Technology	Same as Science and Technology
Follow directions	Takes out materials upon request Gives items in group to partner on request	Takes out materials, puts materials away on request from teacher	Uses markers or paint in requested manner Takes out materials, puts away materials	Same as Science and Technology	Repeats sequence of recipe steps Repeats sequence of large needlework steps
Push self in wheelchair	Pushes self to and from work areas Negotiates around obstacles without help	Moves to desk without assistance	Same as Science and Technology	Same as Science and Technology	Same as Science and Technology

(continued)

TABLE 3.1 CONTINUED

IEP GOALS	MORNING OPENING *SONG/ GREETING	MATH	SPANISH	SIGN LANGUAGE	LANGUAGE ARTS
Use sign language to communicate consistently: yes/ no/ more/eat/drink/ music	Waves to peers Gives high-5 to peers Responds to teacher's questions using sign language Indicates time for music with sign	Indicates desire for continuing work (more) Uses yes to indicate readiness to begin, end.	Responds to Spanish greeting with wave Responds to question in Spanish "What do you want?" with appropriate sign	Responds appropriately to questions from peers Makes requests of adults or peers using sign language	Chooses book to read Signs "Yes" or "More" to indicate desire to continue activity Signs name of book Signs name of peer to work with
Use communication device to communicate wants, needs, answer yes or no	Indicates which song to sing Greets peers with programmed message	Chooses Math activity from choice of 2 Indicates need for break Identifies numeral when shown number of items	Responds with programmed Spanish phrase to questions Greets peers in Spanish Asks "question of the day"		Uses Macaw to respond to teacher's questions Chooses activity in Language Arts from choice of 2
Wait for her turn in games, conversation using communication device	Raises hand to indicate need to communicate Uses Macaw to communicate or request	Responds to teacher's question to ID number using Macaw	Communicates using programmed Spanish phrase in conversation during group work	Waits for speaker to finish before signing response	Waits for teacher's question to be completed before responding with Macaw
Greet friends appropriately with handshake, wave, and eye contact	Looks at peer she is speaking to Uses Macaw to greet peers Raises arm to wave	Looks at teacher when asked question Looks at peer when interacting in groups	Maintains eye contact during conversation in group work	Watches peer or adult sign to completion Greets peer partners	Greets peers in language group Maintains eye contact with peers or adults in groups; conversations
Work independently		Works on Math sorting activity for 20 seconds without prompts			Looks at books independently Works on matching pictures of story covered in class

California Confederation on Inclusive Education, 1996.

FIGURE 3.4   Melissa's Team Meeting

TEAM MEETING FOR:

Student: Melissa

Date/time: 8/27/00 2:30 p.m.

Location: Room 16

If you are unable to attend, please contact: Bill J.

Team members:

Jack S. (father); Norman B.; Steve L.

Ken L.; Sue D. (general education staff)

Bill J. (inclusion support staff)

Communication backup:

Bill will inform Jeanine (learning center coordinator) about using center

---

Agenda for this meeting:	Time limit:
1. Team members vision for the year	15 minutes
2. Evaluating progress	15 minutes
3. Remediation strategies	10 minutes
4. Other	5 minutes

Agenda for the next meeting: Next meeting date and time: 10/2/00 3:15 p.m.

1. Progress update

2. Results of adapting lessons process

3. Other

4.

Roles:

For this meeting	For next meeting
Facilitator Bill	Sue
Recorder Norman	Ken
Timekeeper Steve	Jeanine

(continued)

FIGURE 3.4   CONTINUED

MEETING NOTES	TO DO:	PERSON(S) RESPONSIBLE	DATE TO BE COMPLETED
1. Staff provided an overview to the program focused on the integrated curriculum approach. Melissa's father shared his hopes for Melissa and some of the frustrations she's had with school over the years. Important to find ways for Melissa to demonstrate her skills and knowledge other than by paper and pencil tasks. Also important for her to get direct remedial work on reading and writing. Discussed school learning center and whether Melissa would want to use it.	Introduce Melissa to learning center. Observe in classes to determine best strategies.	Norman Bill	9/15/00 ongoing
2. Evaluations. Team talked about alternate ways to evaluate Melissa's progress. Important to observe first for a while and also to involve Melissa in decisions. Portfolio and student-led conferences?	Complete adapting lessons worksheet.	Bill, Norman, Sue, Ken, Steve	ongoing
3. Direct instruction on strategies for learning. Team discussed SIM (Strategies Intervention Model), particularly DISSECT. Learning center will discuss with Melissa.	Talk with Melissa about strategies.	Learning center staff	9/30/00
4. Frequency of meetings. Team decided to meet once a month. Additional meetings will be set if necessary.	Notes out to all.	Norman	9/3/00

member of groups, working with a partner to make notes as they research or discuss. Through the learning center and tutorial, she will receive help in preparing organizers for her Math work, which allow for her to keep numerals in line as she does Math applications. She will also use the learning center and tutorial period to obtain assistance on her written work and reading for Language Arts or Science.

Accommodations for Melissa are not sufficient for her educational needs, however. They *do* allow for her to continue learning along with her peers in meaningful contexts and to demonstrate her skills and learning style, and this is critical. Her planning team must also address how she will become a better reader and how she will become able to complete written communication in an effective and efficient manner.

The inclusive education support teacher shares strategies for assisting Melissa in developing visual memory skills during educational activities. For example, DISSECT strategies from Strategies Intervention Model (SIM) (Schumaker, Deshler, & Denton, 1984) will be used. DISSECT stands for the following steps: **D**iscover the context; **I**solate the prefix; **S**eparate the suffix; **S**ay the stem; **E**xamine the stem; **C**heck with someone; **T**ry the dictionary. Melissa will learn this strategy during her work in the learning center, and both parents and her classroom teachers will remind her of this strategy as she works in class. For her reading assignments, Melissa will go over an outline of the read-

TABLE 3.2 Adapting Lessons

STUDENT: Melissa   SUBJECT AREA: American Literature (Mr. Howell's class)

LESSON: "The Lottery"

EXPECTED LEARNER OUTCOMES: (Students will be able to…)	PRODUCTS OR DEMONSTRATIONS OF COMPETENCE:
1. Recognize and identify situations of irony.	1. Develop three-page short story in small group with ironic twist.
2. Define and use vocabulary works appropriately.	2. Complete vocabulary quiz on key words.
3. Read story.	3. Use vocabulary works in sentences.
4. Identify how author developed ironic twist.	4. List experiences that were similar in student's life (small group).
5. Identify main or true intent of the story.	5.

ACCOMMODATIONS

INPUT MODIFICATIONS	TIME ALLOWED	SUPPORT STRATEGIES
Read story with Melissa at home before class Story on tape	More time allowed for editing in study skills class	Review vocabulary words prior to class; outside class Word prediction software

DIFFICULTY/AMOUNT	ALTERNATIVE WAYS TO REPRESENT KNOWLEDGE
Dictate story first into tape recorder Writes 1 1/2-page story on computer Dictate sentences to peer; edit on own	Oral vocabulary quiz

TEST ADAPTATIONS	
Spell vocabulary orally for quiz	

Adapted from *Best Practices Workshop*, by J. Bauwens, 1998, Santa Rosa, CA: Sonoma County Special Education Planning Area. Used with permission.

ing material with a peer and a special education support person each day prior to attempting to read the material. This will allow her to more easily read in context without having to read word by word with limited comprehension. The team discussed ideas for finding more motivating reading material for Melissa to practice reading and suggested several magazines for teens.

Taking the time to discuss the implications of Melissa's learning disabilities is important for general education staff. With a better understanding of how they are affecting her attention and her work, teachers are more inclined to structure learning situations for success and to recognize her efforts. For an excellent and practical explanation of learning disabilities from the learner's perspective, readers are referred to "How Difficult Can This Be?" a staff development video (Rosen, 1989).

Joey's initial meeting was held on a district staff development day provided on the two days prior to school starting in the fall (Figure 3.5). Because this is Joey's second year with Mr. Vasquez, there is some familiarity among team members and with Joey. The team discussed how they might operate during the coming year in terms of meeting dates and team process. They also review Joey's IEP objectives, his family's hopes and dreams, and the expectations for the year. Many of Joey's objectives relate to communication, choice, using a picture schedule, participation in classroom activities with adaptation, computer use, beginning reading, writing, and math.

Using the matrix (Table 3.3), his team generated a number of ways for Joey to practice using his communication book with peers and staff to contribute to discussions, make choices, ask questions, and share information with peers. He will use his picture schedule system on a regular basis to keep track of all class activities and to learn to monitor his time. Computer time offers the opportunity for him to work on academic skills, play games with peers and research, and create class reports. Journal writing provides a chance to work on his communication and conversation skills with peers, his learning to copy and write letters, his ability to recognize words and numbers and to share his thoughts. The structure of Mr. Vasquez's class offers many opportunities for cooperative learning, active participation in lessons, and the chance to demonstrate skills in a variety of ways. The high degree of student-to-student interaction allows natural supports from peers to be incorporated within his program.

Raymond's skills appear to be far different from those of his peers in high school. However, he is working on things that are a normal part of life in high school—academics, social interactions, consumer skills, and vocational skills. Raymond's IEP objectives, although at a different level than most of his peers, can still be met in this setting and, in our opinion, have a much greater chance to be met, given the potential of the learning environment. Objectives include improving his communication skills through the use of a conversation book (Hunt, Alwell, & Goetz, 1990) answering questions, using full sentences, requesting breaks, and conversing with friends. His IEP objectives also focus on appropriate behavior and with support from his peers and teachers, he has the opportunity to learn more effective and efficient ways to behave.

Raymond's planning team included two general education team members from the Buckeye team, his inclusion support teacher (who also teaches on the Buckeye team), and his mother (Figure 3.6). The team discussed the objectives that had been established for him at his last IEP, and Raymond's mother shared her hopes for Raymond at the high school. She expressed her frustration about his lack of progress over the years and his limited participation in the activities of other students his age. She hopes Raymond will learn more appropriate behavior from other kids and that he will have some fun in life.

The team examined each IEP objective in regard to each period in the school day and discussed ways to get him involved in some extracurricular activities (Table 3.4). For example, although Raymond has some verbal skills, he has limited conversational skills and finds it difficult to convey his thoughts to others in an effective manner. The connection to his aggression and destruction of property is likely, and any progress in his self-expression may have a great impact on his behavior. The team decides to work with a peer group to help him use his conversation book in class and during less structured times such as lunch, computer labs, and clubs. Providing choices throughout the day should also support Raymond in learning more appropriate behavior by allowing him more control over his life. A more complete functional analysis of behavior is necessary to develop an effective positive behavior plan, but these steps may provide a more positive learning context, which can preclude behavior problems. For more information, see Chapter 4. An

FIGURE 3.5   Joey's Team Meeting

TEAM MEETING FOR:

Student: <u>Joey</u>

Date/time: <u>7/26/00 9:15 a.m.</u>

Location: <u>Room 6</u>

If you are unable to attend, please contact: <u>Luis</u>

Team members:

<u>Jane—inclusion support teacher</u>

<u>Luis—classroom teacher</u>

<u>Marie—Joey's mom</u>

Communication backup:

<u>Provide minutes to Jane Lake—speech and language therapist (Ruben)</u>

Agenda for this meeting:	Time limit:
1. How team will operate	20 minutes
2. Classroom activity analyses to complete	10–15 minutes
3.	
4.	

Agenda for the next meeting:	Next meeting date and time: <u>8/28/00 9:15 a.m.</u>
1. Reading instruction and materials	
2. Computer programs and use	
3.	
4.	

Roles:

For this meeting	For next meeting
Facilitator <u>Luis V.</u>	<u>Marie M.</u>
Recorder <u>Marie M.</u>	<u>Jane R.</u>
Timekeeper <u>Jane R.</u>	<u>Luis V.</u>

(continued)

FIGURE 3.5 CONTINUED

MEETING NOTES	TO DO:	PERSON(S) RESPONSIBLE	DATE TO BE COMPLETED
Team decided to meet before school for ½ hour two times a month to start, with goal of moving to one time a month. We discussed ground rules, ways we like to interact in meetings (e.g., have agenda and stick to it, come prepared, keep others informed with minutes, etc).	Summary of group process to be typed up and shared.	Luis	8/28/00
Team divided up remaining activity analyses that are needed: e.g., Social Studies groups, recess, plan, do, review.	Complete these assessments of Joey's performance and support needs and bring to next meeting.	Luis: Social Studies Recess Plan, do, review	8/28/00

intervention plan with a chance of not only reducing problem behaviors but increasing Raymond's more prosocial, effective behaviors must start with a comprehensive functional analysis of his behavior. This process is congruent with IDEA (1997) requirements when students exhibit problem behavior that interferes with their learning.

Raymond's academic objectives address sight word reading, typing words, and simple addition and subtraction. The team brainstorms ways to have him learn the most relevant words from his Science, Math and English, Humanities blocks; practice reading, writing, and math skills through computer programs and games, and use his conversation book to assist him in communicating his understanding of concepts in academic classes. More functional skills, such as purchasing items, developing vocational skills, and monitoring his daily schedule will be addressed through a combination of on-campus (lunch, clubs, campus jobs) and off-campus (shopping, employment training) activities.

Structuring Planning Team Meetings.   Planning meetings are critical to the success of inclusive education, and the frequency of these meetings depends on the needs of the student. Team meetings might be held as frequently as once a week, although it is more common to hold monthly meetings for approximately forty-five minutes each. Subsequent team meetings may focus on the following items as well as other celebrations, challenges, and opportunities:

1. Developing curriculum adaptations
2. Identifying problems and progress with ongoing functional assessments
3. Adjusting the student's support plan
4. Planning for transitions
5. Celebrating successes and setting new initiatives

It is also important to remember that teachers and parents have a great number of demands on their time, and meetings must be both productive and efficient. We need to spend time learning to work collaboratively, finding ways to respect the contributions of each member of the team, and finding ways to incorporate these contributions into our support plan. It is equally important to maximize the limited amount of time available for meetings and to become very efficient in getting things done. One of the keys to effective and efficient meetings is to organize and document our conversations. The team planning worksheet adapted from Neary et al. (1992) is one way to keep on task and to keep

TABLE 3.3 Joey's Matrix

Student Joey

Grade/Teacher 2nd–Vasquez

School Vineyard Elem.

Date 10/00

SELECTED SCHOOL SUBJECTS AND ACTIVITIES

IEP GOALS	CLASS BUSINESS: JOURNAL—8:30	ACADEMIC GROUP 1: LANGUAGE ARTS—9:45	ACADEMIC GROUP 2: MATH/ SCIENCE AND SOCIAL STUDIES	RECESS	GROUP 3 10:30-10:45	CLASS MEETING 11:30
Use communication book to augment speech in interactions with friends and adults.	Select picture from book; sign words to peer; copy after peer writes them.	Pictures for story ideas; tell partner book choice; dictate story ideas.	Ask for manipulative materials; tell answer; ask questions.	Tell friend choice of act.	Contribute ideas; ask and answer questions.	Contribute ideas; ask questions; share news.
Follow picture schedule and participate in all classroom activities.	Pick up schedule in cubby; check each activity off when completed. (Staff can provide stickers for completion. Eight stickers = choice of activity at home.)			Return on time		
Use a variety of computer software with peer partners; share, take turns, use intelli-keys and overlays for specific subjects.	Could input journal entries with peer at end of week for weekly journal.	Read books (e.g., animal series) with intelli-keys and book series with speech reader—can do in group. Input text handwritten by others in group. Print spelling.	Use Math-Blaster adapted games with peers. Make graphs of survey data, other measurements.		Prepare reports with peers; read material aloud through program. Go to specific web site and download.	
Participate with peer partners in classroom jobs (selected weekly).	Certain jobs happen before journal (e.g., messenger, attendance—do with a partner).	Same	Same	Collect balls.		Put chairs in circle; pass out items.
Express requests, comments, protests, and make choices using combination of words, pictures, signs.	Tell peer what to write in journal; ask for assistance.	Ask and answer questions; brainstorming; take on role in cooperative groups; act as timekeeper; encourage	Ask and answer questions.	Choose activity and ask friend to play.	See 1 and 2.	Tell ideas; ask and answer questions Agree and disagree with others.

(continued)

TABLE 3.3 CONTINUED

IEP GOALS	CLASS BUSINESS: JOURNAL—8:30	ACADEMIC GROUP 1: LANGUAGE ARTS—9:45	ACADEMIC GROUP 2: MATH/ SCIENCE AND SOCIAL STUDIES	RECESS	GROUP 3 10:30–10:45	CLASS MEETING 11:30
Initiate and take turns in conversation with peers.	Tell about event, activity, news, etc., as he's coming into class and setting.	See above.	Check answers with partner; construct pattern together, taking turns.	Tell about weekend or evening.	Give ideas for group project. Draw ideas.	See above.
Copy dictate words into journal, etc.	Peer writes them in, Joey then copies.	Copy sentence from story.	Copy peer's written sentence about subject (e.g., people of Polynesia)		Copy written sentence.	
Develop sight-word vocabulary of five new words weekly.	Select one word per day with him and list in journal.	Point to word for spelling quiz; use Cootie Catcher to practice words with partner.	Follow one-word math instruction, e.g., "add."			Choose job from word or picture cards. Say initial consonant sounds.
Use beginning reading materials and acquire initial word attack skills.	Sound out initial sounds of selected words with him.	Tell beginning sound of word in reader. Listen to taped story and read along.			Listen to peer- or staff-taped materials.	

IEP GOALS	LUNCH AND CIRCLE 11:45-12:30	SILENT SUSTAINED READING 12:35	PLAN, DO, REVIEW 12:50	LIBRARY, PR, COMPUTERS 1:50-2:45
Express requests, comments, protests, and make choices using combination of words, pictures, signs.	Choose drink in cafeteria; choose activity for circle or recess from choice of three.	Select book and partner--reader; express like or dislike for story.	Select activity from words and pictures; use picture (smile or frown) to express opinion of activity.	
Initiate and take turns in conversation with peers.	Use communication book to discuss choices, etc.		Use book to converse during activity, e.g., painting, playing outside, etc.	Share at station with peer partner (e.g., about model airplanes); say one line (two to three words) in skit.
Copy dictated words into journal, etc.		Copy sentence for book review from words selected and written by peer.	Use template and copy in selected words: "I plan to ____ with ____."	Copy short sentences for shareathon poster.
Develop sight-word vocabulary of five new words weekly.	Present word choices for opening circle activity, e.g., Bingo, jump rope.	Highlight targeted words in reader for him to recognize and read aloud to partner.	Use template with known words and blanks for writing his plan.	Peer partner in library; peer partner to assist in shareathon.
Use beginning reading materials and acquire initial word-attack skills.		Use first-level readers for book selection and pair with third grader.	Template for one ____ plan to ____ with ____.	Use repetitive-line books (e.g., Brown Bear)

California Confederation on Inclusive Education, 1996.

FIGURE 3.6   Raymond's Team Meeting

TEAM MEETING FOR:

Student: <u>Raymond</u>

Date/time: <u>1/12/00 7:30 a.m.</u>

Location: <u>Room 206</u>

If you are unable to attend, please contact: <u>Mr. Whitman</u>

Team members:

<u>Don W.—Humanities—Buckeye Team</u>

<u>Angie D.—Humanities—Buckeye Team</u>

<u>Joanna W.—Parent</u>

<u>Nancy H.—Inclusion support teacher</u>

Communication backup:

<u>Nancy H. will inform Bill James, instructional assistant, and Julie Meyer, speech.</u>

<u>Don W. will inform other Buckeye team faculty.</u>

Agenda for this meeting:	Time limit:
1. Getting circle going—need two circles	10 minutes
2. Information to peers	10 minutes
3. Off-campus job	10 minutes
4.	

Agenda for the next meeting: Next meeting date/time: <u>2/12/00 7:30 a.m.</u>

1. Off-campus job

2.

3.

4.

Roles:

For this meeting	For next meeting
Facilitator <u>Don</u>	Bill
Recorder <u>Angie</u>	Nancy
Timekeeper <u>Joanne</u>	Angie

FIGURE 3.6   Raymond's Team Meeting

MEETING NOTES	TO DO:	PERSON(S) RESPONSIBLE	DATE TO BE COMPLETED
The team discussed the need for a different circle or support system for Raymond in classes outside the core where other teachers and students don't know him as well. Decided Ms. Horace would start it and train Mr. James then would give Mr. James a break at a different time.	Inform Bill of new role—provide training on circles. Monitor first meeting. Help recruit students.	Nancy Horace Nancy Horace Nancy Horace whole Buckeye team.	2/5/00 2/5/00 2/12/00
Students in groups with Raymond seem to need more information about his hearing loss, about how he communicates, and how to use a conversation book with him.	Hold Q&A for Raymond and peers. Train peers in using conversation book.	Nancy Horace	2/20/00

records of our discussions and decisions. This process saves a lot of time later as we try to remember what we were supposed to do and why. We have included planning team minutes for our four students to demonstrate their use.

The next time Amanda's team met (see Figure 3.3) the inclusive education support teacher had prepared an agenda containing four items for discussion:

1. Effectiveness of her communication system
2. Upcoming classwork and ideas for adaptation
3. Support in class
4. Friendships

The meeting was held during the regular team planning meeting time and was planned for forty-five minutes. Each team member received the agenda prior to the meeting. The inclusive education support teacher was the facilitator, and one of the general education teachers volunteered to keep the minutes. Each item was assigned a certain amount of time, but the group could negotiate for more or less time.

In addressing the first agenda item, Amanda's communication system, some of her teachers were concerned that she was not using it consistently. It was difficult to remember to ask her to use it, and peers, while they were talking with her, didn't stay long enough for her to use the Macaw. Her support teacher wondered if she was being given enough time to respond, reminding team members that she needed more processing time. One of the team members also questioned whether the most appropriate messages were being recorded on the Macaw. It was also suggested that she get another system that was more flexible. It was decided that the speech and language therapist would do a functional assessment of Amanda's language needs by observing her at various times in the school day and listing the most important words and phrases. She would also provide the team with an objective look at the way staff and students were using the system and offer ideas for improvement.

Amanda's teachers next described upcoming class activities, assignments, and projects. A math project is due in three weeks that involves gathering statistics on professional basketball players. Students are to make predictions about scoring, rebounds, and time played based upon data from at least two weeks of statistics from this year. The team determined that Amanda should be able to choose a team and a player, cut out box scores

TABLE 3.4 Raymond's Matrix

Student <u>Raymond</u>

Grade/Teacher <u>Buckeye Team and Frontier family</u>

School <u>Monroe H.S.</u>

Date <u>1/12/00</u>

SCHOOL SUBJECTS AND ACTIVITIES

IEP GOALS	SCIENCE OR MATH BLOCK	LUNCH AND CIRCLE	ENGLISH OR HUMANITIES	ELECTIVE: COMPUTERS	CLUBS: YEARBOOK
Use conversation book to ask or answer questions, use full sentences, make choices.	Peers to assist in use of book in groups. Teacher aide uses book to facilitate Q&A.	Make lunch choice with conversation book. Order own food.	See Science or Math.	Input and print words or pictures to insert in conversation book.	See Science or Math.
Request a break when needed using speech and break card in conversation book.	Before each class, take a few moments to discuss expectations and routine of the class with Raymond. Begin to involve peers in this process. Remind him of ability to request break if needed. Examine transition between classes. Lots of praise to smooth periods.				
Maintain appropriate behavior across settings, participate in each activity.	(See above also.) Give choices between two activities, groups of materials.	Choices of food purchases, circle activity, peer support. Play ball.	Self-monitoring. Choice of role, etc. Designated partner in groups.	Self-monitoring checklist; rewarding programs, self-paced; peer support person.	Peer partners. Activity choices.
Read twenty-five sight words (functional).	Select science or math operation words, e.g., add, subtract, pour, fill.	Use friends' names put into conversation book with their pictures.	Highlight five key unit or theme words and focus on these during activities.	Input week's list for homework study; Do word-match games.	Carrera words to assist his photography; peer partners photograph other clubs.
Use computer for keyboarding, producing short paragraphs.	Input (copy) additions and subtraction problems, then solve.		Co-writer use on computer in class. Copy short paragraph, summaries dictated by peers.	Use co-writer word prediction program to facilitate this.	If minutes typed by friend in club, Raymond prints from disk and distributes.

Count coins to $1.00 and read price amounts to $1.00.	Do planning for community purchase with peer one day per week. "Price Is Right" game with peers.	Carry money and purchase lunch in cafeteria and community using conversation book.		Count money for film and supply purchases.
Use dollar-up strategy for purchases.		Read price on menu or in storey, count one dollar more, make purchase.		Purchase film and other supplies as part of job.
Complete simple addition and subtraction problems.	Use Math game program during independent work using earphones.	Add purchase with calculator.	Use Math game computer program for this.	
Participate in extra-curricular activity at schools (e.g., clubs).		Take pictures with peer partner for yearbook club.		Work on photography team doing montage pages. Take pictures. Interview peers.
Participate in core, Math and Science and electives with adaptations, direct instruction, and peer support.	Recruit and provide training to one to three peer support students. Circle brainstorm adaptation ideas and ways to instruct each activity.			
Read and use daily schedule for self-monitoring program.	Check off activities on schedule, show teachers at end of block.	Ask peer support person to review schedule at close of each activity.		
Participate with friends at breaks, clubs, lunch, passing, and circle.	Recruit daily partner to transition from class to lunch with Raymond.	Teach friends how to use conversation book. Ask friends to wait for responses from him.	Daily or weekly partner self-selected from his cooperative groups.	Recruit two friends from his circle if none already there.

(continued)

TABLE 3.4. CONTINUED

IEP GOALS	SCIENCE OR MATH BLOCK	LUNCH AND CIRCLE	ENGLISH OR HUMANITIES	ELECTIVE: COMPUTERS	CLUBS: YEARBOOK
Initiate and acknowledge interactions with friends using conversation book.	Tell peers to remind him to use book. Ask about pictures or words in it.	Teacher and paraprofessional begin facilitating circle meetings, teach structures and process, then fade out.	See Science and Math. Ask peers to wait for him to respond for up to five seconds.		Tape questions and play tape when interviewing for yearbook.
Purchase lunch in community with friend one day a week.		Present choices in conversation book before going. Walk to sandwich shop.			
Learn and complete one on-campus and off-campus job (e.g., stock vending machines)		Soda stocker for vending machines with peer.		Tech aide job? Copy disks, print out material and take to copier, etc.	Develop delivery job for yearbook advisor or film-purchasing job.

with assistance from her family or a friend, paste these scores into a notebook, and choose a friend to help her predict statistics. Decisions will be recorded on her Macaw, and Amanda will use the Macaw at the appropriate time in class to report to her teacher.

Support has been adequate to date, and although staff are not requesting that they spend more time with Amanda, her mother wonders if she's getting too much help from the instructional assistant. The team decides to ask the assistant to move back a bit in small-group work to see if peers will provide some support. The assistant, the support teacher, and general education teachers will provide as-needed feedback to peers about how to assist Amanda.

The final agenda item was Amanda's friendships. At school, a consistent group of students make a point of interacting with Amanda and assisting her in moving about the campus. Students are warm and affectionate to her, but their interactions are brief and primarily focused on greeting or help. There are few interactions outside of school unless Amanda happens to meet a peer in the community. The team discusses how to increase her involvement with peers both at school and beyond school hours. One idea is to ask the students themselves. The inclusive education support teacher will ask for volunteers to form a support circle for Amanda. She will report to the team at the next meeting on plans for a support circle.

Melissa's team meetings may be less frequent but are as important. Again, an agenda is established, and a thirty-minute meeting set with her student planning team (Figure 3.4). Team members address progress on her work with accommodations and in remediating her learning challenges.

Melissa's teachers talk about her work and the ways they have accommodated her learning disabilities. She has been allowed to take tests orally as a supplement to her written work, and this change has been helpful. Homework assignments are still a problem, and Melissa is behind on several of her assignments. During discussion, the team determines that she has not been using the learning center or tutoring period and is missing out on the homework assistance she could receive there. Staff also need more information on her SIM strategies so they can remind her to use them. The team decides that the support teacher and Melissa's parents will sit down with Melissa to talk about why she is not using the learning center. The support teacher will also offer a brief inservice talk for staff on SIM strategies at the next house meeting.

Joey's team decided they should discuss how to operate on an ongoing basis. Members felt that the meetings during the last school year were too frequent and too long, and at times, there seemed to be no clear agenda. Team members also agreed that they needed to come prepared for each meeting. Team meeting planning worksheets and accurate notes would be a great help.

A second agenda item addressed gathering more information about Joey's participation in classroom and school activities so that staff could plan a more powerful instructional program for him. The team divided responsibilities for completing activity analyses for specific activities and routines. (Activity analyses will be addressed later in this chapter.) The next meeting would discuss reading instruction and computer programs.

The discussions by Raymond's core team members help to allay fears about meeting his needs by informing team members about what his needs really are and showing how he can be part of the natural fabric of the high school experience. Team members have established a plan for addressing the problems associated with his behavior and a process for further discussion and resolution.

Raymond's planning team set an agenda for their second meeting (Figure 3.6) and listed three items to take up, (a) getting circles of friends together, (b) providing information to his peers, (c) discussing his off-campus jobs.

Roles for the meeting were set with Mr. Whitman, the Humanities teacher, serving as the facilitator; Ms. Dickinson of the English and Humanities section keeping records; Ms. Horace, the inclusion support teacher, keeping time; and Mrs. Weldon, Raymond's mother, encouraging the group as they hit the inevitable barriers and bumps. The discussion focused on the need for two circles of friends so that he would have support in each of his core classes. They decided that training would be provided to the instructional assistant so that both he and Ms. Horace could get these circles started and maintained. The team also talked about Raymond's hearing loss, the importance of informing his classmates about it, and how they might communicate with him more effectively. A question and answer meeting with peers would be held, and these peers would also learn to use his conversation book. Dates and responsible people were noted, and these actions will be discussed at the beginning of the next meeting. The team set a meeting date, and because they didn't get to item 3 (off-campus jobs) at this meeting, it will become the main item at the next meeting.

Following each team meeting, the next meeting is scheduled and the tentative agenda set, along with responsibilities for meeting roles. Sometimes it is assumed that the support teacher will facilitate each meeting; however, this is usually not a good strategy. Each member of the team needs to develop facilitation skills, recording skills, and observational skills in order for the team to become more proficient Collaboration is a skill and, like all skills, it needs to be practiced and can always become better. For more information, see Rainforth & York-Barr (1997) and Falvey (1995).

Developing an Action Plan for Success:
Functional Assessment

The work completed during this initial planning process does a great deal toward preparing educators and families for the challenges of meeting the needs of a student with disabilities. Ideas have been generated; hopes and dreams have been shared; plans have been made for initial support, and team members have gotten a chance to begin collaborating. There may be a tendency at this point to consider the program established. In our opinion, the initial planning is just that: *initial.* Continued success for Amanda, Melissa, Joey, and Raymond requires continued work toward understanding how to support their progress.

For students with disabilities, getting into the inclusive classroom is the beginning. The structure of general education classrooms, even in those restructured schools practicing best educational practices, is not going to ensure that students are learning to the greatest degree possible. For many students, we can measure progress over the course of a year, however for students with more significant challenges, pre- and postevaluations of progress are not sufficient. Waiting until the end of a school year to see if progress is being made is likely to result in missed opportunities for learning. Assessment for students with disabilities must be ongoing. The functional assessment process is designed to evaluate student performance in the context of real activities with natural materials and performance standards. As the planning team continues its regular meetings, members periodically set actions to complete functional assessments and to report on what these ongoing functional assessments are telling them. Adjustments in support and teaching strategies are based on our structured observations, and new objectives are set if indicated. A functional assessment examines student performance in activities and routines to evaluate current abilities, to suggest adaptations and skills in need of instruction, and to make recommendations about ways to increase student competence and participation.

During a science session, Amanda is involved in Astronomy Workgroup, in which students research a person or concept and create a product demonstrating that research information. Staff completed a discrepancy analysis (Table 3.5), showing the generic steps in this routine and noting what Amanda was able to do on each step. For example, the second step is to read the assignment page and questions. Amanda cannot read; however, she did look at the book with her assistant. This demonstrates some interest and some understanding of the expectations of the task. We must now accommodate her and adapt the material so that she can use her skills to gain meaning. An adapted book with pictures was suggested to address the most important points in the assignment. You'll also notice that she will be taught to push herself in her wheelchair to the reference area to gather resources for herself and her team.

Joey's assessment worksheet describes his performance in a Mathlands sorting activity (Table 3.6). The objective of this activity is to make groups from a box of various

TABLE 3.5   Amanda's Activity Analysis

CLASSROOM ACTIVITY ANALYSIS WORKSHEET

☒ As is   ☒ Physical Assistance   ☒ Adapt Materials   ☒ Multilevel   ☒ Curriculum Overlap

Name Amanda   Date 1/16/00

Activity Astronomy workgroup

CLASSROOM ACTIVITY STEPS	STUDENT PERFORMANCE	SPECIFIC ADAPTATIONS	SKILLS IN NEED OF INSTRUCTION
In table groups, listen to teacher directions—create poster about one important astronomer (one per group).	Appropriate behavior, look toward teacher. Tries to push wheelchair away from table (brakes are on).		
Read assignment page questions	Looks at books with assistance from instructional assistant.	Use adapted book with Astronomy section.	Opening and turning pages independently.
Go to resource display shelves for references.	Attempted to push self to display. Desks in the way. Unable to negotiate through crowded areas.	Clear path.	Moving self independently to selected areas.
Make notes in response to questions on assignment.	Unable to read or write notes. Manipulation of paper is difficult.	Use pictures to reflect topic of assignment.	Identifying of pictures of astronomers, astronomical events, objects. Choosing own materials.
Individually prepare contribution to poster about astronomer.	No opportunity to observe. Amanda was looking at books.	Use adapted book with pictures of topic.	Choosing assignment. Pointing to requested items. Showing pictures to peers.
Return items to shelf.	Attempted (see above).	Clear path.	Wheelchair mobility.

Comments/Recommendations:

items and to state the rule for the groupings. Joey was not able to group or to state a rule for grouping. However, his partner in the cooperative team showed him his group of round items. One suggestion for this activity is to ask Joey to find all the round items. This allows the rest of the team to complete the core of the activity–identify rules for certain groupings and allows Joey to work on his receptive language skills as well as his matching skills.

In Raymond's English or Humanities block, staff analyzed and assessed his performance on general classroom routine for group work. It was noted that his lack of skills in terms of reading and copying from the board interferes with his performance. He also periodically gets up from the group to wander around the room. The staff suggested using peers to prompt him to remain with the group or to return to the group, asking peers to

TABLE 3.6   Joey's Activity Analysis

CLASSROOM ACTIVITY ANALYSIS WORKSHEET

❏ As is   ❏ Physical Assistance   ☒ Adapt Materials   ☒ Multilevel   ❏ Curriculum Overlap

Name _Joey_____   Date _10/00_____

Activity _Mathlands sorting activity: grouping and determining rules_____

CLASSROOM ACTIVITY STEPS	STUDENT PERFORMANCE	SPECIFIC ADAPTATIONS	SKILLS IN NEED OF INSTRUCTION
Third grader reads station directions aloud, and others in the group listen and look.	Joey is looking around, picking up the objects on the table.		Attending to speaker. Categorizing. Recognizing common features of objects.
All look at objects.	Picks up items.	Identify one item characteristic (color, size, shape).	Recognizing common features of objects.
Student pairs make groups. All others try to state the rule of the group.	Stays with group, holds items. Doesn't give ideas.	Try to have Joey be first to make the grouping with the rule provided (e.g., all the round ones).	
Students illustrate the rules with pictures, graphs, diagrams.	Watched others. Larry attempted to get him to draw. Joey drew a ball, mirror, round eraser, and Larry wrote the rule.	See above. Do task in reverse with peer. ("Find all the blue ones.")	
Students share groupings and make one drawing.	Joey listened as others shared. Larry assisted in drawing.	Communication prompt (e.g., pictures).	Verbally sharing his results. Completing picture.

Comments/Recommendations: Joey's skills in drawing will be a real asset here. The activity is analytic and difficult for him. Suggest having Joey group with staff direction to find a certain attribute, then draw pictures of the groups.

explain the task to him, allowing him to use his conversation book for whatever part of the task he wants to do (Table 3.7). Working through this process makes it clear how important it will be to keep his conversation book current, and this will probably be a critical point for the planning team to address.

Student Support Planning

One of the most important needs (and often the most immediate need) as students participate in inclusive schools is the *support plan*. General education teachers and parents are

TABLE 3.7   Raymond's Activity Analysis

CLASSROOM ACTIVITY ANALYSIS WORKSHEET

❏ As is   ☒ Physical Assistance   ☒ Adapt Materials   ❏ Multilevel   ❏ Curriculum Overlap

Name Raymond

Date 1/00

Activity English/Humanities Block

CLASSROOM ACTIVITY STEPS	STUDENT PERFORMANCE	SPECIFIC ADAPTATIONS	SKILLS IN NEED OF INSTRUCTION
Arrive on time.	Late to class.	Peer escort for transitions.	Moving from class to class more quickly.
Get into groups.	Needed to be prompted which group.	Peer from group prompts (call to him). Locate in same place daily.	Staying in activity.
Read or copy group assignments.	Couldn't copy from board—fidgeted, requested a break.		
Assign or volunteer for roles in groups.	Roles of notetaker, timekeeper facilitator less appropriate.	If timekeeper, use timer; if notetaker, use tape recorder or pair in roles.	Reading a digital watch or timer. Operating a small taperecorder.
Review written instructions and look over materials.	Couldn't read instructions.	Peer explains task (to whole group) and gives Raymond at least two choices of what he will do (conversation book).	
Complete assigned task: reading assignment research on computer writing	Watched others; got up and gestured; pointed to computer.	Modify written component; peer partner.	

Comments/Recommendations:

interested in how students will be supported in the classroom, and usually this concern is translated into, "Will she have an instructional assistant?" Throughout this chapter, we've spoken about the importance of peer involvement and have provided many examples of peer support as Amanda, Melissa, Joey, and Raymond participate in class and school activities and routines. As we consider students with disabilities, particularly those with significant disabilities, it's difficult to imagine how they could be part of a classroom without extra support from special educators. In many areas, inclusion has translated into an instructional assistant for each student. This is not only prohibitively costly, but it is not the best way to support students—those with and those without disabilities.

One goal of inclusive education is to build communities that naturally support each other in living and learning. Peers of students with disabilities need to learn how to support their friends, and this type of education provides the opportunity to do that. Having said this, it is also important to acknowledge that ultimately, the education support staff is responsible for supporting students with disabilities. Staff members must recognize which responsibilities are theirs alone and which they need to teach others to assume.

As discussed in functional assessments, analyzing activities and routines is necessary, but instead of looking for ways to adapt them and what skills to teach, staff members describe how students will participate in the activity, how support will be provided, and how the students' participation relates to their IEP objectives. Let's look at some examples.

Remember that Amanda is involved in an Astronomy lesson. Her assessment showed that she requires a good deal of support and adaptation to participate in this activity. An instructional assistant is available; however, the team will look for opportunities for more natural support from the teacher and her peers. For example, when it is time to read the assignment, Amanda will listen to peers read the assignment aloud (Table 3.8). Similarly, when it is time for the class to go to the resource shelf to get books, she will receive any necessary support from the other students. Her IEP skills, independent mobility, and attending to conversation are addressed in this manner. When Amanda is locating ideas in her adapted Astronomy book, her instructional assistant will work with her as she finds and identifies the picture and shares it with her peers with the aid of a communication device.

Joey is involved in journal writing during the day. As students begin writing their thoughts, Joey, who is unable to write, will communicate his thoughts to his friend, who will write them down in Joey's journal. Joey will then trace over the letters, thus practicing his writing skills (Table 3.9). Special education support can be available to other students in the class and will be available if Joey needs it.

As Raymond works with his cooperative team on his Humanities activity, he is receiving peer support to use his conversation book as he communicates ideas for the public service announcement they are creating (Table 3.10). Special education staff provided the support to make the conversation book and are responsible for continually updating the material and teaching Raymond's peers to use it with him. As the activity proceeds, his Humanities teacher, Mr. Whitman, supports Raymond by asking him if he wants a break and by reminding him when it's time to come back from the break.

Continually updating these support plans for activities and routines allows the team to continue to encourage independence and natural support from peers and staff. It also ensures that adequate support for learning is available and effective.

Ongoing Revision of Student Programs

Regular planning team meetings keep the educational program and supports on track. Without them, educators and parents are likely to be crisis hopping or drifting along and missing opportunities.

For Amanda, one of the issues constantly addressed by the planning team was the need for practice in using her communication system and moving about in her wheelchair. It becomes easy for staff and students to assist her instead of waiting for her to make a choice or comment on her Macaw. Amanda takes a long time to process information, and staff need to be reminded to wait.

Finding ways for her to meaningfully participate in academic activities is also difficult, especially during times when students are expected to do more complex academic work. It often seems easier for staff to take Amanda off to do something unrelated. The team acknowledges this and promises to continue to try new ideas. The support circle has been very helpful in this regard. Amanda's team has discussed holding a MAPS meeting (Falvey et al., 1994) with her family, friends, and members of her teaching team to ensure that she is being supported appropriately in a rewarding, enriching life style. This process also keeps the team focused on her quality of life now and in the future.

Melissa's team continues to work on her reading and writing. A computer has been very helpful, especially for spelling and grammar. She devotes a tutorial period to her

TABLE 3.8   Amanda's Routine Chart

SUBJECT/TIME
ASTRONOMY 11:00 A.M.

Student _Amanda_   School _Emerson J.H._

Grade/Teacher _Seventh/Spencer_   Date _1/16/00_

CLASS ROUTINE	STUDENT'S ACTIVITIES/ ROUTINE	SUPPORT	IEP GOALS
1) Students in table groups listen to teacher directions.	Same.	None.	Independent work.
2) Read assignment-page questions.	Listen as peers read aloud.	Peer.	
3) Go to resource display and select reference books.	Push wheelchair to display rack (one section has Amanda's adapted books or magazines).	Instructional assistant or student teacher's assistant.	Independent mobility.
	Point to book desired so instructional assistant can remove.	Instructional assistant or student teacher's assistant.	Use of key signs and gestures.
	Push wheelchair back to desk as instructional assistant carries book or Amanda carries it on tray.	Instructional assistant or student teacher's assistant.	Independent mobility.
4) Make notes in response to questions.	Look through selected book.	None.	Independent work.
	Share one or two pages with table group by holding book up for them to see.	Instructional assistant or student teacher's assistant.	Participation in academic activities.
	Students respond by reading passages or commenting on pictures.		Turn taking with peers.
	OR		
	Use communication device to say, "Here's a good idea!" Then show pages.	Instructional assistant or student teacher's assistant.	Use of communication device through day.
5) Individually prepare contribution to poster.	Choose photo or create drawing to add to poster by: a. pushing wheelchair to get materials binder b. bringing materials binder back to desk on tray or strapped to lap	Instructional assistant or student teacher's assistant.	Communicate choices. Independent mobility.

(continued)

TABLE 3.8 CONTINUED

CLASS ROUTINE	STUDENT'S ACTIVITIES/ ROUTINE	SUPPORT	IEP GOALS
	c. opening up binder to get materials out (scissors, markers, rulers, etc.) d. working on individual project		Learn class routines. Improve fine motor skills.
6) Put books and materials away.	Put materials back in binder. Return binder and reference book to shelves.	Instructional assistant or student teacher's assistant.	Fine motor skills. Independent mobility.

California Confederation on Inclusive Education, 1996.

TABLE 3.9 Joey's Routine Chart

SUBJECT/TIME
JOURNAL 8:30 A.M.

Student Joey   School Vineyard

Grade/Teacher second (first to third)/Vasquez   Date 9/25/00

CLASS ROUTINE	STUDENT'S ACTIVITIES/ ROUTINE	SUPPORT	IEP GOALS
1) Students get journal and pencil, sit on chairs or on cushions or rug.	Joey follows routine independently or with prompt by peer or teacher.	Peer to prompt Joey to get items and sit down. (fade)	Use picture schedules to follow routine.
2) Students begin writing in journals, share ideas as writing, tell others what they're writing about, ask for spelling help, etc. First and second grades are encouraged to illustrate after writing.	Joey selects pictures and says words to Larry who writes them into Joey's journal. Joey copies words beneath them as Larry completes his own journal entries. After writing, both get magic markers and illustrate journal.	Peer partner (second or third grade) who is a fluent reader and writer.	Use communication book. Copy dictated material. Conversation turn-taking. Develop sight vocabulary. Initial word attack.
3) Students date and sign entry, bring it to adult to initial.	Joey copies date from paper where Larry has written it and writes his name.	Peer partner.	Copy dictated material.

California Confederation on Inclusive Education, 1996.

TABLE 3.10 Raymond's Routine Chart

SUBJECT/TIME
ENGLISH/HUMANITIES 12:30 P.M.

Student <u>Raymond</u>   School <u>Monroe H.S.</u>

Grade/Teacher <u>Ninth/Whitman; Dickinson</u>   Date <u>2/17/00</u>

CLASS ROUTINE	STUDENT'S ACTIVITIES/ROUTINE	SUPPORT	IEP GOALS
<u>Human rights lesson:</u> Produce public service announcement on human rights issue.	Raymond will be with his regular home cooperative learning group.	Inclusive education support teacher to facilitate peer involvement through circle meetings.	
1) Brainstorm ideas for the announcement and write on chart. (Joe facilitates)	Raymond can brainstorm using his conversation book. Book has pictures of human rights topics. Raymond points to pictures.	Peer support to help him look	Use conversation book to ask or answer questions, speak in sentences.
2) Group selects primary idea: eviction and homelessness.	Raymond can select his idea (picture), remove it, and tape it to the chart. Vote on choices with group.	Peer prompt to put picture on chart.	Participate in core curriculum. Maintain appropriate behavior. Initiate and acknowledge interactions.
3) Choose roles for the announcement.	Choose his role from two pictures.	Peer prompt.	Make choices.
4) Group draws costumes, then listens to music selections for the announcement.	Raymond colors in costumes Joe sketched. Raymond listens to music.	Peer to invite him to select music.	Read sight words.
5) Group chooses background music.	Says "Yes" or "No" to music choices.		

California Confederation on Inclusive Education, 1996.

reading and writing strategies and is increasing the amount of writing she is doing on course evaluations although the team is still helping her with oral responses. As she moves to high school, this planning team will play a key role in preparing high school staff and Melissa for the demands of that environment.

Joey's planning team recognizes that he has untapped capabilities. They are constantly exploring ways for him to demonstrate his knowledge and skills and to deal with the changes and frustrations he experiences. The team is committed to supporting his growth academically and socially.

The challenges that Raymond faces as he approaches adulthood are great. Balancing his needs to learn with his peers with his need to prepare vocationally and to develop independent living skills are important considerations for his team. His parents want Raymond to have a good high school experience and participate in all the typical high school experiences. Ensuring that Raymond has the opportunity to attend the dances, sports events, clubs, and parties and that he will have the support to do so is a major task for his planning team.

SUMMARY

Chapter 3 provides a systematic, comprehensive approach to individualized educational planning for students in inclusive classrooms. Many of the strategies developed over the years by educators to meet the instructional needs of students with significant disabilities are effective in accessing the core curriculum and the wide range of opportunities available when students are fully participating members of the general education environment. Without a systematic, individual planning process and the delivery of systematic instruction, many students in inclusive settings will not completely benefit from these opportunities because of their need for focused instructional support.

Working with families to better understand the abilities and needs of their children is the first step in the planning process. Envisioning the future through this process sets the tone for a long-term collaborative relationship. Reconciling the critical educational needs of individual students with the opportunities available through the curriculum as well as the school and classroom routine provides a focus for planning teams as they determine support needs. Assessing students' performance as they actively participate in school and classroom activities and involving related service providers in this functional approach yields authentic and meaningful information for planning teams.

The importance of thinking through support needs for each part of the school day and ensuring that students learn to rely on natural supports is evident, particularly when resources are scarce. Routine support plans allow planning teams to discuss how individual students will receive any additional support throughout the day and what accommodations and adaptations will be used. Finally, an organized team planning meeting process is necessary to ensure that students (and staff) are successful. Meetings must be regularly scheduled, and specific roles for those involved are very helpful in keeping the group on track.

CHECKING FOR UNDERSTANDING

Mr. Parcells has recently accepted a position at Jefferson Junior High School as an inclusive education support teacher. He has the responsibility for supporting fourteen students with disabilities at the site with the aid of two instructional assistants as well as part-time services from speech and language, nursing, vision, and adapted P.E. He is very excited about his role and wants to be sure that his students' time is well spent. He's also a bit overwhelmed by the amount of work—assessing, planning for curriculum adaptations, developing support plans—but he's young and has lots of energy. In addition to working with a number of general education teachers, he also must coordinate the related services staff and instructional assistants who work with his students. Where does he start?

1. What steps can Mr. Parcells take to get started on the right foot with general education staff?

2. How can he prioritize his time and efforts to develop meaningful programs for his students?

3. How can the team complete assessments in the most effective and efficient manner?

4. What suggestions do you have for finding meeting time?

5. How much support should he provide for his instructional assistants?

CHAPTER FOUR

SYSTEMATIC INSTRUCTION IN INCLUSIVE CLASSROOMS

Walton High School LMC
DeFuniak Springs, FL

Upon completion of this chapter, you will be able to

1. State at least four reasons for providing systematic instruction in inclusive classrooms
2. Describe stages of learning and how they impact instructional strategy
3. Describe how teaching might look from the learner's perspective
4. Describe the discrete trial format and define components
5. Differentiate antecedent and consequent instructional strategies and state when they are applicable
6. Describe at least seven types of prompts and identify advantages and disadvantages of each
7. Describe incidental learning
8. State the rationale for data collection
9. Discuss the process for functional analysis of behavior and describe components of a positive behavioral support plan

THE RATIONALE FOR THIS APPROACH

Recently, a parent who has always been a strong advocate for inclusive education expressed her concerns about her daughter's education. Although she continues to be pleased that her family decided to ensure that Ann remain in the general education classrooms in her neighborhood schools from preschool into high school, she has also found a real lack of direct and systematic instruction, particularly in reference to communication. Staff members have done a wonderful job of adapting lessons and accommodating Ann; however, it appears that her skill level has not improved in many areas. There is a great deal of assistance and support for Ann, but her mother can't help but wonder why she can not become more independent or at least less dependent on the assistance. This situation has moved her to find someone to provide periodic one-on-one instruction at home to allow Ann to practice and become more competent in communication as well as in motor and self-help skills.

Criticisms of Systematic Instruction in Inclusive Education

Many educators are critical of inclusive education for a variety of reasons. In some cases, as described in Chapter 1, inclusive education has been misrepresented and unsupported.

A clear definition of inclusive education and the keys to success will address most of these criticisms. In others, the criticisms may be more closely related to the difficulty of change. Moving from a system of special schools and separate classes in which everyone understood their roles can be disconcerting. General education teachers who have been able to refer students to special education believe they do not have the skills or will not have the resources to serve these students if they remain with their peers. Addressing the personal and systemic changes necessary to support inclusive education is critical and is addressed in Chapter 8.

Others in the field see inclusive education as a movement by advocates of students with severe disabilities who want only to "enhance social competence" of these students and to abolish special education altogether (Fuchs & Fuchs, 1994). These educators, many of whom have been involved in developing the technology of special education and the strategies for supporting learning, see inclusive education as a real step backward to the days when students were set up for failure, particularly those students with learning disabilities and sensory impairments. Citing statements of the Learning Disabilities Association (1993) and the National Joint Committee on Learning Disabilities (1993) claiming that students with learning disabilities sometimes require an intensity and organization of instruction uncommon to general education classrooms, Fuchs and Fuchs (1994) cautioned educators about abandoning systematic instruction and emphasized the need for a continuum of options. They also mentioned their distrust of general education's capacity to provide specialized services for students with sensory impairments. In our view, some of their concerns are valid, and in many situations, educators *have* neglected to integrate the proven effective practices of special education in their movement to inclusive schools. We should listen to these advocates and build an inclusive system that incorporates empirically validated, systematic instruction as a critical part of the service system.

The special educator has two very important roles. In recent years, a great deal of attention has been given to enhancing the image of people with disabilities; supporting involvement in age-appropriate work, living, and school environments; supporting self-advocacy; providing information to community members about disability; and moving the field out of the shadows. We also have another equally important role and that is to increase competence. Ensuring that students have enough instructional support to gain in their motor, communication, cognitive, social, and activity performance should be addressed objectively with time-tested and empirically validated strategies.

In their analysis of program-quality indicators in educational services for students with severe disabilities, Meyer, Eichinger, and Park-Lee (1987) surveyed a number of experts in the field—researchers, state directors of special education, and parents—to determine the most promising practices. Data-based instruction, including attention to instructional cues and corrections, fading strategies, data collection for making program changes, and mastery defined as performance in criteria situations without teacher assistance, was found to be critical to program quality. The fact that students are members of the general education classroom does not negate these quality indicators. These best practices are valid in any setting.

Can We Provide Powerful Instruction in Inclusive Settings?

Systematic instruction for students with severe disabilities has a long history. As long ago as the early 1800s, Jean Marc Gaspard Itard, working in France, laid the groundwork for intensive instructional practices (Blatt, 1987, p. 34). Practices developed over the years, such as task analysis, functional assessment, and applied behavior analysis, have shown that all students can learn and can improve their competence. Gold's (1980) early work in task analysis and his alternative definition of mental retardation refocused our efforts by demonstrating the importance of the *power* of instruction rather than I.Q. measurement as the critical factor in student learning. The important point of his work was that with powerful instruction, all students can learn, and if they are not learning, there is nothing to gain by lowering our expectations. Failure to learn indicates the need for a more powerful instructional approach.

Educational services for students with severe disabilities made great strides, the more powerful instructional approaches being developed through applied behavior analysis. Educators organized learning environments to reduce distractions, and created instructional plans that systematically provided prompts and reinforcers to support discrete skill development. Repeated practice of discrete skills such as identification of body parts; pointing to red, green, blue; and sorting and matching was typically provided in a massed-trial format. A single, discrete skill might be repeated ten times in a learning period. However, as educators saw the need to involve students in more immediately meaningful learning environments and activities, instruction became more functionally based, and the massed-trial approach gave way to instruction in age-appropriate, integrated, community-based, and functional activities. Instructional opportunities, instead of being repeated in a single learning period, were distributed across the day. For example, recognition of a particular color might be incorporated within a board game, during an art activity, in dressing, and in social communication with peers and teachers. Regardless of whether the focus of instruction was discrete skills or functional activities, systematically arranging instructional prompts continued to be critical to the success of learning and provided the power necessary for learning. The discrete-trial format is described in more detail later in this chapter.

In many educational situations, systematic instructional practices appear to have fallen by the wayside. This is not limited to inclusive or even mainstreamed situations but also occurs in the separate special education programs. Often students in resource programs or special classrooms are involved in a watered-down version of the general education curriculum or are simply working at a much lower level without attention to learning strategies that will support their access to the age- and grade-appropriate curriculum (Knapp, Turnbull, & Shields, 1990). As a result, they continue to fall further behind in spite of (or because of) their special education services. Students with more significant disabilities, including those who may be involved in a more functional, community-based program, appear to receive little planned instruction in terms of how prompts and corrections are delivered. There may be a great deal of exposure to interesting, age-appropriate activities and environments, but without attention to the way we deliver our instructional assistance, students' skills will show little improvement.

One result of this lack of specific, systematic instruction is the rapid growth of nonpublic schools and agencies that provide direct, one-on-one instruction in a discrete trial format, particularly for students with autism. Families who believe their children are not being systematically instructed are increasingly opting for this educational approach, often sacrificing participation with age-appropriate general education peers. The discrete-trial approach is not new; special educators have used it as a way of organizing instruction in a manner that ensured success. In recent years, with a recognition of the importance of context, and a movement toward a more integrated, functional, age-appropriate curriculum, this approach has been largely disregarded. Although we question the massed-trial drilling of nonfunctional compliance behaviors in many such nonpubic school programs, discrete trial instruction is a useful tool for planning instruction. Public schools that are losing students to nonpublic schools and agencies that *do* provide this type of instruction would be wise to consider why some families find it so attractive.

Accommodation or Adaptation as the Major Strategy.   In Chapters 2 and 3, we described a number of adaptation strategies for supporting students in classroom activities and curriculum. Providing physical assistance, adapting materials, allowing for alternative ways to receive and demonstrate knowledge, and multilevel instruction are common strategies in inclusive classrooms. With increasing numbers of schools, students, and staff involved in inclusive education, we are building a strong bank of strategies for curriculum adaptation and accommodation. A number of books on adaptations are on the market—for example, Giangreco, Cloninger, and Iverson, 1993; McCarney, McCain, and Bauer, 1995; McCarney, Wunderlich, and Bauer, 1988; Neary, Halvorsen, Kronberg, and Kelly, 1992—and IEP teams are becoming more comfortable with outlining ways to accommodate for students' disabilities. Adaptation and accommodation allow students to participate in and have access to what other students are experiencing, and this is critical. A student who is pulled out for brief periods or given a separate education misses what other students are learning at that time. Even if the separate instruction is of high quality, these students will need to catch up on the material they missed.

However, accommodation is only one aspect of the inclusive educational process. Students can participate in interesting, age-appropriate activities without having all the prerequisite skills and can reach levels at which we *can* instruct new skills. Students need to increase their skills and competence. Educators should support them in such a way that they will need less adaptation and accommodation by helping them increase their motor, communication, cognitive, and social skills. Ann's mother is correct. Ann should be increasing her motor, communication, cognitive, and social skills, needing less support and demonstrating increased participation over time. The functional assessment strategy described in Chapter 3 identifies both strategies for adaptation and targets for teaching. Our instructional plans must use this information as well as additional information about their learning style to establish strategies for providing the specific prompting and reinforcing students need to improve competence. The rich curriculum content and process in excellent general educational environments will support learning for all students. At the same time, because many students with disabilities find it difficult to learn, individualized instruction is necessary, and this systematic instructional approach *can* be provided in the general education classroom. For example, Raymond is learning to carry money and make purchases in the cafeteria and in stores. What instructional strategies will help him move beyond his current ability (handing his wallet to the cashier) to being able to give an appropriate amount of money? When Melissa takes short written exams, she is allowed to supplement her written answers with oral explanations. How can we help Melissa to independently organize her thoughts on paper and use an assistive device, such as a computer with word-prediction software, to increase her written output?

What Happens When Support Is Dispersed?   When students with disabilities are congregated within one special classroom, there is a daily opportunity for staff communication and observation and training of the instructional assistants. As more students have left the special class for integration, mainstreaming, or community-based instruction, supervision and communication become more difficult. In addition, as more staff members—for example general education teachers—interact with students, adults need communication skills as well as time to communicate in order to ensure program consistency. The planning team meetings described in Chapter 3 are one of the best ways to keep the information flowing; however, a more immediate and specific approach is necessary. Inclusive education support strategies as described in Chapters 2 and 3 may involve the support staff in a number of classrooms and school settings. In secondary school programs in which some students are involved in vocational settings, the territory expands even more. Meeting time is limited. Instructional assistants are supporting and teaching students on a daily basis, making instructional decisions, and modeling for other staff and students. The most effective instructional approaches require an instructional plan as well as training for assistants that incorporates periodic observation and feedback on their work. In many schools the general education teacher and the special education support teacher share the training and supervision of instructional assistants. However, in terms of specific instructional strategy, the special education teacher, with her specific expertise, is responsible. Planned instructional strategies, based upon assessments in natural settings, which take into account each student's individual learning style and consider the context of the learning activity, are necessary to establish and maintain consistency in our own behavior as we assist students in becoming more skilled. For example, each staff member involved with Amanda needs to understand the amount and type of assistance she needs to use her communication system. If there is not a clear understanding, she'll be receiving too much assistance from some staff members and too little from others. This is an inefficient use of instructional time and hardly fair to Amanda.

Need for Reliable Standards.   One of the recent changes in programs for students with disabilities is to provide parents with progress reports regarding their children's IEP objectives at least as often as their nondisabled peers receive this (IDEA, 1997). This report, in addition to the annual IEP review, is another opportunity to examine the results of our program to determine if progress is being made. One of the basic tenets of the field of special education is that if the student is not making progress, it's incumbent on the teaching staff to determine why and then to change the approach. On what basis are we determining progress? Far too often, IEP objectives are continued because the objective has not yet been met, or team members believe some progress has been made but have no data to support that determination. When IEP objectives show little or no progress over the course of a year, either the objective was poorly chosen or the instructional program should have been changed long ago. No progress is not acceptable, and continuing the same IEP objective year after year is wasting everyone's time, particularly the student's. For example, if, even though she demonstrates the ability to understand books on tape and can dictate her thoughts to a peer or staff member, Melissa's abilities to deal with the written word are not improving, we need to find a better strategy for her decoding. It is reasonable to expect that in some situations progress will be slow, and small gains may be made over time. An objective record of student performance is critical for determining if progress *is* being made rather than reporting how we feel about it. And when we can show progress, we need to know under what conditions the student is demonstrating the skill. When staff have a well-thought-out plan for providing instructional prompts and corrective feedback and keep track of how the student progressed with that assistance, they can decide how to best support learning and when to change the program. Instruction should build competence. When it does not, we need to determine why and make changes.

Besides the obvious need to ensure that students are learning, staff also need reinforcing when gains are slow and difficult to see, especially on a day-to-day basis. Gathering information to see how our strategies are working is critical to our own satisfaction. Families also need to know that their children are learning and growing and that everyone working with their child is following the plan they had a part in establishing.

In defining inclusive education, we identified those practices that provide the best possible environment for success. Membership in the general education classroom, training for all involved, support systems, and regular planning meetings all set the stage for successful inclusive education. Students' growth in all areas depends upon instructional strategies that are individually designed for each student. The general and special education teachers must collaborate to ensure not only that the student participates as a regular member of the classroom and that core curriculum and materials are adapted but that the student's IEP objectives are systematically taught.

EFFECTIVE INSTRUCTIONAL PRACTICES

It is difficult for most of us to remember exactly how we learned all the things we have over the years. Of course, we remember some activities in school—the texts, workbooks, experiments—but that is such a small proportion of the enormous amount of information and skill we've somehow retained. Most of what we've learned has probably been from exposure, models, trial and error, and repeated practice. It would be safe to say that, for the most part, we didn't even try to learn most of what we know. This is one of the reasons many students surprise us in inclusive settings. There is a whole host of interesting, motivating, and powerful things to experience and to incorporate. In our national discussion about the influence of the media on our children, there is at least one point of general agreement. Models have a powerful influence in terms of assisting students to learn. Joey observes how his peers communicate; problem solve; initiate, maintain, and terminate interactions; use materials; deal with conflicts; and many other skills. As he continues to shape his own behavior, he has a variety of models to use.

Natural Consequences as an Instructional Tool

Our own learning process is typically facilitated in a very natural manner. We learn by practicing and extending skills in new settings and situations. The use of those skills is reinforced (or not) by natural consequences: what people say or do, the feeling we experience, whether we gain or lose. And if we choose or have the opportunity to continue using the new skill, it becomes part of our repertoire. When exposure, practice, and natural consequences do not result in learning, other strategies must be used. For people with disabilities, particularly those with severe disabilities, learning is more difficult, and those of us who support learning need to use the strategies we have learned to assist them. Ford and Mirenda (1984) described a decision model for community-based instruction that is applicable in any setting. We must first decide whether the natural consequences of an action will be sufficient to support learning. Sometimes the consequences are reinforcing, but sometimes they are not and can serve as a correction. When do we allow natural corrections to occur? Natural corrections are defined as "the stimuli generally available in an environment after a response has already occurred which serve to weaken or eliminate an inappropriate response" (Ford & Mirenda, 1984, p. 80). Ford and Mirenda emphasized the importance of the likelihood that natural consequences will be of sufficient magnitude or immediacy to be effective, how the public may perceive the situation, and the safety of the individual. It is not likely that Amanda will be able to benefit solely from natural corrections in order to use her communication system, move about in her wheelchair, or reach and grasp items. Melissa will also need more than poor scores on her written work to support her learning. She needs assistance before she will be able to receive any benefit from those natural consequences. Direct instruction on a variety of learning strategies to better access the core curriculum would help ensure that Melissa becomes more competent in demonstrating her abilities. These learning strategies are techniques, principles, or rules that enable a student to learn to solve problems and complete tasks independently, emphasizing steps to take and when to use the strategy (Friend & Bursuck, 1999, p. 344).

When students with significant disabilities are not learning a particular skill, there are five basic reasons.

1. They are unable to physically complete the motor requirements of the skill.
2. The skill is too complex in its present form.
3. They do not know when (or not) to perform the skill.
4. There is insufficient reinforcement.
5. There is insufficient practice.

The educational support staff has to determine why a student is not learning and incorporate strategies to

1. Support the ability to perform the motor task.
2. Break the skill down into parts that are more easily learned.
3. Assist the student in recognizing the natural stimuli for the skill.
4. Provide sufficient reinforcement to support learning.
5. Provide sufficient opportunities for practice.

A word about reinforcement is important here. The natural consequences that are reinforcing for many of us may not be particularly reinforcing for some individuals. An artificial reinforcer is often more meaningful and immediate. In separate educational settings, we have typically chosen reinforcers that often do not support the image of a student as competent. Primary reinforcers, such as food or exaggerated social reinforcers, present a harmful image of students with disabilities and are not necessary. However, when these types of reinforcers are naturally a part of the activity, there may be a way to use them. For example, students who stock the soft-drink machine at school do this as part of a work program. When Raymond stocks the machine, work experience credit is not particularly meaningful and reinforcing to him, so he also receives a Coke and a "Nice job, Raymond." Even these extra reinforcers can and should be faded to approach the natural consequences of this activity more closely. Providing a Coke every other day or script or money to purchase a Coke may be one strategy. We should also consider other forms of reinforcement that acknowledge student preferences. For example, free time or time to do something with a friend may be earned by success in learning.

Reinforcement is a powerful tool in assisting individuals to learn. Its use depends on the ability of an individual to respond in the correct way. Very often a student may not know how to respond in a correct way and will never get an opportunity to experience reinforcement—artificial or natural. Clearly, in such cases, additional instructional information should be provided so that students can experience the natural reinforcements that maintain skills.

Organizing Our Instruction

Many practitioners and researchers have outlined important considerations to guide us as we prepare our instructional plans. First, there is a need to balance formal, context-based teaching with less formal, and less structured time with peers (Snell, 1993). Sailor et al. (1988) also remind us of the importance of activity-based instruction and of teaching in context. Inclusive classrooms can provide these opportunities, particularly when schools are focused on meeting the needs of all students.

It's also wise to consider some additional guidelines from Snell's (1993) principle of parsimony. Methods should (a) suit the student's age, (b) be nonstigmatizing, and (c) reflect the student's learning mode and preferences. It's critical that these methods be effective.

Wolery, Ault, and Doyle (1992) reminded us of the importance of student-directed teaching as opposed to adult-directed teaching (p. 36). Students who are motivated to participate are more likely to learn. Choice in what and how they learn is a powerful factor in motivation. Joey's interest in using the computer offers enormous potential for learning a multitude of academic skills, including reading, math, writing, and research. As noted in Chapter 2, his ability and interest in drawing give him a valued role in his cooperative team and offer a way for him to learn attributes of categories of items in Mathlands activities.

Stages of Learning.　　When we learn a new skill, there are common stages of that learning process regardless of who we are or what the skill is. We begin with the difficult task of *acquisition*—acquiring the new skill and learning the motor, cognitive, or communicative subskills involved. Anyone who has taken on a new challenge, for example, playing piano or guitar or learning karate, understands how challenging this stage can be. We may need a great deal of support during this phase. A second phase of learning, *maintenance,* is best described as the stage at which we practice our new skill, still not perfectly but somewhat independently. We can play a song or complete a form but still make mistakes (particularly when we are demonstrating for our instructor, it seems). Opportunity to review, practice, and be reinforced is important in this phase of learning. In the third phase, *fluency,* we develop the quality of our skill, the speed, accuracy, the ability to perform our skill with increasing perfection. We develop confidence in using our new skill and are able to begin to extend it to other settings. The intrinsic motivation of being skilled supports the continued use of it. In the final phase, *generalization,* we are demonstrating our new skill across settings, people, and activities. It has become part of our repertoire of competence. (For a more detailed examination of these stages, see Figure 4.1; Wolery et al., 1992; Snell, 1993).

Characteristics of Systematic Instruction.　　What are the defining characteristics of systematic instruction? Anderson, Mesaros, and Neary (1996) offer some suggestions. First, instruction occurs on a regularly scheduled basis. Particularly during the acquisition

FIGURE 4.1   Stages of Learning

STUDENT: Joey

SKILL: Using communication book to augment speech in interactions with friends and adults

STAGE: ACQUISITION

Until this school year, Joey's communication skills involved gestures and some vocalizations. Although his ability to verbalize some of his needs is improving, and his gestures more closely approximate sign language, he needed an additional communication tool to augment these two communication strategies. A picture communication was developed using pictures of items, people, activities, and places he was familiar with. The communication book is changed periodically to reflect changes in his life as well as interesting things he might want to talk about.

During the first month using this system, Joey was assisted to use his communication book when he was sitting with peers, during morning business, and during his circle of friends meeting. Staff prompted him to point to pictures during each interaction using a verbal cue, ("Joey, use your book") at first and then moving to a gesture.

STAGE: MAINTENANCE

As Joey began to remember to take out his book whenever he was involved in these three activities, staff initially used a time delay to give him the opportunity to respond before a prompt. Joey quickly learned to open the book, although he periodically forgot to use it unless someone reminded him ("Joey, use your book").

STAGE: FLUENCY

Joey's communication book continually expanded as his experience with it grew. The contents of the book also expanded to reflect his growing experiences as a second grader. Activities, events, trips, and friends from school and home provided more conversation topics to use in conversation. Joey became more efficient at using his book to communicate during his time with peers, in morning business, and circle time. The book has become a natural part of these activities.

STAGE: GENERALIZATION

Joey's family has reported that he is using his communication book at home, particularly when he wants to share something about school. He also carries it with him when he is at recess, lunch, and on any school related trips. He has used it with the school office staff on several occasions when he was delivering materials to the office.

and maintenance stages, students need the opportunity to learn and practice. Because many of our students have a difficult time learning new skills, long periods between opportunities to practice will likely mean that they have to start over each time. Second, instruction results in continual student progress. If students are not learning, what do we need to change to support their learning? How can we make our instructional strategies more powerful? Plateaus are not acceptable. Third, objective data are used to modify or maintain our instructional program. Progress may be slow, but the only way we'll know if we are getting anywhere is if we keep a record of the instructional support provided and the result. Fourth, teaching techniques are individualized on the basis of learning style and the setting. Each of us learns in a different way. Some of us may depend on visual information: "Show me an example; draw it for me." Others may learn more effectively with auditory information: "Tell me how to do it; put it in a song." Some need a more hands-on approach: "Let me do it once; then I'll understand it." Many of us work better alone, but others work better in a group. We have different times of the day when we're in a learning mode; we have differing amounts of time that are productive for learning. There are so many variations in our styles. Consider these.

1. Student characteristics: What's our student's motor style, social orientation, current abilities?
2. Student performance characteristics: Is our student independent or more dependent? What about his or her rate, precision, consistency?
3. Learning characteristics: What types of cues are most salient? How does she or he problem solve? What strategies does our student use to learn?
4. What preferences in terms of environments, settings, activities, people does our student show?
5. Learning history: What has worked in the past? What skills has she or he learned and maintained?
6. How much time on a learning task is productive? How do we know when a break is needed?

Amanda has always shown a definite interest in music, and her family knows that from an early age she responded very positively when they sang to her. She maintains interest in an activity longer, tolerates some therapies for longer periods, and retains information better when presented in musical format. Melissa has a flair for the dramatic and demonstrates her abilities more successfully when she is involved with a group that is active, artistic, and performing. Knowing this gives her teachers avenues for motivating learning. The information in Chapter 2 regarding multiple intelligences (Gardner, 1983) is particularly applicable here.

Fifth, instruction is provided in each situation where skills need to develop. The school day is a series of connected learning opportunities. Each organized learning activity offers the chance to use communication, cognitive, motor, and social skills to interact with peers, teaching staff, and materials. The transitions between organized learning activities also provide opportunities to learn and practice new skills. Students may need support during these times and our support should be consistent with our instructional plan. Raymond, Amanda, and Joey use augmentative communication systems to inform others about their thoughts. They should use their augmentative systems throughout the day. Therefore, these systems must be readily accessible at all times, and everyone, including peers, should understand how they are used.

Finally, instruction needs to be focused. We need to attend to the student, without allowing ourselves to be distracted by all the other things going on around us. This is difficult to do, and we should consider delaying an instructional sequence if we can't stay focused. When we're distracted, we may inadvertently be teaching things we didn't intend to. In practical terms, when students with disabilities are involved in group work, staff will be facilitating participation, making accommodations to allow participation, and providing direct instruction. When direct instruction is provided, the support staff has to be able to concentrate on the instruction.

Planning Individualized Instructional Programs

It helps to view learning in a simple paradigm. We learn to do things in certain situations because we are reinforced sufficiently for behaving that way. We also learn to *not* do things in situations because we are not reinforced or are punished in some way. Situations contain stimuli that help us decide how to respond (or not), and the reinforcements or punishments we receive either strengthen (reinforce) or weaken (punish) our behavior. When we arrange our instructional time, we try to organize assistance so that students learn how to perform a skill and how to recognize and act on specific discriminative stimuli. We also reinforce or correct them on their performance, further strengthening demonstration of skills in the appropriate situations. However, a student may see something different from what we had in mind. For example, Donnellan et al. (1988) described a possible student learning experience in Figure 4.2.

If we don't pay attention to our prompting and correction strategies, we may be simply confusing students and possibly teaching behaviors we do not intend. Our instruction must be organized, structured to provide the best possible chance for learning. Support must be sufficient for students to be successful but not so much so that students become dependent on it. We need to consider a "Goldilocks rule" in identifying how much instructional assistance we provide—"not too much, not too little, just the right amount." Response-prompting strategies, based upon current student performance and the natural cues and corrections inherent in the activity, provide that support. They are intended to support the transfer of *stimulus control,* reliable or predictable responding in the presence of one stimulus and the absence of the response when the stimulus is not present (Wolery et al., 1992, p. 37), from our instructional prompts to the natural stimuli (Billingsley & Romer, 1983; Wolery et al., 1992). An example is instructive. In Joey's school, students must learn to perform periodic emergency drills. When the fire alarm rings, Joey and his peers are expected to stand up, push their chairs in, walk to line up at the door, and follow the line leader outdoors. The alarm is the natural stimulus for initiating this procedure, and Joey (and all the students) must respond to this signal without any additional prompting. While he is learning this behavior, staff provide instructional prompts that not only help him learn the safety procedure but help him make the connection to the natural stimulus, the alarm.

We can organize our instructional support through a careful consideration of the natural stimulus (or stimuli), the desired response, and the natural consequence for correct responding. This process is commonly labeled a *discrete trial format* (cf. Donnellan et al., 1988). (See Figure 4.3.) For example, when Amanda's cooperative group is working on a research task, the group decides it's time to gather research materials, and team members begin to move in that direction (natural stimulus). Amanda unlocks her wheelchair brakes and moves toward the resource center to gather books (response), bringing them back so as to share pictures with the group (consequence). As educators, we need to continually assess what signals inform us that a certain response is called for. We need to clearly define the response we expect. What are the natural consequences for responding

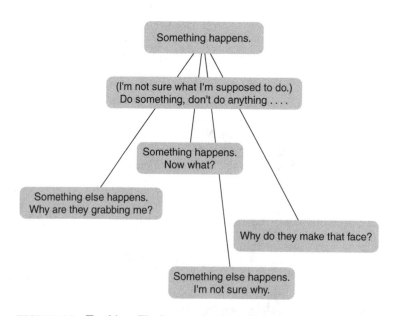

FIGURE 4.2 Teaching: The Learner's Point of View

Adapted from *Progress without Punishment,* by A. M. Donnellan, G. W. La Vigna, N. Negri-Shoultz, and L. L. Fassbender, 1988, New York: Teachers College Press. Used with permission.

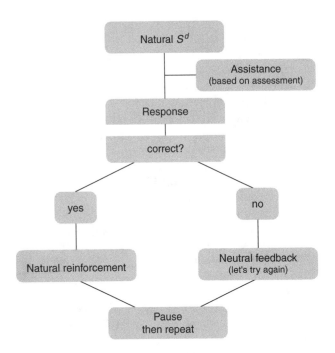

FIGURE 4.3　Discrete Trial Format

Adapted from *Progress without Punishment,* by A. M. Donnellan, G. W. La Vigna, N. Negri-Shoultz, and L. L. Fassbender, 1988, New York: Teachers College Press. Used with permission.

in that way? Once this basic sequence is identified, then we can focus on the support our student will need to be successful.

Natural reinforcement is available only when a response is correct. Our behaviors are continually reinforced naturally throughout the day; however, when a particular skill is not yet in our repertoire, we may not experience these natural reinforcers. During the acquisition stage of learning, a student will not be able to receive natural reinforcers. This may inform her that she's incorrect, but repeated failure does not teach what she is supposed to do. *Antecedent prompting,* providing assistance *before* the student responds, is necessary if she is to respond correctly. The amount of assistance and the type of prompt are determined through the functional assessment process described in Chapter 3. That assistance becomes the starting point for our instruction. For example, during Mathlands, Joey's functional assessment showed that he did not provide ideas on sorting rules for the group. Joey needs a verbal prompt ("...all the round ones") to be successful. Because Joey enjoys drawing, an appropriate reinforcement would be to be able to demonstrate the idea he provides through a drawing.

What additional reinforcement will our student need to let him or her know that a response is correct? If the natural reinforcement is not particularly reinforcing or is not immediate enough, an instructional consequence will have to bridge the transition from response to natural consequence. This discrete-trial approach is success oriented because it teaches what is expected before errors occur and ensures reinforcement. In many programs, the discrete-trial format is delivered in a massed-trial manner, with a sequence of repetitions of the same response. Typically, the discrete-trial format includes a relatively short pause between trials. For example, some teachers work on identification of numbers, letters, colors, or shapes by drilling students repeatedly in this manner:

"Show me M." (Stimulus)
Student points to letter "M" on table. (Response)
"Good pointing to M!" (Consequence)

Pause

Repeat

It's important to understand that the pause can be longer, so as not to be in a "drill and kill" mode, and can be distributed across the instructional day in a more natural manner. For example, Joey is working on tracing letters so that he can develop written language skills. One strategy may be to have Joey practice once a day during journal-writing time. Another strategy that may result in more effective learning would be to ask him to do a small amount of writing as part of *every* activity, even if simply signing his name to materials. For example, when students are generating story ideas during Language Arts, Joey can copy a portion of the ideas he and his peer generated and that his peer helped him to articulate, as was depicted in Figure 4.1.

Our instructional programs must also be effective and efficient. Effectiveness refers to whether students learn. Efficiency relates to how long a strategy takes to be successful. This is a consideration for both the instructor's time and for the student's use of the skill. If a particular strategy is effective but takes a long time for students to learn, there may be a better way. If a student can use two equally effective skills to obtain a desired item, one a socially appropriate behavior that is time and labor intensive and the other a socially inappropriate behavior that is quick and easy, which will be used? Horner and Billingsley (1988) demonstrated this by using an augmentative communication strategy. Students who had been using tantrums to obtain items were taught to use a communication tool instead. However, a tantrum required less effort, and the students tended to revert to the more effective means (tantrum) to gain what they wanted.

When Raymond needs a break, he has learned to strike out. In the past this behavior has meant a time-out. Although this is certainly not the best way for him to get a break, it is effective. Teaching Raymond to request a break is far more socially acceptable, but we must listen to him when he makes his request. Making the communication process easy for him and clearly and quickly understood by others may also make it more efficient for him. This does not mean that staff will no longer help Raymond learn to attend for longer periods on task. Learning to stay on task longer is also critical for him and will be part of his instructional plan.

Implications for Inclusive Education.   A number of strategies for systematic instruction in inclusive settings exist. Some strategies developed and implemented in separate settings in which stimuli can be more readily controlled do not transfer to general education or inclusive community settings without some modification. Inclusive settings provide far more variety in activities, and stimuli are not so easily controlled. The pace of a general education classroom is typically faster and more spontaneous. Ensuring that students have the opportunity to practice skills sufficiently in such an dynamic environment is critical. The selection of prompts that are effective as well as nonstigmatizing is also an important consideration.

Billingsley and Kelley (1994) surveyed project directors, professors, administrators, and researchers who provide direct or indirect services to students with severe disabilities and identified a number of appropriate and inappropriate strategies in general education settings. Many of these were considered inappropriate mainly because of the logistics of implementing them. Strategies identified by at least 20 percent of the respondents as inappropriate included massed trials, physical assistance, one-to-one instruction, stimulus shaping, and graduated guidance. The age of the student was a consideration in the use of certain strategies. For example, physical assistance was more acceptable for elementary school students and less acceptable with high school students.

With so many people involved in instruction, communication of our strategies must occur regularly and frequently. We propose the following guidelines in considering instructional strategies for inclusive settings.

1. Employ repeated practice to ensure that skills will be reinforced throughout the day by all—staff, students, and parents.

2. Provide nonstigmatizing instructional prompts and consequences.
3. Select instructional strategies that are natural, yet still effective. If natural consequences are sufficient to support learning, don't use any other prompts or consequences.
4. Ensure that all staff have the information and skills to instruct systematically.
   a. Communicate the instructional plan to all.
      (1) Provide a written record of the plan.
      (2) Provide a method for recording student progress.
   b. Supervise and train all staff involved with the student.
5. Establish regular opportunities to review the program's effectiveness.
   a. Hold collaborative team meetings with data review.
   b. Modify written plans in accordance with data review and team decisions.
   c. Ensure that all staff are aware of changes.

Making Prompting Effective

When Do We Prompt?   Instructional prompts are delivered either before a response to ensure accuracy of the response or after the response to correct an inaccurate response. If before a response, an *antecedent* or *cue procedure* should provide just enough information to ensure success. This approach has also been referred to as errorless learning (Touchette, 1971). As was mentioned in Chapter 2, Madeline Hunter (1982) noted that "practice makes permanent." It is critical to minimize students' practicing mistakes. When Raymond is learning to copy computer disks and print out materials, it would be unwise to just let him use a trial-and-error method. Support staff will provide assistance in the form of modeling, gestures, and partial physical assistance immediately, without waiting for him to make errors. How are the prompts selected? Each prompt is selected based upon what Raymond demonstrated during our functional assessment of this activity.

The second prompting strategy, a *correction procedure,* assists a student in correcting an inaccurate response. As noted, at different learning stages, each of these strategies is applicable. For example, during acquisition of a new skill, the cue procedure makes most sense so that a student can learn the correct response. When the student has learned the skill but is working on maintenance or fluency, the correction procedure is more effective and efficient. Corrections consist of providing the amount and type of assistance a student needs to complete a skill or a step in an activity. The assistance is always the smallest amount necessary. In order to provide this assistance, educators typically provide a very nonintrusive prompt, for example, "What are you forgetting?" "What's next?," or as Gold (1980) suggested, "Try another way." If that is not sufficient, a bit more assistance is provided until a student is able to correctly perform the skill.

When Amanda is answering a question from a peer or one of her teachers, although she has demonstrated the ability to operate her Macaw, she does not always remember to use it. When she forgets, her peer or teacher glances down at her Macaw as a first corrective prompt. As Melissa works on understanding a story she is reading, she is learning to use the CAPS strategy (Leinhardt & Zigmond, 1988). A mnemonic device prompts students to consider:

C   Who are the *Characters*?
A   What is the *Aim* of the story?
P   What *Problem* happens?
S   How is the problem *Solved*?

Staff prompt Melissa to remember her steps by rehearsing the strategy as she begins.

What Types of Prompts Are There?   Prompts come in a variety of forms. We use physical, verbal, proximity, gestural, contextual, visual, and within-stimulus prompts in our everyday teaching (Falvey et al., 1980). Many times we don't even realize we're prompting because it's such a natural part of our interaction with students. But when we prompt in a manner that is not systematically planned, we are likely to reinforce a dependence on our assistance and inhibit independence. For example, many of us provide repeated prompts that increase in intensity until the student responds correctly. We may actually be teaching our student to expect this chain of prompts before the final response. Our teaching effort might be perceived like this: "Let's see, she does that; then I do this; then she does that, and I do this; then she does this other thing and I do this, and she gets happy about it and I get what I want."

The selection of prompts is worth consideration for a number of reasons. Prompts are additional information provided to assist a student to learn a skill, not adaptations that are meant to continue. For that reason, once we introduce a prompt, we must consider how we're going to ultimately remove it. This removal process must be done in a manner that continues to allow for student success. Continually and systematically fading the intensity of our assistance or the amount of information provided allows a student to approach natural performance contingencies. It is also very important to remember that a prompt must not detract from the natural stimulus but rather highlight it. Amanda has to learn to look at whoever is speaking. When a prompt is provided for this skill, it should come from the speaker, possibly enhanced by adding her name ("Amanda, which group will you join?") or in increasing the volume, *not* from another person reminding her to look.

Pros and Cons of Prompt Types.   *Physical prompts* are provided by touching or guiding a student's body through a movement or series of movements. They are typically used to assist a student in learning a particular motor pattern when correct responding is important. They allow motor patterns to become established by repeated practice. Students with motor and sensory impairment may need physical prompts as a support when learning motor tasks. However, some people do not like to be touched or manipulated. Physical prompts can also be stigmatizing and age inappropriate and may not allow students to learn from their errors. Many things we want students to learn, such as verbal communication, are not primarily motor tasks, and physical prompts are not useful for these activities.

Graduated guidance is a form of physical prompting that involves providing full physical assistance in the beginning, typically using a hand-over-hand strategy to move the student through the task. Assistance is provided as needed to move through the task and reduced as the student becomes more familiar with the specific movements required. There may be fading criteria established as described by Demchack (1989), or the instructor may reduce assistance based upon student performance each instructional period. Reduction of assistance may involve using a lighter touch, touching less surface area, or moving further away from the hands. Shadowing, following the movement of the hands without touching, may be a third stage of assistance.

For example, helping Raymond learn to operate the mouse on a computer when he is copying disks or printing material may require some amount of hand-over-hand assistance at first. However, the instructor should quickly move away from this assistance both to help Raymond learn to use natural stimuli (the location of the cursor and icon) and to avoid stigmatizing him.

Verbal prompts involve talking to the learner to provide assistance. This instructional strategy is probably the most-used strategy and often the one least likely to be useful. Describing an action sometimes doesn't supply enough information. Verbal prompts are more useful when assisting a student in recognizing when to take an action or when to model a desired communication and are also useful in social or group situations because modeling is also present. Verbal prompts are not typically stigmatizing, as they are commonly used for all students. They *do* require auditory skills, and for persons with little language ability, they will not be as useful. They may also distract a learner and can be overused. We often spend so much time telling people what to do that we ignore other, more effective and less intrusive, ways to convey information. Verbal prompts should contain only the information necessary to support correct responding. Long, complex explanations describing steps to take and rationales for taking them are not useful and, in fact, are counterproductive.

There are two types of verbal prompts, direct and indirect. Direct verbal prompts describe an action to take, for example, "Show him your break card, Raymond" (as Raymond's agitation indicates he needs a break). This verbal prompt describes what Raymond should do. An indirect verbal prompt provides information but does not specifically describe what to do. The individual needs to interpret the prompt and take action. For example, Raymond knows how to use the break card but does not always remember to use it. We might change our prompt to "What do you need to do, Raymond?" When Melissa is learning to organize her Math worksheets, verbal prompts may describe specific actions for her to take as she completes these practice sheets. Initially, staff members prepared Math worksheets with boxes for her answers. This strategy allowed her to keep numerals in line and helped avoid confusion about carrying and borrowing. Melissa is learning how to prepare these organizers herself now and needs periodic reminders that range from, "Make your boxes" to "What's your first step?"

Proximity prompts, in which the teacher positions herself near the learner or near desired materials, assist a student in recognizing that a response is called for and also in identifying what a teacher may be expecting. Moving closer to a student may prompt him to initiate a response, and moving closer to another person or item in the room may show the student which response to make. Proximity prompts depend on contextual cues to make any sense. When Amanda needs materials from the resource book area, her peer or a staff member moves to the area and waits. This prompt tells Amanda that she is expected to push herself over there to bring back items. When it is time to leave the classroom, support staff or peers again move to the door and look back at Amanda to prompt her that she needs to do something. One problem with proximity prompts is that students may pay more attention to the person providing the prompt than the natural discriminative stimuli.

Gestural prompts involve directing the learner's attention to stimuli without physically touching the person, perhaps with a nod to indicate direction or by pointing at something. Gestures are common, natural, nonstigmatizing prompts that are easily used and effective in groups and across distances. They may be difficult for students who do not pick up subtle cues well or need much more information. Staff members use gestural prompts to remind Joey and Amanda to use their augmentative communication system. They gesture toward Joey's book when it is time for him to share his thoughts by using his conversation book. When it appears that Amanda wants to communicate, staff (or peers) look at her and gesture towards her Macaw to make her remember to use the tools that she has.

Contextual prompts provide information through the context of the situation. Materials, actions, communication, and other environmental cues assist the learner in making a correct response. A student who is placed in a context that demands a skill is encouraged to respond in order to participate. Haring et al. (1987) demonstrated this process through a modified incidental teaching procedure, in which staff organized the classroom environment so that students needed to communicate to obtain items or activities they wanted. Inclusive educational and community environments offer a rich variety of contextual prompts. Students must be able to pick up more subtle cues and perform the skill in their repertoire to benefit from this strategy. One of Joey's primary goals is to express himself in terms of choice, making comments, protests, and requests. He needs to practice continually over the day, and staff look for any opportunity to allow him to use his words. When his schedule shows that it is time for Math work on the computer, he knows he must select a peer to work with. This encourages his use of language as well as his choice-making skills.

Visual prompts provide a model of a desired response. Demonstrating what is expected of the learner, providing an example to copy, or describing an outcome or response through pictures or words are examples of visual prompts. They are naturally available, typical in school and community environments, and nonstigmatizing because they are so common. Visual prompts require that students be able to imitate or copy what they see.

Picture and word schedules remind students of tasks they need to complete. Several examples of this process can be found in all school and community programs and throughout the literature. Wilson, Schepis, and Mason-Main (1987) provide an example. Visual prompts can be easily faded by reducing the amount of visual material available. Melissa benefits from this strategy in much of her work. Staff have found that with a model, she is better able to complete written work. For example, staff always provide a model of a math problem on her worksheets. The model demonstrates exactly what she will do to complete her problems, with organizing boxes included. When she is completing written papers in American Literature, she is given a model outline to use.

Raymond also uses a visual system to advise him of the next steps in his schedule. This picture system shows him what to do and is coordinated with his digital watch. Each picture shows a task and the time he is to start it.

Within-stimulus prompts involve exaggerating some dimension of the natural stimulus to increase its salience. Making something brighter, bigger, more defined, louder, or more tactile assists a learner in recognizing the critical stimulus that will discriminate correct responding. Joey is practicing his writing skills by tracing over words printed by staff or peers. Initially, the letters of the words were large and dark enough to be easily seen. As he became more proficient, the letters were reduced in size and made lighter. Joey needs to concentrate more with these prompts and make his letters with more precision. Another example involves the size and amount of information on the icons on Amanda's communication system. As she becomes more proficient in locating the specific icon she needs to press, more messages can be included on the system and less information provided on each icon.

Within-stimulus prompting is easily faded simply by fading the exaggeration. It may be difficult to find ways to exaggerate some stimuli, particularly in the community. Making a street-crossing signal brighter may be problematic unless we consider that the saliency of a street-crossing signal tends to be greater at night. The use of Frequency Modulation (FM) systems is a good example of increasing the volume of verbal information while keeping other auditory information constant.

Sequencing Prompting.   Specific prompts based upon good assessment information are necessary to ensure that students have enough information to be successful but not more information than they need. Learning means stretching a bit away from support. Because of their intrinsic nature and the nature of specific skills, activities, and contexts, prompts will have varying strength in different situations and with different learners. Certainly visual prompts are not very informative for students with visual impairment or visual processing difficulties. Similarly, verbal prompts may not be helpful for students who find auditory input confusing. Selecting a prompt requires that we also plan for fading it, either to a less intrusive variation of that prompt type or to another, less informative, prompt.

The stage of the instructional planning and implementation process is also important in the selection of prompts and prompting strategies. For example, during the assessment phase we are interested, in part, in the amount of information needed to successfully complete a skill or task. Providing the least amount of information at the start and then adding more if necessary is the best strategy. As soon as we provide enough (as indicated by the learner's ability to perform the skill), we stop prompting. This *increasing assistance* approach allows us to plan our instruction for success. In contrast, during the acquisition stage, it would be wise to use a *decreasing assistance* approach, in which we provide the assistance required for a student to be successful and then decrease assistance as the student learns. When a learner has acquired a skill and is practicing it for maintenance and fluency, the increasing assistance approach is again useful but only to correct errors in skills already learned.

Joey has difficulty categorizing items by attribute in Math. Initial attributes should be highly contrasting, and the number of categories should be few in number so that he can experience success. At first, staff pointed out the specific attribute for each item he was handed and pointed to the location of the category. Later, they simply pointed out the attribute and, finally, began to decrease the contrast.

Time-Delay Strategies

The success of our instructional programs lies in finding ways for learners to move from dependence on prompts to the ability to perform skills in an effective way at the right time. Decreasing-assistance models, of which graduated guidance is an example, are one way to make this transition. To implement *time delay,* the appropriate prompt is first provided concurrent with the natural stimulus or instructional cue to ensure correct responses and access to the natural reinforcement or to an arranged additional reinforcer. As the student becomes more proficient, a delay between the natural stimulus or instructional cue and the prompt is arranged. Initially, the delay is very short, with the planned prompt delivered almost immediately. If the learner does not initiate a response, the prompt is provided after the determined delay, for example, two seconds later. The delay is progressively increased based upon student performance, as in a progressive time delay, or at regular intervals (i.e., zero seconds for the first five opportunities, two seconds for the next five opportunities, three seconds for the next five, etc.) in a constant time delay. Time delay increases the likelihood of learner success and supports the transition from instructional prompts to natural stimuli. McDonnell (1987) found time delay to be more efficient than the increasing-assistance prompt strategy in a study of purchasing skills. A number of other researchers have also been very successful with this procedure in a variety of settings and activities (Halle, Marshall, & Spradlin, 1979; Snell, 1982; Snell & Gast, 1981).

Raymond is learning to use money to buy his lunch at school. Staff have established a prompting program to support his independence in telling the clerk what he wants, remembering to pay, and collecting his change. He is given a variety of verbal prompts and gestures. Initially, the verbal prompt ("Tell her what you want") was provided as soon as the clerk looked at him and said, "Next?" The gesture toward the clerk was provided as a prompt as soon as she said, "That'll be $1.75," and a gesture was also provided immediately when change was handed to him. After one week, the prompts were delivered approximately two seconds later. Further increases of the delay will be made as the program continues.

Incidental Teaching Strategies

In recent years, there has been a great deal of interest in integrated therapy—the integration of communication, motor, social, and cognitive skills within functional activities. This contextual approach attempts to organize instruction in a relevant way. The contextual cues naturally provided within the activity assist a learner in discriminating the appropriate stimuli for specific responses.

Incidental teaching refers to an interaction between an adult and a child that arises naturally in an unstructured situation and is used by the adult to supply information or give the child practice in developing a skill (Halle, 1982). It allows educators to benefit from a learner's interest in some topic, event, situation, or item. Research by Hart and Risley (1982) provides a basis for incidental language learning, outlining nine components of incidental teaching for language development:

1. Arranging the setting with attractive objects
2. Involving someone in the environment who is important to the learner and to whom the learner can relate
3. Waiting for the learner to initiate
4. Looking into the learner's eyes and focusing on the topic
5. Asking if not sure of the topic

6. Asking for elaboration or improvement
7. Prompting if there is no response or it is inappropriate
8. Modeling the response and asking the learner to say it, too
9. Confirming the response and providing the requested item or action

Because students with severe cognitive and language disabilities may require additional support when learning in an incidental manner, Haring et al. (1987) adapted Hart and Risley's model to increase salience, finding an increase in spontaneous responses. The four strategies they utilized were

1. Providing opportunities for choice by offering a clear presentation of two or more objects to select
2. Placing objects out of reach and waiting for three seconds to prompt
3. Blocking access silently or passively for a minimum of three seconds
4. Intentionally giving students materials that were inappropriate for the situation (p. 220)

In incidental teaching, the occasion for instruction arises naturally in unstructured situations and is used to enhance skill competence and provide an opportunity for practice. The occasions are always student initiated; however, as noted, environments and activities can be modified to encourage initiation. The teacher should determine exactly what response is expected. Prompting is typically provided in an increasing-assistance model.

The importance of this information is that opportunities for learning occur spontaneously throughout the day, and educators need to have a plan to ensure that students increase their skills through these opportunities. In the inclusive classroom, there are far more such opportunities because of the number of students, activities, and interactions. For example, consider the communication opportunities with peers and staff, using augmentative or alternative communication systems if necessary. Moving from activity to activity, getting to and from class, getting around the campus, or simply manipulating materials and equipment allow for continual practice of both fine and gross motor skills. Cognitive skill development can be facilitated using a variety of materials, exposure to information, and interactions with peers that provide rich opportunities for incidental teaching.

For example, Amanda's peers and support staff make a point of asking her questions or talking with her throughout the day so that she can practice with her augmentative system. These social occasions help Amanda learn how to interact. She has good models for social and communication skills among her peers. Opportunities for communication and choice making, critical skills for Raymond and Joey, occur throughout the school day. In each of these occasions, the adults will provide assistance in accordance with an instructional plan, remembering to use the agreed-upon prompting and fading strategies.

Many empirically validated instructional strategies have been generated over the years. They are all part of the repertoire of tools to support student learning. Finding ways to incorporate those strategies in a natural nonstigmatizing manner while continuing to develop new strategies is our responsibility.

Writing It All Down

The importance of communicating our instructional plan to all involved as well as keeping track of progress has been noted. This is best done through written instructional plans and recording sheets. With these in place, it is more likely that all staff are on the same page, providing the same assistance, corrections, and consequences. We can also be sure that we're addressing the objectives established for the student. Communication among team members and in our quarterly reports and annual IEPs will be more objective and relevant.

One of the most common critiques of written instructional plans and recordkeeping is the paperwork requirements. Our system must be simple enough to be implemented on a consistent basis and sufficiently detailed to describe an effective instructional program.

Student: _Joey_   Activity or routine: _____ Mathlands sorting: grouping and rules _____

Objective: When involved in math sorting activities, Joey goes to the appropriate station, sorts into two attributes with prompts to identify attribute and place item, draws picture of activity, and shows picture to teacher.

Teacher does	Student does									
Indirect verbal—"Where is your group?" three seconds after direction to whole class.	Identify Bats group. Go to station. Listen to station directions.	**date**	10/23	10/30	11/6					**%**
		steps in routine								100
Provide circles drawn on mats. Use one attribute (color, size, shape) only. Increase to two attributes after three sessions at 80 percent. Prompt—"What (color, size, shape?) Where does it go?" Fade to "Where does it go?" only after three sessions at 80 percent.	Picks up items to sort, places each item in circle.	Goes to station.	–	–	+					90
		Looks at reader.	–	+	+					80
		Initiates task.	–	–	+					70
		Sorts by attribute.	–		–					60
		Uses picture to communicate.	+	+	+					50
"What do you need to do now?"	Points to picture of pens, paper.	Draws picture.		+	+					40
Prompt only if Joey does not start. "What do you want to do?"	Takes out materials, draws picture of completed sorting activity.	Shows picture when completed.		–	–					30
										20
If Joey does not show picture by the end of the time block, prompt "Time's up, Joey."	Shows picture to teacher when done.									10
										0

FIGURE 4.4   Instructional Program: Joey

Examples are provided in Figures 4.4, 4.5, and 4.6. Figure 4.5 addresses Amanda's participation in cooperative workgroups and describes the strategies for increasing her competence in using her lesson materials, moving in her wheelchair, communicating to her peers and staff, and making choices. Although the prompt is shown at a specific level, staff will use a prompt fading strategy as Amanda demonstrates skill at this level. The data collection section includes space to record (+) or (–) for responses at the prompt level. The data sheet is also self-graphing.

POSITIVE BEHAVIORAL SUPPORT

One of the concerns about inclusive education for all students regards students who exhibit behavior problems. Educators are reluctant to open their doors to students they see as disruptive or a danger to other students. This is understandable; however, one cannot automatically assume that a student with a history of disruptive behavior will demonstrate the same behavior in the general education classroom. Some also assume that students who exhibit behavior challenges will be better served in special classrooms where

Student: _Amanda_   **Activity or routine:** _Cooperative workgroups_

Objective: When involved in cooperative workgroups, Amanda will use her wheelchair to gather materials, choose materials, open and locate pictures of related materials by pointing with staff or peer support to lift only.

Teacher does	Student does	date	10/23	10/30	11/6					%
Indirect verbal—"What do you need?" Icon is on last page. Staff or peer reads assignment.	Picks up assignment book, turns pages to assignment icon.	steps in routine								100
		Turns pages.	+	+	+					90
Partial physical—if chair gets stuck by light touch on one hand. Provide choice of two. Direct verbal prompt, "Point to the one you want."	Moves wheelchair to resource section, selects books, returns to group with books.	Moves to area.	+	+	+					80
		Points to book.	–	–	–					70
Ask, "Show me_____." Provide assistance at elbow to prompt touching picture. Direct verbal, "Show this to your group."	Identifies pictures of related items. Shows selected pictures to peers.	Points to picture.	+	+	+					60
		Shows to peers.		–	–					50
Gesture toward Macaw to remind Amanda to call for group members' attention. (Eventually fade to glance.)	Activate Macaw to let peers know she has something to share.	Uses Macaw.	–	+	+					40
										30
										20
Data: + for correct at prompt level; – for incorrect at prompt level.	Returns items to shelf.									10
										0

FIGURE 4.5   Instructional Program: Amanda

there are "highly trained staff to meet their needs." In our view, this approach simply moves a problem from a setting with the greatest potential for learning appropriate behavior to another setting in which inappropriate behavior is the norm. Students who exhibit problem behavior in special education classrooms or schools are rarely if ever moved to the general education setting as a solution, even if they continue to have behavior problems in the special class. Behavior problems are not placement issues, but issues of understanding the function of the problem behavior, then developing and implementing a support plan to make it less likely, and teaching better strategies for achieving the same function.

Raymond has a history of problem behavior, including striking out, destroying materials and equipment, and getting up and leaving activities. Staff in his special education programs have typically addressed his behavior by reducing demands on him and avoiding confrontations. Although his former teachers felt he could not be successful at the high school, his parents felt he was not making any progress in the separate program anyway and wanted to offer him a more stimulating environment.

The staff at Monroe High School considered his hearing loss and difficulty in communication important factors in his behavior. By listening to his family, talking with

Student: Raymond   **Activity or routine:** Purchasing lunch at school

Objective: When purchasing lunch at school, Raymond will order and pay using correct change, remembering to take his change with no assistance.

Teacher does	Student does	date	10/23	10/30	11/6					%
Indirect verbal, "Tell her what you want" when clerk acknowledges Raymond.	Orders choice for lunch using verbal skills and communication book.	**steps in routine**								100
		Locate line; stands in line.	−	+	+					90
Gesture toward wallet.	Take out wallet, gives money to clerk.	Takes out book.	−	−	+					80
		Uses verbal skills and book to order lunch.	−	/	−					70
Gesture toward change.	Reach for change. Put change in pocket before taking food.	Takes out wallet, hands money to clerk.	−	+	+					60
		Takes change.	+	+	+					50
		Puts change in pocket.	+	−	+					40
Select food items before going to the cafeteria using communication book.										30
										20
Start at 0 second time delay. After 5 days with correct responding, time delay = 2 seconds; then 4 seconds; 6 seconds.										10
										0

FIGURE 4.6   Instructional Program: Raymond

former teachers, and observing him over the course of the day in a variety of activities and with a number of people, they developed a hypothesis about the functions of his behaviors. Raymond is more likely to strike out or destroy things when he can't get his point across or when he needs to wait. When others attempt to discipline him, he typically strikes them. He is not likely to demonstrate these problem behaviors when he is engaged in familiar routines, listening to music (through headsets with high volume), drawing, and looking through books. He seems to enjoy being around others his age but will not attempt to initiate communication with them. Raymond seems to use these behaviors to avoid activities, possibly because he is not successful in them.

This functional assessment process gives his team the best chance for designing a successful support plan for Raymond, because it recognizes that his behavior is meaningful and makes sense for him. His support plan, outlined in Figure 4.7, involves adapting his classwork to accommodate for his learning problems, providing a way to ask for a break, and interspersing easy with difficult tasks. The staff have also built a peer support group to assist Raymond in class and on the campus and have worked with his peers on how to communicate with him. Raymond needs intensive work in learning to communicate, and staff are providing instruction in signing as well as speech.

FIGURE 4.7   Positive Behavioral Support Plan

STUDENT: Raymond

TARGET BEHAVIOR(S): Striking out; property destruction

SUMMARY OF FUNCTIONAL ANALYSIS OF BEHAVIOR

An extensive review of the history of these behaviors, including interviews with past teaching staff, parents, and peers and observations at school and home indicate that Raymond is more likely to use these behaviors when he is being pressured to participate in nonpreferred tasks, particularly those that are unfamiliar to him. It appears that his initial strategy is to leave the area, and when staff continue to try to get him involved, he strikes out at them or throws, tears, or breaks an item nearby. These communication strategies have been successful for him as his parents and staff have tended to reduce demands on him. When Raymond wants something, he has a difficult time waiting for it and will strike out or damage property in these circumstances. When Raymond is involved in certain activities of his choice, he is not likely to have these challenging behaviors.

GOALS

The primary goals for Raymond are to learn more ways to communicate his preferences and choices, to extend the time he is able to wait for something he has requested, and to expand the range of activities he is comfortable in. A major goal for the educational team is to find ways to involve Raymond meaningfully in school and classroom activities in a way that is interesting to him.

POSITIVE BEHAVIORAL SUPPORT PLAN

A. Quality of life enhancement: Educational staff and peers involved in his support group will generate a list of activities and events occurring on and off campus that he might be interested in and set up a plan for introducing him to those opportunities. Pictures of those that are most promising will be included in his conversation book for choice making.

B. Antecedent changes: The educational team will examine classroom activities for ways to adapt so that Raymond uses his skills and interests. For example, because music and drawing are such important parts of his routine, these will be incorporated when possible. Raymond will also have the opportunity to have some measure of choice in learning activities. All choices offered will relate to the activity.

C. Teaching new skills: Training in the use of Raymond's conversation book will be provided. In addition, staff will provide daily training in manual sign language with special emphasis on communicating those messages he communicates with his behavior. Verbal speech will also be encouraged (not required) when he is signing. Raymond's peers will also receive training on his communication system, including the conversation book and sign language. Peers will be shown how to encourage Raymond to use these tools during class work and during school activities.

The staff at Monroe understand that Raymond's behavior will not change overnight and that he will continue to challenge his family, the staff, and his peers, but with support, these behaviors will be less likely to be Raymond's only strategies.

SUMMARY

Chapter 4 provides a rationale for the application of systematic instructional strategies in inclusive educational settings and an overview of strategies that have proven effective in supporting learning for all students with significant disabilities. There has been strong criticism of inclusive education regarding what some feel will be the loss of direct instruction. However, inclusive education should mean better and more effective instruction. The strategies developed over many years in home, school, and community settings can be applied to inclusive classrooms, particularly if educators ensure that methods (a) suit a student's chronological age, (b) are nonstigmatizing, (c) reflect a student's learning mode and preferences, and (d) are effective. Prompting strategies must be based upon assessment information and should also reflect the particular stage of learning (acquisition, maintenance, fluency, generalization) at which the student is operating. Considerations of student learning style are also important in selecting instructional approaches.

A number of prompt types (physical, verbal, proximity, gestural, contextual, visual, within stimulus) were reviewed, with variations within these types. Each prompt type has advantages and disadvantages, depending on the learner, situation, and natural stimuli. Selecting instructional strategies is truly an individual matter. One size definitely does not fit all.

Communicating progress on instructional programs requires organization. Writing down the specific prompting strategies allows staff to be consistent and to communicate effectively and objectively about how the plan is working. It also encourages educators to modify plans that are not effective.

Finally, many students' behavior interferes with their success in learning and interacting with others. Systematically analyzing the functional basis for behaving provides teams with relevant information to (a) design a positive support plan that will allow students to learn new ways to behave and to (b) remove some of the stimuli that contribute to problem behavior.

CHECKING FOR UNDERSTANDING

Kennedy High School has restructured its program over the past three years for students with IEPs and for students labeled as at risk for school failure. As part of schoolwide reorganization, special education staff belong to teaching teams with their general education peers, and all students are part of teaching "families." Staff have made enormous progress in finding ways for students to participate in all aspects of the core curriculum and school activities. There is a very positive feeling at the school, particularly about the way that students are supporting each other.

Although students are actively participating in the learning opportunities in the school, the level of their participation does not seem to be increasing in many situations. Staff wonder if they are just becoming more creative in finding ways to keep students involved and have begun to think seriously about how they can support students. The way they assist students varies from person to person, and students' abilities seem to vary from day to day.

1. Do staff have a valid concern? Why? Why not?

2. How can educators evaluate the effectiveness of their support?

3. How can teaching strategies be individualized for each student?

4. How can direct instructional strategies be implemented without stigmatizing students and interfering with the natural flow of this creative learning environment?

5. When should teaching occur rather than adaptation?

6. How can staff be consistent with support strategies?

CHAPTER FIVE

PEER RELATIONSHIPS AND SUPPORT

Upon completion of this chapter, you will be able to

1. Delineate components of positive classroom climate and strategies to achieve peer support

2. Describe how classroom meetings can be utilized for proactive planning and problem-solving

3. Identify and describe a variety of peer support and collaboration strategies and systems, including circles of friends, "pit crews," and MAPS

4. Describe informal as well as structured strategies for peer support and distinguish situations in which each is appropriate

Sapon-Shevin, Dobbelacre, Corrigan, Goodman, and Mastin (1998) note an inherent conflict in our attempts to enhance the social acceptance and inclusion of students with disabilities: the concentration of our strategies on the disabled student. They suggest that this focus on the "targeted" student may reinforce a lack of reciprocity and promote the image of that student as the one always in need of assistance and, at the same time, may result in too little attention to the *overall* classroom climate or context (cf. Kohn, 1996).

Clearly, we must attend to both fronts. Students with disabilities will require specific social skills instruction and facilitation of interactions and relationships, and all students require a positive classroom climate in which they can grow. Alfie Kohn (1996), Mara Sapon-Shevin (1990), and many others have written effectively on this topic, and we first outline some of these contextual strategies before proceeding to specific examples from inclusive classrooms.

BUILDING COMMUNITY

In Kohn's wonderful book, *Beyond Discipline* (1996), he posed a critical question for teachers: "What do our students need in order to flourish and how can we provide this?" rather than the traditional query, "How can we make them do what we want?" (p. xv). This question is essential if we wish to create real community in our classrooms, not merely "pseudo-community." Kohn emphasizes that classroom community does not mean simply giving students input into rules and consequences for disobeying them. He notes that the process is important, looking *with* the students for the ways we want our classroom to work. The desire to create classroom community requires a positive view of students, an understanding of the research that has demonstrated student needs for *autonomy* (self-determination, being an originator of decisions), *relatedness* (connectedness to others), and *competence* (taking pleasure from learning and putting learning to use).

Community is not automatic, it is constructed over time by people who recognize a common purpose. In addition to time, factors that facilitate its development include small groupings, teacher inclusion in the larger school community, multiage classrooms, and teachers being able to work with students for more than one year. Kohn makes an important distinction between *community* and *collectives,* noting that communities nourish and preserve individuals and individuality and stress the relationships among individuals. Collectives focus on conformity and are actually much more traditional in this respect with their focusing on obedience or "loyalty to the school order" (p. 108). In contrast, communities are compatible with the personalized learning emphasized in the corollary school reforms of Sizer (1992) and others.

Sapon-Shevin (1990) has suggested some environmental changes for a cooperative, positive climate. For example, she encourages teachers to use the "visitor test." If by looking at the walls, bulletin boards, etc., a visitor can determine who is doing well, who are the classroom "stars," then something is amiss. Sapon-Shevin directs us to remove the star charts and the displays of "A" papers only and, instead, display samples of *all* students' work. Further, student-created murals, mobiles, or other group products related to course content, unit themes, seasons, and so forth, can provide vehicles for all students to participate in classroom design. Sapon-Shevin (1990, pp. 66–70) delineated several additional examples of positive stage-setting techniques

- Use inclusive language, for example, "our class," "students," "kids."
- Eliminate competitive classroom symbols (star charts, etc.).
- Use literature to teach cooperation.
- Encourage recognition of each other's accomplishments (e.g., a "good deed tree," to which students affix classmate's name and brief description of the situation).
- Restructure games in cooperative ways (e.g., musical chairs).

When we enter classrooms in which a community is under construction, we are continually struck by the enthusiasm of students for the process and the generosity of spirit that is demonstrated. We want to share with you some examples we have witnessed of the following strategies that Kohn (1996) articulated so well. A caution: Remember that this is not a list of things to do but rather of the kinds of things that classrooms working toward community engage in. They don't "make" community; they result from that community.

Ask Students What Can Be Done to Put Them at Ease

Kohn suggested a variety of questions to pose to students early in the first month of school, such as: What were good things that happened last year? Tell me about a really awful day. What was happening then? How can we deal with this in a new way?

We know a teacher, we'll call him Mr. V., who has several "appointments" with his elementary-age students throughout the day to discuss questions such as these, to ask how they can make the classroom work, and to check on how things are working for them. He reinforces the notion that students should feel free to come up with ideas that might sound "weird," to make mistakes, to not be afraid of humiliation. He accomplishes this partly by sharing aspects of his own vulnerability at appropriate moments. For example, while the students were writing their own New Year's resolutions, he shared his resolve to wash his dishes daily instead of letting them pile up in the sink for a week.

A fourth grader told us recently that, "There is no time-out or time-out chair in Mr. V.'s class, you know." She went on to explain that when there is any kind of problem, Mr. V. has the class help define the problem, and he writes it on the board. They then brainstorm solutions, which he puts up there as well. Students discuss the solutions and select the most workable, making an action plan. From the outset, these students are becoming originators of decisions and seeing the connectedness of others' actions with their own. They also have live demonstrations of their teacher's very real respect for them, which engenders their mutual respect.

Foster Connectedness among Students and Between Students and Teacher

Common endeavors foster students' interdependence and respect for each others' unique talents or contributions. These class and schoolwide activities cut across both academic and nonacademic periods. Students can construct murals, collages, or quilts; write a class song or a play; make their own student resource or "Yellow Pages" highlighting their talents (Sapon-Shevin, 1990; Kohn, 1996), conduct polls (e.g., What's your favorite ice cream? Sport? Drink?); publish newsletters; conduct research on the Internet; use the Internet to communicate with students in a class across the country or across town; or engage in community service as a group (e.g., beach clean-up day). Activities such as these serve the dual purpose of engaging students' multiple intelligences at the same time as building community.

Teachers foster their connectedness to students when they remember details of their students' lives and make a point of sharing these. In Mr. V.'s class, when students are conducting shareathons, Mr. V. plans with the assigned group a few day's prior to the event. He remembers, for example, that Larry is a whale enthusiast and suggests that he bring in materials about whales to share. He helps Larry think about what he could have the students do in their time with his station, such as drawing a particular type of whale from an illustration or partner-reading from pertinent book selections. While studying Italy, Mr. V. recalls a recent trip that Joey's family made there and asks his parents to help Joey assemble a photo book of the experience for his station. Joey's group composes a spot quiz of facts about Italy for students to play in the station.

A favorite example of ours occurred in a fifth-grade class that conducted presidential elections for the whole school during an actual election year. They composed speeches directly from actual speeches and platform content, conducted debates open to all, registered voters, and put on miniworkshops for other classes regarding the electoral process. In their own class, students considered and researched questions such as the changing role of the media and campaign contributions to the process. On Election Day, all 600 students voted, and results were tabulated for comparison with local, state, and national percentages: democracy in action. Berman (1990) noted that we teach reading, writing, and mathematics by doing them, but we have "taught" democracy by lecture. Community-building and class-school extensions such as these begin to teach students the practice of democracy.

"To Meet Our Needs, We Need to Meet"

We agree with Kohn (1996, p. 87) that this is perhaps the most significant and useful tool in fostering classroom community. In increasing numbers of classrooms, teachers utilize class meetings for a vast array of activities: obtaining student input on how a particular unit is proceeding, problem-solving behavior, homework, or procedural issues. Some of the questions teachers might pose are:

- How can we make sure everyone's homework gets done?
- How can we get our line in order in the morning at the school meeting so we can earn points?
- What do you think about the products I have asked your groups to develop for the Math portfolios?
- How could I improve this assignment for you?
- What do you most want to understand about the Vietnam War?
- What was confusing in last night's assignment?

These meetings extend the community across academic areas as well and ensure that community is not something that occurs only during social periods, or in the "cooperative group time." We cannot assume that students will know how to collaborate any more than we can assume adults—teachers—know this unless it is modeled for them with their direct participation. In many inclusive classrooms, these meetings have grown out of initial work geared to support the inclusion of a particular student with disabilities.

For example, in Amanda's sixth grade Humanities block, a circle of middle school classmates she selected met periodically to discuss curricular adaptations and ways to increase Amanda's participation. Over time, other students began raising their own issues in these meetings, and the adults came to realize the importance of this strategy for all students. Students were encouraged to submit an issue or "challenge" in advance by telling a teacher or writing it down. Anonymity was a part of the process in this classroom, so that students could discuss the issue without being inhibited by personality issues or potential peer conflicts. Two issues that came up were: the problem of having homework assigned right before a big event and people who dance too closely at the dance and how to say no to them.

Use Academic Instruction

Class meetings and group projects of all sorts need not be distinct from academic instruction; in fact, there should not be a false separation. Fairness, a frequent topic of class meetings, may be tied to a whole realm of academic pursuits, depending on the age, grade level, and curriculum to be studied in a given year. The high school public service announcement assignment in Chapter 2 is a good example. Students studying equity as it relates to the U.S. Census and resulting resource allocation can consider the ramifications in their own communities. In a closer-to-home example, Monroe High School students learned about the Americans with Disabilities Act (ADA) and then pursued group investigations of their own school's physical and social access for students with disabilities. The outcomes of this project included a determination that after-school activities were really not available to many students who required lift-buses, because there was no late bus so equipped. Students requiring this form of door-to-door transportation had to leave at the close of the school day. Class advocacy with the school district resolved this situation, while demonstrating both the power of and the need for the legislation. It is also a great example of "ability awareness" embedded in school curriculum.

When classes engage in academic pursuits such as these, where there is a convergence of social or moral issues with curriculum content, important student growth occurs.

A powerful example of this type of peer advocacy occurred in a southern California community. Several years ago, a middle school student, we'll call her Lorraine, was attending a special class for students with severe disabilities in her local school. Lorraine had multiple disabilities, including cognitive delays. She used a wheelchair, had diabetes, and communicated nonverbally. Her special education teacher had initiated a peer involvement program, during which general education students came into the class to provide assistance and to socialize with the students. Several students became friendly with Lorraine and began taking her with them to their classes until she was gradually and "unofficially" included throughout her day, with adaptations and natural supports for her instruction.

When they all moved on to high school, every one of Lorraine's friends, as well as her family, assumed she would attend her home high school with her friends. However, they were informed that this would not be the case. The special education administration cited Lorraine's medical needs as well as her significant disabilities as the rationale for her expected special class placement at another high school, because services were not available at her home school. Her friends, a group of primarily Hispanic boys and girls, said no, this was not acceptable. This was discrimination. And they initiated on their own a campaign to bring Lorraine to her local high school. They encountered and successfully addressed a sequence of obstacles, beginning with obtaining training to administer Lorraine's insulin and receiving physician clearance to do so. They engaged in fund raising through car washes to obtain money to publicize the problem and to acquire legal representation; they approached the local media and received positive coverage on the news for Lorraine's situation. They heard about the state chapter of TASH (The Association for Persons with Severe Disabilities) and came to the Cal-TASH board meeting to request assistance from the organization, including a chance to present at the statewide conference nearby. At their presentation, they performed an original rap song about friendship with Lorraine and, by their networking, obtained free legal representation through a nonprofit organization.

When Lorraine finally obtained admission to the high school, they all rode together that first day in a limousine that they hired for the occasion. A year later they returned to the Cal-TASH conference, still together.

So we have a community of learners growing in our classroom or school. You may be thinking that these represent ideal situations that are too difficult to achieve in the world of our schools today. We would remind you that these ideals brought each of you to teaching; it is the love of children and our belief in their abilities, our valuing of their characters and their potential to grow that called us to the field. However long we have been teaching, each of us can still stretch to achieve these communities of children. We can and need to collaborate with our peers to help our schools become the kinds of communities we value. Let us now examine what else needs to happen to ensure that students with disabilities are active participants and equal beneficiaries of this community. The following pages delineate tools to facilitate real social inclusion, using the situations of Amanda, Joe, Raymond, and Melissa and processes known as circles, MAPS, and "pit crews."

We would like to remind you, as you explore these examples, to keep in mind the importance of the convergence of these strategies with the individualized planning and the delivery of systematic instruction to included students as discussed in previous chapters.

AMANDA'S CIRCLE

You'll recall that we reviewed Amanda's individual student planning team's process and agenda for the future in Chapter 3. All of the items in the team's previous agenda—communication system, adaptation, in-class support, and friendships—are related both to what the adults do as well as to Amanda's interaction with peers. Concern was voiced by her mother at that meeting about possible overdependence on the instructional assistant. In addition, the team noted Amanda's lack of involvement with her peers outside of school and decided to brainstorm with her classmates on ways to facilitate heightened participation both in and out of school.

Amanda's inclusion support teacher, Linda Bonds, has photographed each of the students that Amanda regularly interacts with and has worked with the speech and language therapist to facilitate Amanda's choice of friends to be a part of her circle. Amanda has selected two girls she has known since kindergarten and the six boys and girls who are a combination of new and more recent classmates. In class, Ms. Bonds invites each of the students to come to an initial circle meeting and provides them with a written invitation as well. The group will have its first meeting at lunch. She also gives each student a letter about the circle to share with their parents.

For Tuesday, when the group has its first forty-minute meeting, Ms. Bonds has prepared an initial agenda that includes an opening activity, brainstorming, and action planning as well as a minutes form (Table 5.1). She has also brought some snacks for the group. She begins with an opening activity for the sixth graders, in which students are asked to tell the group about two things they really like (activity, sport, music, TV show, class, book, web site, etc.), except that one of the two is to be something they actually do *not* like. Their peers have the task of guessing which is the false preference. Amanda uses her Macaw with Ms. Bonds's assistance to take her turn.

This type of opener provides students with a positive, interactive start to the meeting. After this five-to-ten minute activity, Ms. Bonds explains that Amanda selected each

TABLE 5.1   Minutes Form: Amanda's Meeting

Date: _____

Recorder: _____   Recorder's Helper: _____

Facilitator: _____   Facilitator's Helper: _____

Timekeeper: _____   Timekeeper's Helper: _____

Reporter: _____   Reporter's Helper: _____

Members Present: _____

_____

Opening Activity: _____

_____

What's Working—Successes! _____

_____

Anyone Need Help—Things Not Working? _____

Ideas & Plans: (WHAT?/WHO?/BY WHEN?/NEEDS?): _____

_____

_____

Closing Activity: _____

NEXT MEETING AND WHERE: _____

Adapted meeting minutes form from L. Triulzi, 1995, Willard Jr. High 7th Grade Support Network, Berkeley, CA: Berkeley USD. Used with permission.

of them and tells the purpose of a circle. She then asks for a volunteer note-taker to record any plans they make. For this first meeting, in the sixth grade core classroom, she is also using an easel and chart paper on which she can record ideas for all to see. She explains to the students that Amanda and her team are hoping that she will develop more activities with friends in and, especially, outside of school. She asks students how they experienced the transition from elementary school, and they generate a list of adjectives and phrases that describe their feelings about it.

- Anxious to get there
- Worried about new teachers
- Uncertain
- Afraid to fail
- Wondering if I'll be with any friends of mine
- Concerns about the work
- Excited about new social life and relationships
- Worried about dating, etc.
- Wondering about after school activities (clubs, sports, etc.)
- Unsure about all the rules

After this three-to-five minute brainstorming, she asks the students to brainstorm the things that helped them get through any of these concerns. The students make a list.

- Visits to Emerson in fifth grade
- Meeting teachers, then finding out who was in my classes that I knew already
- Finding time to see old friends that aren't in same classes
- Joining a club
- Making new friends
- Hanging out with friends after school

Ms. Bonds points out how many of these strategies have to do with their classmates and friends, particularly with seeing friends away from class time. She asks students to list some of their activities outside of school.

- Soccer at the Y
- Horseback riding lessons
- Going to the library
- Being on the Internet at home
- Web site access and design club
- Ice skating
- Swimming
- Basketball team with Parks and Recreation
- Spanish club
- Girl Scouts
- Watching TV, videos, and hanging out
- Piano lessons
- Talking on the phone
- Doing homework
- Playing with or taking care of little sister

At this point in the meeting, she asks how they would envision Amanda getting more involved in these or similar kinds of activities. One student, Cherie, asks Amanda if she has a computer with email and Internet access at home. Amanda responds "yes" with assistance from Ms. Bonds. Cherie suggests that, although phone conversations might be more difficult, they could email each other if Amanda's parents could assist her. She also wonders if Amanda would like to join the school Internet web design class. Susan suggests that they could also meet at each others' houses to watch videos and hang out periodically. Several students discuss possible days of the week for this, and Susan says she will call Amanda at home to discuss this with her and her parents so they can schedule a few dates. Stewart suggests that Amanda come to some of the basketball or soccer games to see her friends who play on these teams and to be with other school friends who come to watch. He and Maria will bring the fall schedules in for Amanda to take home. Maria, who plays soccer but not basketball, says she will call to invite Amanda to meet her at one of the basketball games to get this started.

Diana wonders if Amanda likes horses. Amanda isn't sure because she hasn't been around them, so Diana tells her about the local stable that she and her Girl Scout troop have gone to and suggests that she come to their next group trail ride in three weeks. Ms. Bonds gets the date, and Diana plans to write a note for Amanda to take home about the Scout troop as well.

Ms. Bonds shifts the conversation to activities and relationships *at* school. Students point out that before and after school and lunch–recess are the most interactive times as well as classes in which cooperative or partner structures are utilized. Jim suggests that one friend might be Amanda's lunch partner each day for a week, and another might be her in-class partner in Drama for a week at a time, so that they can each really get to know each other better. Ms. Bonds will bring the Drama suggestion to that teacher. Students decide to sign up for lunch weeks to try that out with Amanda. Students have begun the action plan, and Ms. Bonds notes each suggestion on the charts while Maria is taking notes (to be copied for all). Each activity has dates and people responsible, including Amanda. The group sets the next meeting date in two weeks, at which point they will look at what's working and what other activities they want to pursue.

JOEY'S CIRCLE—A "PIT CREW"

In Chapter 2 we noted that Joey, now in second grade with Mr. Vasquez, has a circle of friends—six students from first to third grades who meet with him and one of the teachers every two weeks at lunch. The focus of Joey's group is more academic this year, because this is his second year with Mr. Vasquez, and he was already well acquainted with two thirds of the class—the other second and third graders. The multiage environment has afforded Joey and the other students a terrific opportunity to form sustained relationships over time.

As a result, Joey's peers are able to take an increasing interest in his school progress and have wonderful ideas to share about his participation in specific academic activities. Several years ago, educators and students in Wheaton, Illinois, developed an approach for this which they called "pit crews" (*Choices,* 1991). Their video documentary illustrating the process (Comforty Media Concepts, 1991) demonstrates clearly the ability of elementary-age students to plan together.

Joey's pit crew, which includes his close friend, Larry, as well as Suzanne, Bill, and Latisha from second grade, Daria from first, and two third graders, Kevin and Tory, are meeting today with Ms. Ruben, the inclusion support teacher, to plan further for Joey's participation in their Social Studies unit on our neighborhoods and communities.

Ms. Ruben opens the meeting of this established group by asking Joey and his classmates what is working for Joey, what activities are successful right now in the neighborhoods unit. Students volunteer statements, which she writes on the easel chart in their room:

- Joey likes looking at the maps of streets and shops on the Internet.
- Joey participated in brainstorming about the neighborhood using his communication book to help him talk.

Ms. Ruben asks them what's *not* working and asks Joey where he might need to do things differently or have another type of assistance in order to contribute and complete his assignment. Here are their responses:

- Joey needs to know what to *do* with the maps he pulls off the Internet.
- He needs help with the template (fill-in form) he is using to write about his neighborhood

Now the group talks about their ideas. Tory suggests that maybe Joey could get the map with his street on it and have it made larger for his book. Larry says that Joey could probably draw it himself (from that model). Daria says that perhaps that would help Joey with the rest of his project; because he is such a good artist, he could label things on his street and draw houses, trees, and so forth, on the map. Kevin asks, "Why doesn't part of Joey's group build a 3-D neighborhood from their maps and descriptions?" Other students are enthusiastic about that idea, and someone suggests that each group member take photos around their neighborhoods to help them decide what to include and to build. Ms. Ruben asks Joey if he would like to do this, and he says yes and points to pictures of his house in his conversation book.

The group then begins planning how this can take place in their classroom unit's group. Together they dictate a note for parents about picture-taking. They then discuss who can bring in or find various building materials. Larry says that he has plastic trees and some other buildings from his train set at home that he can bring in. The students decide to

1. Take photos at home around their neighborhoods.
2. Select four or five streets from the Internet maps and ask Ms. Ruben to enlarge these.
3. Work in pairs to make layouts of each street from the maps and photos (Tory and Joey, Larry and Daria, Kevin and Suzanne, Latisha and Bill). Joey will do most of the drawing in his partnership with Tory. Tory will write labeling words for Joey to copy onto street signs and other structures.
4. All of the pairs will work on building, after item 3 is completed.
5. When the streets and neighborhood are completed, students will then write about their neighborhood. The students agreed that this will assist all of them, including Joey, in their descriptive passages.

The meeting ended with a specific plan to which all students had made valuable contributions. "Pit crews" were so named by *Choices* (1991), borrowing from the race car terminology, because they complete rapid "tune-ups," "oil changes," and the like as a team to help ensure that their entry has a good chance of success. That's what Joey's team is all about.

RAYMOND'S MAP

We last saw Raymond, who is fifteen and in the ninth grade, in his high school Humanities class, working with a cooperative group on a human rights public service announcement activity. As you'll recall, Raymond is included for the first time this year after spending his previous school years in a special public school. He had been given to disruptive behaviors there, and those behaviors had interfered with his having greater independence in his life, despite his good adaptive daily living skills. Raymond has a hearing loss and has never had a well-developed augmentative communication system to bolster his limited verbal repertoire. Communication is a priority for his team this year because both his family and the educators at Monroe have observed that his lack of effective communication skills has contributed significantly to his difficult behaviors in the past. He now has a conversation book (Hunt, Alwell, & Goetz, 1990), which has increased his interactions with peers both in groups and during free time. Raymond has been supported by circles not unlike Amanda's and Joey's, but at this point in his life his planning team has decided to begin the process of *transition planning,* sometimes known as personal futures planning, with a process known as *MAPS,* student-centered action planning involving the individual, peers, family, support staff, and friends (Forest & Pierpoint, 1992; York-Barr, 1996). The family-friendly, jargon-free MAPS process is designed to occur in a comfortable setting and to focus the group on a series of questions as a framework for planning. These seven questions, adapted from York-Barr (1996), are

- What is Raymond's history?
- Who is Raymond?
- What are Raymond's strengths, interests, gifts, abilities, and capacities from which to build?
- What are Raymond's areas of need?
- What is his and our dream for him? What would Raymond like to be doing in the future, and where would he like to live? What kinds of relationships does he want to have?
- What are our nightmares? What do Raymond, his family, friends, and support staff want not to happen?
- What learning opportunities do we want to make available for the student throughout the week?

The MAPS process is based on several inclusive assumptions—that individuals will be active participants in their schools and their communities, that future plans will be personalized, that family and friends are centrally involved, and that all are working collaboratively to develop and achieve meaningful goals. York-Barr (1996) noted that it is *not* a quick fix but rather a "point of new beginning…" a way to "address the complex personal and social issues…for individual students" (p. 26). They have adapted the original order of the questions (Forest & Pierpoint, 1992) to address who Raymond is, his strengths and preferences, before proceeding to dreams and nightmares, to assist those students who have just gotten to know the individual.

Table 5.2, Raymond's action plan, presents a graphic depiction of the outcomes from Raymond's MAPS with many of his ninth grade friends and classmates, family members, school staff, and other friends. Ms. Horace is facilitating this MAPS meeting at Raymond's home, and she begins the process by asking, "Who is here?" and "Why did you come?" Mr. Whitman is recording participant responses on large chart papers that are placed in strategic locations on the walls of the living room. Jose, Maria, Josephine, Suzanne, Raymond, Charles, Bill, and Alana are sitting together on the floor. They offer a number of responses to Ms. Horace's query.

Jose: I wanted to see if there was more I could know about Raymond since he's my friend.

Maria: I've been wondering if there's more we could do to help Ray learn in class.

Raymond: (With conversation book and Charles's assistance) Meeting friends. Talk about me. Good time.

Suzanne: We just met Ray this year. I want to know more about where he's been going to school, what he wants to do and stuff.

Ms. Horace facilitates responses from school staff and family as well segueing from "Why are you here?" to questions about Raymond's history. She speaks to Raymond in preparation for this meeting, to ensure that he feels comfortable about the meeting and with discussion of each of the questions. At that time she explained the rationale for each question and advised the students that anyone can "pass" on any of the questions. If they are not at ease with sharing historical information, their history could be restricted to education or they could edit out that area. The Weldons all felt that some information about Raymond's life to date would be good for all to share.

What Is Raymond's History?

Raymond's dad talks a bit about the family's early concerns that Raymond couldn't hear them, which led to hearing tests that showed an impairment, and to other assessments, which led to discovery of some delays in his development. Raymond subsequently went to a special preschool, and a special education school was recommended when he turned five, because he was beginning to "act aggressively" around other kids. At this point, says his mom, Raymond seemed less and less happy. His behavior got worse and it was hard to go anywhere together. The school couldn't seem to help him communicate better. However, his family was convinced by the strong arguments from the school personnel that this was the best setting for him. At the time there were no inclusion classes in any schools in the district; they did not begin until he was of middle school age. Then his parents started to hear about inclusion from other parents. They went to a meeting held by the area's Family Resource Network and began to consider this for Raymond. At his IEP's annual review last year, they heard about Monroe's inclusion classes. At first they couldn't believe it could happen right there at their local school! Now they are just so glad. Thanks to everyone, Raymond is learning; he has friends; he is getting assistance with talking. His behavior is better! It's all making sense—"We just wish we knew sooner about all this." Raymond adds, "I like Monroe."

TABLE 5.2   Ray's Action Plan

WHAT?	HOW?	WHEN?	WHO?
1. Go to high school team games (football, soccer, track, basketball)	With friends who invite him by calling home on Thursday–Friday before the weekend	At least two times a month	Jose, Maria, Charles, Bill
2. Develop improved ways to converse and communicate with friends, teachers, and others	**a.** Communication reassessment by district augmentative communication team (ACT); explore Dynavox or other means and instruct Ray in its use	**a.** This month	**a.** ACT meeting with IEP team
	b. Revise conversation book to have expanded content of interest to him	**b.** This month	**b.** Ray and friends, Ms. Horace, Mr. Whitman, parents
	c. Training for peers in conversation book to have expanded content of interest to him	**c.** Within three weeks of completing (a) and (b)	**c.** Ms. Horace, friends, and Raymond
3. Instruct Raymond in email use with partner	During Internet use time at school and at home		Mom and Dad, Maria, Alana, Suzanne
4. Raymond will get involved in the *Community Service Elective* as a means of starting job exploration and training	Ms. Horace or Mr. Whitman will meet with ninth-grade counselor and Raymond to schedule him for this next semester. Find out if SPCA is one of the current community service work options	Before school scheduling process begins	Ms. Horace, Ray, Mr. Whitman, Mr. T., counselor
5. Raymond will participate in a Monroe Frontier Team peer counseling group	Work with Mr. T. to set up group interested in weekly meetings	In next two weeks	Jose, Charles, Alana, Bill, Ray
6. Ray will participate in developing the transition plan for his next IEP	Develop transition plan by beginning to look at (a) next year's classes and activities, (b) potential summer job training, (c) self-advocacy training, (d) other areas to be identified using district IEP planning processes	Over the next eight weeks	Ray, friends, Ms. Horace, parents, Mr. T., representative from rehabilitation

Who Is Raymond?

The group engages in a rapid round robin to share adjectives or phrases that each feels describes Raymond. York-Barr (1996) suggests asking people for the first word that comes to mind when they think of the individual. Here are some of the responses Ms. Horace obtains about Ray.

- Funny (Suzanne)
- Caring (Maria)
- Wants to say stuff and can't always do it (Jose)

- Like all of us (Charles)
- Happy to be here (Ray)
- Tall (Bill)
- Athletic (Alana)
- Trying hard (parents)
- Friendly (Maria)

What Are His Strengths, Gifts, Abilities?

Ms. Horace asks Raymond about his favorite things, and Ray uses his conversation book pictures to assist him to tell the group things he likes: soccer, the Loderunner computer game, his friends, school, his parents, and home. She brings others into the conversation by asking the same question. Maria says that Ray likes to show her pictures of things he does outside of school, such as watching sports on television and that he really listens when she tells him about things she likes such as her favorite music groups. Raymond's parents mention that he likes to turn the car radio on to rock stations now, too, and they have gotten a Walkman with headphones for him. Jose talks about how Raymond always wants to be active and move around, and that's part of what makes him do well in P.E. in some of the games.

What Are Raymond's Areas of Need?

Ms. Horace asks Ray and the group what are times of the day or parts of his life in which he needs more help or support either in or outside of school. Some suggestions are more group activities besides soccer on weekends or after school (Dad); invitations to go to games at school with a friend (Mom); better ways of telling us what he wants or wants to do (Maria); ways to calm himself down instead of acting out or getting mad (Alana); other ways to talk to friends outside of school without pictures (e.g., on the telephone?) (Charles).

What Is Our Dream?

Now it is time to discuss the future. To help the group with this question, Ms. Horace suggests some related questions: "What would you like to do in the future, Raymond?" "What kind of work do you think you would like to do?" "Where would you like to work or live when you are older?" "Who would you most like to do things with now or in the future?" Ms. Horace starts by suggesting that, after hearing initial thoughts from Raymond, other members contribute their own dreams as well as their dreams for Raymond.

Because Raymond appears somewhat confused by the questions about the future, Ms. Horace suggests that his friends start the process by talking about any of their own hopes and dreams after high school. Jose starts by telling them he wants to go to a good college and eventually be a doctor. Alana says she hopes she can get a scholarship to go to college; she wants to teach. Suzanne wants to have her own business; Charles hopes to play baseball. Ms. Horace encourages them to continue sharing what they want their lives to be like, which results in a variety of responses.

- Lots of friends and have fun with them
- Get married but not until later
- Live with friends after college
- Have enough money to go to things like games and concerts
- Have my own car
- Still be friends with each other
- Have a good job

She then asks Raymond, as she reads the list, if any of these choices are things he also wants, and he says, "Yes. Money, friends." Jose asks, "Raymond, how will you get money?" Raymond says, "Work." Mrs. Weldon tells the group that Raymond seemed to really enjoy helping to take care of the pet animals at his former school such as rabbits, hamsters, birds, and the like. Ray nods as she says this. Suzanne suggests that Raymond get a summer or afterschool job volunteering at a pet store or with a veterinarian. Charles says maybe he would like working somewhere like the aquarium.

Nightmares

After more ideas are generated with Raymond regarding where he might want to live and what he'd enjoy doing, Ms. Horace shifts the group to talking about their fears or nightmares. "What worries you when you think of your own and especially Ray's future?" Several people speak, with comments like

- If he had no friends or family and he was alone
- No good jobs for him so he stays home
- Being homeless with no money
- Being with people who don't like him
- Being segregated again

She then moves the group to an action plan, which she explains will help them keep their fears from being realized. She reminds them that to make any of our dreams happen, we all have to plan, and Raymond and his family will need extra supports to make sure of a smooth transition when he leaves school. "First, though," she points out, "we need to plan for his needs now, the things that need to happen in the present to address high school life, some of which will help us with the future."

Action Plan

The group looks back to the needs they generated earlier, and Ms. Horace suggests they take a break, get drinks, think about this, and then come back in ten minutes to do the plan.

The group reconvenes and develops Raymond's action plan, depicted in Table 5.2.

As he records, Mr. Whitman illustrates the plan with simple drawings of figures representing Raymond and his friends at games, using computers, Raymond with animals at the ASPCA, etc. Ms. Horace closes the MAPS by asking everyone to remember one thing about the meeting that they found enjoyable, and Mr. W. writes down their final comments.

- Inspiring
- Fun
- Cool to hear all the ideas
- Amazing!
- Eye-opening
- Made me feel good to know we're all together
- Good to meet everyone
- Looking forward to all these things happening
- Understand Raymond better

A MAPS such as this one is another example of community building that is value based *and* can facilitate very specific outcomes for the individual who is the recipient of this support.

MELISSA: CONTEXTUAL ARRANGEMENTS

Hunt, Alwell, Farron-Davis, Wrenn, and Goetz (1996) have described proven strategies to facilitate and support student relationships in inclusive settings. Many of those strategies have been highlighted here in our descriptions of classroom meetings, circles and MAPS. These authors also researched and presented less formal methods for utilizing the *classroom context* to facilitate interaction and relationship development. You will recall that in Chapter 2, we described several ways that Melissa is supported by her peer partners and through the activity-based, multiple-intelligences-oriented instructional strategies that are employed by her middle school team.

These *natural supports* (cf. Nisbet, 1992; Jorgensen, 1998) have proved sufficient to ensure Melissa's active participation as a member of her peer group and to guarantee her access to the general education curriculum. Melissa will not require additional specialized mechanisms beyond those that have been built into her school community experience.

Ford et al. (1995) have suggested that teaching teams look at each of their students as the school year begins and they become acquainted in order to determine what types of peer supports may be required for *any* student. Decisions are made by the team as to the nature and extent of support required, and plans are made accordingly, always with the least intrusive means in mind. These processes of determining the need, defining possible peer support strategies and implementing them are the key. What the process is called (e.g., MAPS, circles, "pit crews," or meetings) is less important than the individualization of an approach that fits the student in the context of their school experience. We encourage readers to explore this area further through resource books, manuals, and training materials available, many of which are cited in the reference section.

SUMMARY

In this chapter, we review aspects of positive school and classroom climate that set the stage both for productive learning and for development of student relationships. The chapter outlines positive stage-setting techniques, providing illustrations from the students profiled throughout the book. Specific techniques and activities for building relationships among included students and their typical peers were provided. Selection and tailoring of these strategies to meet individual students' needs are emphasized. Examples include a circle of friends with Amanda, a "pit crew" with Joey, and a MAPS for Raymond. Development of both structured and informal natural supports were emphasized.

CHECKING FOR UNDERSTANDING

1. Provide a secondary example of how a teacher might utilize classroom meetings in developing positive classroom climate.

2. Think about a student you teach (who may or may not be receiving special education services), who appears somewhat isolated from his or her peers. How would you select the type of peer intervention you might employ? Which of those discussed in the chapter seems most appropriate to you for this situation?

3. How would you respond to parents or educators who might be concerned about too much instructional time of their students being devoted to peer-support activities?

4. How could the MAPS process be integrated with a student's individualized education plan?

5. What would be the most difficult aspect of implementing school climate and peer collaboration strategies reviewed in this chapter. Why? What would be three possible approaches to resolve this difficulty?

CHAPTER SIX

COLLABORATION

Upon completion of this chapter, you will be able to

1. Define key characteristics of collaborative consultation
2. Identify key components of co-teaching and a variety of approaches for implementation
3. Define collaborative teamwork and state difficulties in achieving it
4. Identify key characteristics of a collaborative team
5. Describe strategies educators and families can use to facilitate collaborative teamwork
6. Describe a process for effective team meetings

COLLABORATIVE CONSULTATION
AND CO-TEACHING APPROACHES

Idol, Nevin, and Paolucci-Whitcomb originated and defined the concept of collaborative consultation in 1987 as a service delivery approach for supporting students in general education, particularly students with IEPs, students at risk for school failure, and students who experience cultural or linguistic differences. A primary stated goal was ensuring students maximum interaction with both grade-level curriculum and grade-level peers (1994, p. 6). In this way, collaborative consultation is one vehicle for operationalizing the interactive teamwork required when schools strive to improve their practices for the benefit of all students.

Nevin, Thousand, Paolucci-Whitcomb, and Villa (1990) characterized the approach as having these five features.

1. Group members agree to view each other and their students as possessing unique and necessary expertise.
2. Frequent face-to-face interactions among members occurs.
3. Leadership responsibilities are distributed among members, and the group holds its members accountable for their specific commitments,
4. Reciprocity and interdependence are practiced.
5. Members agree to practice and increase social interaction and their task or achievement skills through consensus building.

Collaborative consultation contrasts sharply with traditional consultative models. We recently read a mystery in which the sleuth encounters an "educational consultant" and calls her friend, who has worked in the schools, for a definition of this elusive term. Her friend tells her that such a person is someone who gives your kid a lot of tests and recommends that they go to school somewhere else (Dawson, 1997). This notion of the expert with a briefcase coming down from on high to advise the "consultee" and then leaving has been a common feature of traditional medical consultation models, and, too often, this has been duplicated in classrooms throughout the nation. Teachers have complained at length and with justification about the person who swoops in and out, leaving often unwanted and sometimes irrelevant suggestions, because he or she has not understood the ecology of the classroom. Collaborative consultation is an intentional interaction of two or more equal partners who bring different skills, expertise, and backgrounds to the table and who wish to work together to increase their effectiveness as teachers.

Let's think about Vineyard Elementary for a moment. Ms. Ruben, the inclusion support teacher (special educator) and Mr. Vasquez, the multiage classroom teacher (general educator) have been co-teaching and building a collaborative relationship over the past two years. They begin their work together by considering a series of questions.

- Why are we here? What are the goals and needs of our students?
- What is working? What do we need to change? Who will be our team members, and how do we function as a team?
- What do we need to do in terms of organizational structure (e.g., role change, classroom structure, planning meetings, materials) and curriculum to achieve co-teaching in the same classroom?
- How much time will we teach together, and what model or approach will we use, for example, one teaching, one supporting; station teaching; parallel teaching; complementary teaching; etc? (Adapted from Friend & Cook, 1996; Harris, 1998)

Now let's look in on a meeting of Mr. V. and Ms. R. as they plan the Social Studies neighborhoods unit.

Mr. V.: As you know, part of the third grade standards involves students learning about their community.

Ms. R.: You know, that is such a great vehicle for integrating Writing, Math, everything across the curriculum. There's so much we could do that would be a great learning experience for the first and second graders too, including Joey.

Mr. V.: I agree. What are some of your ideas? Let's brainstorm the central questions and how to approach them with activities.

Ms. R.: I think one central question to build on would be, "What is the best thing about my neighborhood or community?"

Mr. V.: Yes, and some others might be, "What are the different parts of my neighborhood? Who lives there? Who works there?"

Ms. R.: What kinds of jobs do they have? What kinds of activities are there for kids to do? What kind of things can you buy and where? What's the architecture like?

Mr. V.: How do people get around the community? What kinds of transportation are there? Are there bike lanes? Busses? Okay, we have over ten questions now—that's a good start. I've got them all recorded here—let's talk about our learner objectives. I think I'd like to see them be able to present information about their community in an organized way across these categories, like transportation, architecture, businesses, leisure activities.

Ms. R.: And they could present this exhibition or whatever we want to call it in such a variety of ways. Could students work together?

Mr. V.: It makes sense, because some of them live near each other, and it's such an interactive activity by nature. They could even interview people in their neighborhoods in pairs if we can work that out with parents—or take small groups out during the school day.

Ms. R.: You know, I'd like to see several possible products presented to them as alternatives. For example, a book, a 3-D map....

Mr. V.: A game where you move from place to place! This is great, we can really capitalize on kids' stronger intelligences. Do you have that book we got with Gardner's ideas put into classroom practice?

Ms. R.: I'll bring it in tomorrow. Let's talk for a minute about grouping, so we can be sure to be heterogeneous across grades as well as abilities. Should students be able to work in pairs, trios, or just groups of four?

Mr. V.: I think we can have some flexibility here in conjunction with the day's activity for the unit. I see this going on for about three or more weeks with kids rotating during the academic block each day.

Ms. R.: I'm not sure how the flexibility in group size will work. Give me an example of what you're thinking.

Mr. V.: Well, for example, let's see—we could first group by who lives where, being sure to mix across grades. Then see if groups are uneven anyway—like a group of five, and so during a time when they might be using the Internet to pull up maps, they could split into groups of two and three. With twenty-four kids, and with you in the A.M., Ms. Lopez in the P.M., and Daria (instructional assistant), we can make a workable structure. What kinds of adaptations do you think Joey will need, if any?

Ms. R.: Well, he's so good with maps; he should shine in that part of it. I think I'll need to either talk with his Mom about getting photographs from the neighborhood, or maybe even take a few kids out one day to take some. I think I might also take the guide book and develop some templates for him to use on the computer or for written work.

Mr. V.: That sounds like something that some of the *other* first and second graders could use, too! Good idea. Okay, let's start with the grouping plan—I have the address list here.

This example illustrates some essential components of the collaborative relationship. Mr. Vasquez and Ms. Ruben are consultants to each other, and you'll notice that as they have been sharing their individual expertise over the two years, each has begun to learn and assume parts of the other's role. Bauwens and Hourcade (1995), Friend and Cook (1996), and others have delineated guidelines for maintaining these working partnerships. They remind us that:

- Collaborative or co-teaching is an *evolving* relationship; don't expect it to work perfectly!
- Structure your roles to ensure that all students are the responsibility of both teachers during the co-teaching periods.
- Utilize active learning strategies and thus take advantage of the teaching capacity of each adult.
- Evaluate your co-teaching practices on an ongoing (formative) basis as well as in a more summative manner, examining student outcomes.

These authors also suggested developing your rules for classroom routines such as:

- *Organizational structures*—from how students request going to the restroom to whether they line up singly, in pairs, or not at all when moving as a class.
- *Instructional routines*—from how students work together, use the room, and are grouped to what comes first each day and how students use free time.
- *Classroom climate and community*—from how you will address individual student problems to whether you will have specific rules or consequences and who will de-

velop these. How will students participate in rule design and problem-solving? (See Kohn, 1996, and Chapter 5 for a discussion of this area.)

Co-Teaching Schedules

Mr. Vasquez and Ms. Ruben are currently engaged in a *dyadic stable schedule* (Harris, 1998). Ms. Ruben, the support teacher, works with Mr. V. on a fixed daily schedule, which facilitates both their planning and student learning through its predictability and opportunities for each to focus on specific student needs and small groups during Math period. Ms. Ruben also works in other classrooms where students who have IEPs are included. She also has a stable schedule with two other classrooms and a "rollover schedule" with three others. In the rollover schedule, she rotates a period, going to classroom A on Monday and Tuesday, classroom B on Wednesday and Thursday, and classroom C for a longer period on Friday. Each marking period, she meets with her partners in these classrooms to decide whether they would like to change the scheduled times.

The approach to co-teaching also varies across Ms. Ruben's six classrooms. Seven structures for co-teaching have been described in the literature (Friend & Cook, 1996; Harris, 1998):

Co-Teaching Models

One teaching, one supporting, is a method in which the second or supporting teacher supports the lead teacher's work. The lead teacher designs and delivers the lesson, and the supporter provides assistance where needed. We advise that teaching pairs alternate these roles, so that the support or special education teacher is a full partner and doesn't wind up functioning as a paraprofessional.

Station teaching occurs when the partners divide instructional responsibilities by having students rotate among stations they have designed together. This works especially well in, for example, primary classrooms engaged in developmentally appropriate practices, in which centers are designed for students' active learning. Two adults may rotate among four stations, and students move after designated time periods. This provides for movement and variety in instruction but can result in confusing or noisy transition times, especially at first.

Parallel teaching takes place when teachers co-design instruction but deliver it separately to two heterogeneous groups within the room. This lowers the ratio but does require close coordination and equal content knowledge.

Alternative teaching involves providing small group instruction for the purpose of "pre" or "re" teaching of content. It should be noted that this approach can begin to resemble within-class tracking if it is overused, and may signal a greater need for multilevel instruction. See Chapter 2 or other interventions if this is the case.

Team teaching means that teachers jointly present the material they have co-designed, and it is most common among teachers from the same discipline (e.g., two Math or two History teachers), elementary grade level (where curriculum is in common), or with a special educator who also has general education certification or experience and a general educator. This is the approach used by Mr. Vasquez and Ms. Ruben in the Social Studies unit. You will recall the example of Monroe High School and the ninth grade Buckeye team. Ms. Horace, the special educator on the team, has become a specialist in Language Arts or Social Studies, and team teaches for this block. She works in a supporting teacher role in Math and Science. Each of her peers from special education has developed a specialty in at least one specific area at that grade level and team teaches for those subject areas.

Two additional structures presented by Bauwens and Hourcade (1995) and Friend and Cook (1996) are *Complementary Teaching* and *Supportive Learning Activities.* In complementary teaching, the general educator teaches the subject matter, and the special educator assumes primary responsibility for addressing student needs such as study and organizational skills, development of appropriate adaptations of materials, etc. Supportive learning is supplementary instruction provided by the special educator to reinforce and enrich general instruction. This has similarities to the alternative teaching approach. Its main difference is that supportive learning activities take place for *all* students (e.g., small group discussions following a lecture by the general educator), and both teachers are present for the full sequence of activities.

It is not surprising that co-teaching and the collaborative relationship that informs it have been called a "dance" by researchers and practitioners alike. Like all dances, we must first hear the music, then learn the steps, maintain our balance, and coordinate with our partners. The actual "messiness" of our collaborative interactions probably compares more to 1960s rock and roll than to a stylized ballet, but the synchrony is there, nevertheless.

The following sections describe the specific collaborative teamwork practices engaged in by individuals working with students through individual student planning team meetings. Let's look first at an early meeting of Joey's team when he was beginning kindergarten.

JOEY'S FIRST PLANNING TEAM MEETING

Joey's team, including his mother, his kindergarten teacher, Ms. Gordon, the special education inclusion support teacher, and an instructional assistant are meeting for the first time as a group to discuss how things are going. The meeting was called by his general education teacher, because she had some concerns that she wanted to share. The meeting was held after school at around 2:45, and the instructional assistant agreed to stay for a bit.

By 3:00, everyone had arrived, and Joey's teacher opened the meeting by thanking people for coming. She wanted it known that she understood why Joey's family wanted him included and that she too, believed he was benefiting from the social contact he had with other students. However, she felt that he was getting frustrated with the work in the class, and it was showing in his behavior. It seemed that he was distracting the other students and taking all of Ms. Adam's (instructional assistant) time to keep him busy. She closed her comments by saying, "Are we doing the right thing for Joey?"

Mr. Lewis, the inclusion support teacher, asked what he was doing in class, how he was disruptive. Ms. Adams said that she had to go but wanted to say that she didn't think it was all his fault. Some of the students were "getting him going" and something needed to be done about them. She worked with him on his projects, but it seemed that he wasn't always interested in the materials he was using. Joey's mother asked whether he was made to feel welcome in the class and whether he couldn't be more involved in what the others were doing. Maybe he felt out of things. The team members continued stating their positions, and Mr. Lewis did his best to give everyone their say while trying to get a sense of the problem. At about 4:15, Ms. Gordon said she needed to leave, but she wanted to get this out on the table. Mr. Lewis said he would come in the next day and see if he could help. The meeting ended with a promise from all to try some different things.

Learning to Work as a Team

Meetings like Joey's team had are common, particularly in situations in which inclusive education is new or if individual students are included when inclusive education is not a central value and practice of the school. People who are interested in Joey's success and who are really concerned about doing their part can still have a difficult time putting all this collaboration into practice. We've all been involved in meetings like this, where the reason for the meeting is a concern; the process of the meeting is to hear what everyone thinks about that concern, and the resolution of the meeting is to try harder or even to consider a more restrictive placement. It doesn't take long for people to avoid meetings because they never seem to accomplish anything. When that happens, people give up, just do the best they can do personally, or go underground to complain about this "inclusion stuff." It would be easy to say, "Well, they just weren't really committed to inclusive ed-

The Collaborative Team Structure

Who should be involved in the individual student planning team? We have found a wide range of planning team structures, each of which carries advantages and disadvantages. At times, team meetings seem to be designed less for effectiveness than for ensuring that everyone hears the same information. We have worked with teams that included parents, the principal, general and special education teachers, instructional assistants, speech and language therapists, a vision and hearing specialist, an occupational therapist, and a behavioral specialist. With one of us also attending as a district consultant on inclusive education, such groups were overwhelming and, not surprisingly, accomplished very little except talk, which is all that is possible among twelve people who don't know each other well.

At the other end, some planning teams involve only the special educator and the classroom teacher. Certainly, these teams can be more productive but may be not as creative. Core planning teams should involve those directly impacted by decisions on a daily basis. The classroom teachers, cooperating special education inclusion support, staff, and parents are key members of the core individual student planning team. Others, for example, related services staff can be invited to the meeting as their expertise is needed. Keeping the size of the team small facilitates scheduling. It also allows team members to remain focused on important issues for the team. As long as members are open to new information and can keep ancillary staff informed and involved, this composition can work.

Tools for Collaboration

Time to Communicate. "To meet our needs, we need to meet" (Kohn, 1996). It is clear that as more people become involved with a student, the need for more communication among all is critical to success. People need to talk—to share information, expertise, perceptions, concerns, ideas, and questions. Problems need to be talked about because that is the only way to begin to understand how we might surmount them. The logistics of providing time for these conversations is daunting, particularly when large numbers of people are involved.

Consider a secondary school campus organized in a traditional manner into separate subject areas. A student may have six to seven general education teachers in addition to a special education teacher and related services support staff. Scheduling time to talk is very difficult, and attempting to coordinate with family members makes setting up planning meetings almost impossible. It is clear that when we do create the time, we need to use it efficiently and effectively. The best way to facilitate communication about meeting the needs of students with disabilities within the core curriculum is to ensure that communication is not arranged solely for that student but for all students. When schools commit to continued discussion about teaching, finding ways to support learning for students who happen to have disabilities is a natural part of the discussion. Jorgensen (1998) provides an excellent view of schools that have made this commitment.

How Do Teams Operate? Even when teams are able to establish time to meet, we often do not have the communication skills to make our meetings effective. Putting ten experts in a room together does not automatically equal success or solutions. The strategies we encourage among students in terms of cooperative group structure are required for success in our own team planning meetings. For example, how often in a meeting among staff do team members assume the specific roles we expect in our cooperative learning groups? Who facilitates? Is there a recorder of the discussion and action steps? Do we keep track of time so that we are most efficient and not prone to spend all our time talking about something we are not going to be able to resolve? Is the administrator always the leader of the discussion? Who designs the agenda? When we look at Joey's meeting, there appears to be little organization.

One of the first things each collaborative planning team must address regards how they are going to operate. The logistics of meetings include when and where meetings are held, how long they will last, who will be involved, how the agenda will be established, the roles of members of the planning team, and how planning team members will interact. For example, meetings are typically held after school when teachers are free from students and are supposedly able to focus. However, this may actually be the most difficult time for teachers to focus. In the first place, their energy may be depleted, and ideas may not be as creative as at other times of the day. Teachers often have a number of competing activities at that time, for example, coaching or club sponsorship. That may be their time for meeting with families or for being available to students. Many teams arrange to meet before school when people have more energy and when family members might have time before work.

Tying team planning meetings to curriculum planning meetings may allow teams to address some specific student issues as they meet to articulate instruction. These meetings are typically scheduled during the school day or during minimum-day schedules. In terms of where meetings are held, the location may also make a difference. It makes sense to remember a student with disabilities is first a member of the general education class, and meetings related to his success belong in that location. It's also important to consider the responsibilities of a host and rotate meeting locations to spread the responsibilities.

Meetings that drone on and on are of no value to anyone. There are many things every team member needs to get done, and meetings cut into the time available. Team meetings must be efficient. They must maximize the time used or they will become counterproductive. Members will begin to skip meetings in order to get other things accomplished if the meetings are seen as monopolizing the limited time they have available. Successful meetings start and stop on time. Those arranging them consider the time available, the amount of time members can focus on an issue, and the time necessary to accomplish something. Meetings that are too short run the risk of being a waste of time because nothing can be accomplished except a review of the problem. The most successful meetings incorporate an agenda that can be accomplished within the time available.

Establishing a Meeting Agenda.   How is the meeting agenda established for an individual student planning team meeting? There may be numerous things to discuss and a number of critical issues to resolve but, as we have noted, limited time to operate. We can't stress too much the importance of a clear and concise agenda to set the parameters of the meeting. It keeps the team focused and may also support preparation for the meeting. When team members know what is to be discussed, they are able to obtain the critical information to best understand the issue and reach some resolution. Of course, additional issues may arise that may be of more immediate importance in a particular meeting, and the team may need to adjust the agenda by group consensus at the start of the meeting. Time is allotted to those issues, at times shifting an established agenda item to the next meeting. The key is to agree to a specific number of items that can be addressed within the time available, providing adequate time to discuss each item and to establish actions and responsible team members for completing the actions.

The cooperative learning structures discussed in Chapter 2 have definite benefits for students who are learning core curriculum concepts, specific instructional objectives, and social interaction and collaborative skills. The benefits are not limited by age. In terms of learning, problem solving, and collaboration skill development, benefits can accrue to adults too. If the student planning meeting is approached as a learning opportunity, cooperative learning structures can support more creative and positive discussions and outcomes. The roles used in cooperative learning—facilitator, recorder, timekeeper, and reporter—can ensure a more efficient use of time and may increase the chance that the agenda will be carried out. One of the key understandings of cooperative learning is that members of a cooperative team sink or swim together. This approach will help motivate teams toward resolution of issues by joint action rather than by expecting one or two team members to carry all responsibility for the student.

Dealing with Conflict. "Two people can see the same thing, disagree, and yet both be right" (Covey, 1989, p. 40). Clearly teams will need to learn ways to resolve conflicts in a way that members perceive as fair and effective. It may be that if a team discusses an issue for enough time, the members will come upon a solution that is so right and unanimous it will satisfy everyone. However, this is usually not the situation, and teams must have a plan for deciding on actions when everyone is not completely satisfied or sure. Several frameworks for problem solving typically involve some method for clarifying the issue, identifying the interests of the parties involved, generating ideas for resolution, and selecting one or more to implement. When members of a team can agree that there is one idea that has the best chance to be successful, common action is more easily taken. The team must also agree on a strategy for selecting the best alternative when all can't agree. Choosing an idea that everyone can at least live with may be the best alternative. This alternative must also be carefully discussed to avoid selecting something that none of them wants, but everyone thinks the others want.

Jerry Harvey, in *The Abilene Paradox* (1988), provides an excellent discussion of this experience in action, pointing out that the management of agreement, not conflict, is one of our greatest challenges. The student planning team must discuss this as they begin to work as a team so that when these situations occur, there is a strategy available. Teams are dynamic entities, and the interaction among members is important to success. If a particular team member, because of force of personality or role, guides the team process to their agenda, decisions made by the team will not be fully supported, and team members will not allow truly creative ideas to flourish.

Another Look at Joey's Team Meeting

Let's look again at Joey's team meeting. How could this meeting have been restructured, and what could the members have done to lead to a better outcome for Joey and the team members? His classroom teacher believed Joey was distracting other students and taking too much of the time of the instructional assistant. She interpreted that to mean that he was frustrated with the work and questioned whether it might be better for him to be in another type of program.

For a start, this is quite a conversation to be having at the first planning team meeting. When teams meet because a problem exists, there is only one thing for the team to do—try to solve the problem. All their efforts have to focus on assuring his classroom teacher that some new things will be tried and that Joey will come around. Planning teams need time to learn how to work. They need to establish a way of talking with each other and to learn to deal with conflicts and differences in perceptions. It is also helpful if they have some early successes to celebrate. Joey's team should have met prior to his involvement in the class. One of the best practices in inclusive education, described in Chapter 1, is to plan for the transition of students to next year's classes and schools. Sharing strategies and successes from Joey's preschool experience begins the process of informing his new teacher about his capabilities as well as ways to support him most successfully. The transition team would have begun to discuss how his IEP objectives could be met within the structure and curriculum of his new class.

A schedule for individual team meetings would have been established, and the team would have begun to have some practice planning together. By having these initial discussions, the team can initiate actions that will help avoid the problems his staff are now facing. Ensuring that Joey's work is meaningful and achievable is an important task for the team. Involving his peers in his success is also called for, particularly if he or they are acting in ways that cause problems. Ms. Adams' role should be continually examined to make sure she is facilitating his involvement, rather than simply teaching him in the classroom. Each meeting should have an established agenda, a definite beginning and ending time, established roles for the meeting, recording of determined actions and responsibilities, and a plan for the next meeting.

Let's look at another example of a planning meeting for Joey (see Figure 6.2).

Joey's mother arrives for the planning meeting in his kindergarten classroom. His classroom teacher, special education inclusion teacher, and support staff are already there, talking about how Joey seems to be doing so far. His classroom teacher has expressed some of her concerns to Mr. Lewis about his behavior. Mr. Lewis listened to Ms. Gordon and asked questions to be sure he understood.

Ms. Gordon thanks the team members for getting together and reminds them that they have until about 4:15 today to work together. She notes that Joey seems to be doing better in some groups than others. He loves recess and looking at books, especially ones with maps. She reminds the team that they'd set three agenda items at the last meeting: (a) getting him more involved in activities with other students, (b) communication skills and strategies, and (c) developing friendships. In light of some recent behavioral problems, she asks if the team can discuss those. Mr. Lewis suggests that these problems be addressed through the other items on the agenda because they may be connected.

Ms. Gordon and Ms. Adams describe how Joey is working in learning center groups. He has recently begun to misbehave by teasing other students in the group, throwing materials and getting off task. The team talks about how he is involved in the group and identifies several ways for him to be successful by starting with expectations they are sure he can meet and adding new expectations very slowly. They also decided to address the third agenda item at this time.

Ms. Adams suspects that Joey's behavior is a way to gain attention from his peers. His mother adds that he's always tended to misbehave to get others to notice him. She advises the group that he spends his weekends with family members and typically doesn't see any of his classmates except in school. The team decides to ask for assistance from his peers about how to get him more involved in groups and with friends inside and outside of school. Ms. Gordon and Mr. Lewis will ask for peers to be part of a circle of friends for Joey. The purpose of the group will be to generate ideas for how he can participate more fully in classroom learning and play.

The group decides to begin discussion of the third agenda item in the remaining ten minutes available. Joey's mother asks if he's talking more in school, because she doesn't hear him using more than one or two words when he speaks. Other team members also have noticed this. The team brainstorms ideas to encourage him to use his language skills more and use longer sentences. Staff and his family will model longer sentences for Joey and prompt him with, "Say the whole thing." Mr. Lewis will ask his speech and language therapist how she's working on articulation and ask her to demonstrate for classroom staff. They also decided to provide Joey with a conversation book containing events, people, and activities in his life that he could share with classmates. Joey's mother will gather some photos and put some memento of a weekend activity in the book so Joey can talk about it.

It is now 4:10, and Mr. Lewis reviews the actions determined and asks for items for the next meeting. Members are reminded of the date. Joey's mother expresses her appreciation for the meeting and the way team members are supporting him.

How Do We Learn to Be Better Collaborators?

People who collaborate well have a common goal, work on their communication skills, and schedule time for this important activity. They recognize that collaborators are not born, they are made. Typically little attention is paid to training in the area of collaboration, particularly regarding the communication skills necessary to be a good collaborator. It is imperative that university teacher and administrator training programs and staff development committees address these skills so that all educational staff and each collaborator can take responsibility to increase their own skills in this area. A large part of this skill development must include problem-solving strategies and conflict resolution. Simple ways to move beyond barriers, real and perceived, must be part of each collaborator's repertoire.

FIGURE 6.2   Joey's Team Meeting

TEAM MEETING FOR:

Student: <u>Joey</u>

Date/time: <u>9/14/96 3:15 p.m.</u>

Location: <u>Room 23</u>

If you are unable to attend, please contact: <u>Ms. Gordon</u>

Team members:

<u>Betty G. (kindergarten)</u>

<u>Ken L.(inclusion support teacher)</u>

<u>Lori A. (instructional assistant)</u>

<u>Marie M. (mother)</u>

Communication backup:

<u>Ken will speak with Ms. Newberry (speech) about demonstrating for peers and staff how to get him to use longer sentences.</u>

Agenda for this meeting:	Time limit:
1. Joey's participation in classwork	25 minutes
2. Communication skills	20 minutes
3. Friendships	10 minutes
4.	

Agenda for the next meeting:	Next meeting date/time: <u>10/16/96</u>
1. Update on progress in group work	
2. Circle of friends activities	
3. Class overnight at school	
4.	

Roles:

For this meeting	For next meeting
Facilitator <u>Betty G.</u>	<u>Ken L.</u>
Recorder <u>Lori A.</u>	<u>Betty G.</u>
Timekeeper <u>Marie M.</u>	<u>Lori A.</u>

FIGURE 6.2 CONTINUED

MEETING NOTES	TO DO:	PERSON(S) RESPONSIBLE	DATE TO BE COMPLETED
1. Joey's behavior in group work: Some teasing, off-task behavior. Start with material and activities he can be successful with. After two days of success, add one more new task. Pair Joey with Jackson when new task is added. Check with group about how to get him more involved in task. Joey can be responsible for keeping track of time for groups. 2. Peer interactions: Some behavior appears designed to get others to pay attention to him. Joey is not seeing friends outside of school, and his mother feels he really looks forward to seeing them. Suggested to involve peers in problem solving to see how Joey can be more involved with things they do. Circle of friends? 3. Communication: Joey is using his speech, but not progressing beyond a couple of words. Discussed ways to get him to use longer phrases, sentences. Considered conversation book. Important to teach other students how to communicate with Joey.	Identify which materials and activities Joey is most successful with. Plan for upcoming activities re which new part to add to repertoire. Ask peers in group to decide how Joey can be involved as first step of task. Ask for peers who want to be in a support group for Joey. Check with Joey re preference. Initiate first meeting at lunch. Model longer sentences: "Say the whole thing." Speak with speech therapist to demonstrate for staff and students. Develop conversation book using pictures from home and school. Take pictures and send in important mementos.	Ken/Lori Betty Betty Betty/Ken Betty/Ken/ Lori/ family Ken Ken/ family Mom	9/22/96 9/22/96 9/22/96 9/29/96 9/22/96 9/22/96 9/29/96 9/26/96

SUMMARY

Chapter 6 provides information regarding collaborative consultation, an effective vehicle for the teamwork required when schools provide inclusive educational services for all students. Collaborative consultation is characterized by agreement by group members that students and staff possess unique and necessary experience, frequent face-to-face interactions among members, distribution of leadership responsibilities among members and accountability for commitments, reciprocity and interdependence, and commitment to skill building through consensus building.

Several approaches to co-teaching are also provided, including one teaching, one supporting; station teaching; parallel teaching; alternative teaching; team teaching; complementary teaching, and supportive learning activities. These strategies require continued learning among participants as well as frequent communication.

Chapter 6 also examines the difficulties and benefits of collaborative teaming. Effective inclusive education services for students with special learning needs require all those involved to work together in a manner that builds on the creativity and skills each member brings. Collaborative teamwork is deceptively difficult, however, and requires continual work to unlearn behaviors that interfere with working in this manner. Team members are also required to learn how to interact with each other through conflicts and how to problem solve so that students succeed.

A number of critical considerations in establishing and maintaining collaborative team meetings are provided, including finding time for meetings, knowing how and when to schedule meetings, setting the agenda, determining who should attend meetings, operating in an effective and efficient manner in meetings, and problem solving. Meetings should be held at times that are most convenient for all and at times when members are best able to accomplish the tasks of a planning meeting. The atmosphere of team meetings must be collaborative, and each member must welcome the contributions of all.

Finally, well-planned meetings include a clear and achievable agenda, specific team roles in the meeting, specific actions to be taken, and a record of meeting discussion and action steps.

CHECKING FOR UNDERSTANDING

1. Joey's team is interested in his success and, at the same time, is dealing with the realities of school life—competing demands, learning new skills, finding time to collaborate, and trying to meet a variety of needs. Individually, each member of his team will try their best to make this work for him; however, if they can learn to work as a real team, they can expand their creativity beyond the sum of each individual's contribution. You have been asked to observe his team meeting and assist the team in becoming better collaborators. Looking at Joey's meeting described at the beginning of this chapter, consider the following questions.

   a. What suggestions might you offer for how to organize these meetings?

   b. What things could be done to enhance the affective atmosphere of team meetings?

   c. What strategies might team members learn to move beyond statement of the problem to solutions?

   d. How can team members experience and celebrate success?

   e. When a challenge is particularly difficult for the team and solutions are not readily evident, what would you recommend?

2. Think about a teacher with whom you are working toward a more collaborative relationship. Which aspects of a collaborative-consultative relationship do you have now, and which, if any, need to be developed? How would you go about facilitating this?

3. Imagine that you are embarking on a co-teaching relationship with a colleague. Which approach to co-teaching would you be most comfortable with? What would be some of your necessary first steps? Make a hypothetical action plan to discuss the areas and issues the two of you would need to address and resolve.

CHAPTER SEVEN

EVALUATION: A MATTER OF CONSEQUENCE

Upon completion of this chapter you will be able to

1. Distinguish between system-accountability and student-outcome data, describe how they intersect, and relate to each other in the evaluation process
2. Select from several possible strategies, including needs assessments, surveys, interviews, focus groups, best-practice indicators, and cost analysis in planning for evaluation of program quality
3. Provide the rationale for community-referenced, performance-based assessment approaches and describe several types of performance-based measures for students with and without disabilities
4. Suggest ways to adapt exhibitions and portfolio expectations for a student with specific disabilities

Let us consider the essential question: Are our inclusive efforts producing the results that we expect and want? *Accountability,* described by Erickson (1997) as systematic methodology that informs both those within and those external to the system about progress in desired directions, is inextricably linked to educational reform. In their evaluative framework to analyze state and school district policy in relationship to inclusive practices, the Consortium on Inclusive Schooling Practices (1996) identified six major policy areas: curriculum, student assessment, accountability, personnel development, finance, and governance. In this policy context, accountability appears to equal *system* or *program* integrity. In other words, did we do what we said we were going to do? Did we provide the service, the educational experience, as promised? Did that service meet the standards? And how do we know this?

Servatius (1995) reminded us that we must stop saying "we provided the service; we can't help it if he failed…"; "we tried to teach him; he just didn't get it…." Educators must take responsibility not just for the *teaching* but for the student *learning* that does or doesn't occur.

In this chapter we will consider some ways districts, schools, and individuals can examine the effectiveness of their work on school *and* student levels. We will consider what we want or need to know and how the data can be measured or obtained.

SYSTEM ACCOUNTABILITY

We begin with system or program accountability. Over the past decade, numerous educational organizations, university-based research projects, and systems change efforts have produced "best practice markers" to serve as guideposts for evaluating our program and school effectiveness. We can begin, of course, with the guidelines delineated in Chapter 1 of this volume, where the essential components that form the foundation for inclusive education were laid out in detail. Halvorsen and Neary (1996a&b) have further specified these practices in the form of both district and school-site level needs assessments to assist districts and schools with planning and with formative evaluation of their progress toward best practices. The areas tapped by each of these surveys are summarized in Table 7.1, and the complete instruments are contained in the appendices. The interested reader may also wish to refer to Simon, Karasoff, and Smith (1992), and to McGregor and Vogelsberg (1998) for the research base of specific practices for district and school program effectiveness.

These two surveys have been utilized to date by fifteen California school districts and more than fifty urban, suburban and rural schools, including five of the top ten districts in enrollment in the state. The process for their use has been consensus based, with a representative group of stakeholders (administrators, parents, teachers, support personnel) participating. These players work with an internal or external (e.g., university faculty) facilitator to pinpoint their level of *implementation* of the specific practice as well as the level of their *need for assistance* to accomplish further implementation. Once consensus has been reached regarding current status, the group uses the information to develop an action plan. For evaluation purposes, the survey is revisited approximately eighteen months later, to determine whether and how the level of implementation and need for assistance have changed and how successful their plans have been in meeting desired objectives.

Here then is an example of *formative* or ongoing program evaluation, which is used to inform the planning process as well as to support implementation. Through this process, the players are examining as well the resources that are needed to accomplish their plans (e.g., planning time, personnel development) as well as structural supports such as policy or procedural changes (e.g., teacher contract language, board of education policy on inclusion). This type of formative evaluation has both *quantitative* and *qualitative* features. We can see how our numerical rating of implementation has changed (*quantitative*), and we are at the same time engaged in reflection on our practices and the supports that encouraged us to reach this point, as well as the barriers that are discouraging or preventing further development (e.g., lack of collaborative planning time, rigidity of bus schedules, need for more in-classroom technology). The latter can be viewed as a form of *qualitative* evaluation. It may not yield numerical scores, frequencies, or sums that can be graphed or compared statistically; rather, qualitative data help us form new hypotheses about the reasons for our progress or the challenges that remain.

We are thus presented with a picture of how we are doing, one which can then be shared back the larger school or district community, through vehicles such as faculty meetings, site councils, PTA forums, school newsletters, school report cards and web sites, district board of education meetings, PTA and parent advisory groups. Here we are demonstrating our *accountability* to the community we serve and beginning to engage others in our problem-solving processes.

TABLE 7.1   District- and School-Level Needs Assessment Areas

DISTRICT	SCHOOL
Policy	Environment
Resources	School Climate
Personnel	Staff Integration and Collaboration
Preparation	Student Integration
Students	
Parents	
Transportation	

Another quantitative aspect of system or program accountability frequently employed by districts and schools is *consumer satisfaction* or *consumer attitude* measures that tap multiple perspectives on implementation. From the district level, the organization may survey individuals in specific roles such as principals, teachers, parents, and paraprofessionals to determine each group's overall attitude toward or satisfaction with the innovation. This input is particularly useful in validating the first measures of program progress described earlier, as it helps determine whether the larger population reflects a similar perspective on our growth and change and lets us know where there is more work to be done in terms of support and training.

Each of these and any other methods for program evaluation should be participatory in nature, encouraging families and school personnel to provide their input at critical steps of the formative process (Duchnowski et al., 1995). Table 7.2 defines the key program evaluation terms discussed in this chapter. Duchnowski, Townsend, Hocutt, and McKinney (1995) noted that "researchers who wish to study the restructuring of the nation's schools need to be prepared to board a moving train" (p. 373). In other words, when we evaluate our efforts, we are doing so in the midst of the change process; we are attempting to evaluate a moving picture as well as the "snapshot" of this point in time. For this reason, Sailor and Skrtic (1995) challenged educators and researchers to utilize a constructivist approach to our evaluation, one which is grounded in qualitative methodology that can inform us about the culture of the school and will promote "…understanding of how teachers interpret their practices in context, how these interpretations affect their practice, and the manner in which they change" (p. 421).

With this in mind, program evaluators need to encourage and employ qualitative approaches such as those employed by Hunt et al. (1998) in their work with an inclusive school. These investigators utilized *focus group research methods* (Krueger, 1994) to examine the alignment of the school's inclusive education with other reform efforts, specifically, with an innovative bilingual program, and the contributions of the combined reform efforts to positive outcomes for students and the school community. Multiple themes emerged, including singular benefits to the respective inclusive and bilingual programs as well as joint benefits experienced by them. These joint benefits included student familiarity with cultural, language, and ability differences through their relationships with other students; student feelings of competence and self-esteem; and a sense of unity and equality with their schoolmates. In addition, the researchers noted that students learned to work through their differences to complete collaborative tasks.

As Hunt, Hirose-Hatae, and colleagues noted (1998a), perhaps the most important contribution of the study is "…the emphasis the participants in the discussions placed on the establishment of a school 'community' *as the foundation for, rather than the outcome of,* the design of collaborative structures and the implementation of inclusive educational practices" (p. 37). These researchers have developed a *Needs Assessment for Building a School Community* (Hunt et al., 1998), which will be a valuable planning and evaluation tool for sites looking to explore the unification of inclusion with concurrent reforms at the school level.

In any discussion of program evaluation tools and strategies, one area that is frequently raised but less often addressed is that of cost and cost-effectiveness. Do inclusive programs cost more or less in actual dollars spent than segregated services? And, what is the relative "bang for the buck"?

Halvorsen et al. (1996) conducted a pilot study to examine these questions within a single California district. The unique feature of this study was an instrument developed by Piuma (1993) to tease out the actual *cost ingredients* of each respective program, the real resources spent in personnel, time, materials, space, and transportation rather than simply examining budgeted costs. The inclusive cost analysis scale or INCAS (Piuma, 1993), provided a format for obtaining data including: (1) documented or reported general education teacher time spent with included and mainstreamed special class students; (2) special educator time with included and with special class students; (3) paraprofessional time in each situation; (4) per-pupil space, materials, and transportation costs for each setting.

TABLE 7.2 Key Evaluation Terminology

Program Evaluation

The practice of examining a program that has the specific intent of "…influencing decision-making and facilitating change" (Stevens & Folchman, 1998, p. 203). Patton (1986) advocated that program evaluation emphasize utility, relevance, and practicality and strive to meet the decision-maker's specific information needs.

Formative Evaluation

The collection and sharing of data/information for the specific purpose of program improvement. Formative evaluation is a useful strategy to provide a feedback loop while a program is in its developmental or initial stages and is often characterized as an "ongoing" mode of evaluation.

Summative Evaluation

The collection of data and information to examine the impact or overall value of a program. This is a useful tool once a program has moved beyond its developmental stage and is perceived by designers, providers, and consumers to be operating as intended. Summative evaluation also serves to identify future needs to be addressed in the next phase of operation.

Quantitative Methods

Collection of data and information that has or can be assigned a numerical value, such as percent, rate, frequency. Quantifiable data are usually utilized in experimental research designs utilizing the scientific method. Quantitative data are often one component of a program evaluation that includes qualitative data as well.

Qualitative Methods

Collection of descriptive information through naturalistic methods such as interviewing, focus groups, observation, and review of documents. Evaluators "triangulate" multiple sources of data and seek to identify themes within and across the different sources of information. Qualitative methodology developed from the anthropological research tradition of gathering and interpreting "rich" descriptive data in order to obtain a deeper understanding of an experience or a culture rather than to "answer" a specific question or hypothesis.

Participatory Action Research (PAR)

A process in which the participants or "subjects" of the study participate actively with the researcher *throughout* the investigation, from its initial design to the final presentation of results and discussion of their implication for action (Whyte, 1991). PAR evolved from formative evaluation and action research (Singer, 1997) and is seen as related to qualitative research because it is concerned with understanding from within, from the subject's perspective, as opposed to examining from without.

Focus Group Methodology

A qualitative research process sometimes used within PAR that provides a nonthreatening environment in which stakeholders can share their perceptions of a specific phenomenon, listen, and exchange views with others through "carefully planned discussion" (Krueger, 1994, p. 6). Nondirective interviewing techniques (Krueger, 1994) are utilized to stimulate participation of all involved.

The investigators first identified two elementary programs within the district which met validated site criteria for integrating students with disabilities. One of these schools integrated students from a special class for an average of 17 percent to 47 percent of instructional time. The second program, in another school, included students with disabilities within general education, bringing support services to them. Each program had the same number of special education teacher and paraprofessional support personnel, and the general education class sizes were equivalent. Students with disabilities were matched according to age and level of disability across the two programs.

Four students from each school and their classrooms were targeted for the study, which included document review (IEPs, teacher schedules, student schedules, salary schedules), observation and time sampling utilizing the Educational Assessment of

Social Interaction (EASI) with an engaged time measure, structured teacher interview, and an instrument developed for the study to examine IEP team members' perceptions of student achievement of IEP objectives (Halvorsen et al., 1994).

The outcomes of the study were provocative, although results cannot be generalized to other situations, given the single district nature of the study. However, the investigators demonstrated a *process* for determining actual costs, and the results in this district were helpful to administrators and others in the planning process. The inclusive program cost less in terms of actual resources expended. This was a result of multiple factors: lower per-pupil space costs for included students who were one of twenty-five to thirty, not one of ten in equivalent space; lower (in some cases zero) transportation costs for included students who attended neighborhood schools rather than being bussed away from their area. Personnel costs also presented an interesting picture. Although general education teachers were spending additional planning and instructional time with included students, their nondisabled students were also receiving instruction and support from special education teachers and paraprofessionals. This situation contrasted with that of special class students. When the latter were integrated, the paraprofessional or special education teacher tended to stay only with those students, by their own report, and then faded their presence out of the classroom entirely, returning to the special class to work with other students.

The student outcome measures did not yield significant differences across programs in terms of engaged time, social interaction, and achievement of objectives. However, one anecdotal report that surfaced in general education teacher interviews bears mention. The general education teachers of included students were well versed in the students' IEP, in what they were working to achieve, and their progress. The general education teachers of students who were integrated from the special class had not seen the students' IEPs and had no knowledge of their objectives prior to the meeting of the core team, which was held to discuss objective achievement.

This study occurred several years prior to IDEA 1997 reauthorization, which requires general educator participation in IEP development for students who are or may be participating in general education. However, the implications of this report appear to underscore a critical difference between schools and classrooms that include and those that do not: teacher "ownership" of the student. It is alarming to consider that a student might be spending a quarter or more of instruction time in a classroom in which the educator in charge has no inkling of his or her instructional needs and expectations, and yet no specialized support personnel are present for the majority of that integrated time.

This brief examination of costs associated with specialized and inclusive models of support has introduced this area of program evaluation, and the reader is encouraged to examine other resources, such as Parrish (1997).

STUDENT OUTCOMES

Grant Wiggins, who popularized the term *authentic assessment* (1989), notes that when we compose our tests of tasks we value, then the very act of test preparation is desirable and is, in fact, educationally sound.

Thus, the most salient accountability question is, How are the students doing? In this brief overview of various program evaluation tools and strategies, we have seen that some data on student performance, student relationships, and student achievement will emerge as a part of program review. However, a concurrent focused look at student outcomes is necessary to truly evaluate whether these "best practices" are *producing* as expected.

Statewide Assessments

In an invited commentary on Kentucky's Alternative Portfolio Assessment System, Sailor (1997) stated that "methods to evaluate student progress drive curriculum and instruction as much as they reflect the results of their application" and further noted that "inclusive education absolutely requires inclusive assessment" (p. 103). The inclusion of students with disabilities in statewide assessments was a policy goal of the 1994 Goals 2000 Act, the School to Work Opportunities Act, and a mandate as well of the recently reauthorized Individuals with Disabilities Education Act (IDEA, 1997). Modifications that the student with an IEP typically requires for instruction are permitted, such as calculators for mathematics, increased time, oral questioning in cases not involving a test of reading comprehension, braille use, testing in a separate room (Kleinert, Kearns, & Kennedy, 1997; Fisher, Roach, & Kearns, 1998). These adaptations must be delineated on the student's IEP and cannot abrogate the purpose of the test, in other words, one cannot be read *to* and then assessed for comprehension (Kleinert et al., 1997). This new mandate, which states had to implement by July 1997 for all students who could participate in the statewide measures sprang partly from the dearth of outcome data stemming from special education. The Council for Exceptional Children (CEC) reported in 1995 that fewer than half of students receiving special education services were participating in statewide assessments. Other data indicated that no students with disabilities participated in six states' assessments in 1993, and that the range of participation was from 5 percent to 100 percent across 44 states, with only two states, Maryland and Kentucky, reporting 100 percent participation (Lipsky & Gartner, 1997).

The logic of inclusion in measures used with the general education population is twofold: If students are to be tested, then we must ensure their access as well to the general education *core curriculum* on which the test is based. If we do not test students receiving special education services in the same ways as their peers, then how can we measure the effectiveness or appropriateness of their education? As Sailor said (1997), students must be included in the assessment. But what about those students for whom the assessments, even with adaptations, are not a meaningful measure of performance, students whose severe intellectual disabilities prevent their participation?

As a part of its comprehensive Education Reform Act of 1990 (KERA), Kentucky has developed a mandatory performance-based assessment system that provides for an Alternative Portfolio assessment for students with moderate to severe cognitive disabilities (Kleinert et al., 1997). Although implementing such a statewide innovation has been a daunting task, Kentucky is to be admired for its commitment to holding schools responsible for *all* students' learning. Kentucky uses both standardized statewide assessments and performance-based tools for its total population. The performance-based assessments are portfolios in math and language arts. Specific accommodations can be made to the standard portfolio system as delineated in the student's IEP. The alternative portfolio system is available for those who cannot participate either in standardized measures or in the typical portfolio process. The decision to opt for the alternative portfolio is an individual one, usually utilized by students with moderate to severe disabilities. The reader may wish to explore Kleinert et al. (1997) and Fisher et al. (1998) for more detail on the portfolio's components, the research base, and for a discussion on issues such as interrater reliability in scoring portfolios. The system is evolving and many questions remain. However, there are several noteworthy aspects of this work as summarized by Elliott (1997), of the National Center on Educational Outcomes.

1. The authors reviewed the literature to obtain indicators of the best practice.
2. Assessment was connected with real-life demands and contexts.
3. Generalizable skills were incorporated into the rubric of the portfolio.
4. The alternative portfolio did not evolve separately but was unified with the regular system from the start, for example, the schedule; and it is aligned in terms of content and procedures. Scoring is aligned as well: Students' portfolio scores are combined with all students' scores in their school, and an "accountability index" is used to compare schools' past and current performance, to determine needs for technical assistance, and to provide specific awards or sanctions (Fisher et al., 1998).

Here we see the critical link between *system* and *student* accountability: If students are not performing to our expectations, then let's look at the system or program that they have been provided. What is unique about Kentucky and a handful of other states to date is their development of a method for examining student outcomes that is based on student learning.

This sounds like a commonsense approach, doesn't it? Yet for decades special education's accountability has been determined only by measuring whether a school or district is in compliance with a set of procedural safeguards or requirements as mandated by IDEA. This was necessary but highly insufficient. As many have said, a school may be "in compliance" but offer little or nothing in terms of quality education that results in meaningful student learning. Several policy efforts are underway nationwide to work on the compliance aspect of our state accountability systems. Their goal is to develop quality-assurance reviews that will measure the presence of best practices as well as student outcomes (Consortium on Inclusive Schooling Practices, 1998). The reader should also note that IDEA 1997 requires all states to have alternative student assessment systems in place by July 2000. It is our hope that these systems will be well integrated with general education statewide assessments and other categorical program review processes.

Ongoing Measurement Strategies of Student Outcomes

There is growing consensus among educators and families that students should receive instruction that enables them to function well in the real world and that we must measure *that* capacity when we collect outcome data (Ford, Davern, & Schnorr, 1992; Peterson et al., 1992; Jorgensen et al., 1998; Sizer, 1992).

Osnosko and Jorgensen (1998) tell us that evaluation and grading are distinct processes with very different purposes. Evaluation's purpose is to assess what students know and can do and, therefore, should be based on multiple pieces of evidence examined by many observers, of whom the student is one. In Osnosko's and Jorgensen's view, grading is one step removed from evaluation in that it is simply the assignment of a shorthand symbol to represent the quality of student work (p. 98), for the purpose of communicating with parents, the school community, and the community at large. However, they argue that grading is unreliable and not particularly informative in communicating what students can do, have learned, or how much they are motivated to learn and serves mainly to rank students in comparison to others. The interested reader may wish to refer to Osnosko and Jorgensen's guidelines for evaluating and grading (1998, p. 100) or to practices presented by Falvey et al. (1997).

Performance-Based Assessment.   So how will we evaluate and how will we communicate about students' performance? Performance is key: we want to be able to see the student using their skills and knowledge. Sizer (1992) noted that "using knowledge assumes a student to be markedly active, inventive...[whereas] displaying knowledge can be done with relative ease by a passive student" (p. 85). As we discussed in Chapter 2 on effective instruction, it makes sense then to utilize authentic assessment strategies, including exhibitions, and portfolios containing a sequence of demonstrations selected to illustrate competence or proficiency in a specific area (e.g., Jorgensen et al., 1998; Falvey et al., 1997; Boggeman et al., 1996). To further link both our instruction and the assessment of learning to the real world enhances our confidence that students have actually acquired the skills on which our curriculum is based (Comer, 1988).

Peterson et al. (1992) provided several examples of how problem-based instruction can be community referenced and student exhibitions linked to the real world. In this way, both students with disabilities, who may experience difficulty transferring skills from the classroom to life, and their typical peers are afforded the opportunity to do so.

Indeed, community-referenced instruction, including aspects such as community service learning (Martin, Jorgensen, & Klein, 1998), is a major emphasis of educational reform for *all* students (e.g., Benjamin, 1989; Fitzgerald et al., 1997). These approaches range from a K–8 magnet school's *microsociety,* in which all students attend morning academic classes and in the afternoon operate a range of business and governance functions from legislative to marketing, manufacturing, sales, and a newsroom (Ford et al., 1992) to a high school law class in which student teams take turns serving as juvenile juries in the local court system (Peterson et al., 1992) while other sophomores in a Humanities block prepare videotaped news reports for their classmates' critiques (David Rice, personal communication, July, 1998).

In each of these cases the connection between learning and its outcome is clear. Modifications for students with disabilities are facilitated by the active nature of the activities, both in terms of the instruction and our measures of performance or competence. Teachers and students from New Hampshire to California are engaged in (and by) activities leading to exhibitions such as those depicted in Table 7.3. Again, these demonstrations extend from a constructivist view of learning in which all students are expected to be *active* participants. Table 7.4 provides an example of how Raymond's portfolio of work might be adapted to address his IEP objectives and expectations for proficiency.

Friend and Bursuck (1999, pp. 408–409) outlined instructive guidelines for portfolio use that are summarized on page 150.

TABLE 7.3   Sample Exhibitions and Products

HUMANITIES (LANGUAGE ARTS/SOCIAL STUDIES)

Detailed or 3-D map

Diorama of event or place

Dictionary or glossary of words specific to an event, time, or place

Diary of important historical figure over a specific time period

Election process: campaign speeches, debate, platform, votes, and tabulation

Illustration or painting representing work of literature

Invented correspondence based on what is known of two historical figures

Live debate or taped debate on specific issues

Menu developed for specific place or time

Mobile

Mural, e.g., to depict an historical timeline

Newspaper "from" specific time or date

News report from specific time or date

Original song (lyrics and music) representing a time period or artistic work

Oral report

Play—script, production, scenery, costumes

Poetry readings on videotape

Poetry volume

Paraphrased or summarized books, chapters (written or taped) for use by readers having difficulty reading

Slide show and narration

Short skits, stories

Storyboard for film or play

Videotaped interviews

Web site design and use

MATHEMATICS AND SCIENCE

Computer-assisted design (CAD) architectural plan or blueprint

Demonstration of a planned experiment

Game involving math operations in order to progress; facts on cards

Graphs and 3-D graphs

Lesson plans for teaching fractions (or other) to a peer

Original experiment using scientific method

Plants grown

Puzzles

Score of musical composition illustrating aspects of time and rhythm

1. Because a portfolio is designed to assist students to learn about their own learning, the product should contain examples of students' self-reflection.
2. The portfolio is completed *by,* not *for* students, and so they should be directly involved in selecting included work.
3. The portfolio is in addition to students' cumulative folder and is, therefore, separate from test scores and other personal, confidential information.
4. Portfolios should clearly delineate the goals, contents, standards (rubric for acceptable, proficient, outstanding performance), and judgments or ratings of work contained in them.
5. The portfolio is a work in progress throughout the year, containing unfinished work at times, but its final version includes only work the student wants to display or make public.
6. Information included should illustrate students' progress from their vantage point as well as those of teachers, parents, and the district.
7. Growth should be illustrated by the portfolio over time with examples of school or real-world activities that show how the students' skills have improved.
8. Students should have models of portfolios to work from and direct teacher support as well as guidelines for their development.

These authors also provide information on the use of *technology* for portfolio development and organization, such as the Grady profile portfolio assessment (Aurbach & Associates, 1991, cited in Friend & Bursuck, 1999, pp. 410–411). Students build their portfolios with electronic cards, which can store typical print information as well as

---

TABLE 7.4   Components of Raymond's Portfolio

---

1. *Student Information*

   *A. *Student's Primary mode of communication* and augmentative or alternative system(s) used

   *B. *Student's daily or weekly schedule*

   *C. *Student comments* to reviewer explaining rationale for selections and indicating level of assistance from peers, parents, and teacher with (C)

2. *Projects and Investigations*

   A. *Oral Presentation of Content*

   Four ten-minute audiotapes of group discussion, one from each quarter; include questions posed of Raymond and his responses

   Three videotaped exhibitions (e.g., public service announcement, news report) showing Raymond's role

   One oral report (with level of peer assistance noted)

   B. *Written or Illustrated Presentations or Demonstrations*

   Timeline and illustration or storyboard sequence

   Favorite drawings

   Scrapbook of written entries (writing samples)

   Typed (wordprocessed) writing samples from three or four points during year

   C. *Self-Evaluation and Monitoring*

   Sample monitoring checklists drafted by Raymond (with level of assistance noted)

   Checklists utilized at various points in year

   Dictated comments by Raymond for work selections

---

*Adapted from "Accountability for All Students: Kentucky's Alternate Portfolio Assessment for Students with Severe Cognitive Disabilities," by H. L. Kleinert, J. F. Kearns, and S. Kennedy, 1997, *Journal of the Association for Persons with Severe Handicaps, 22*(2), pp. 88–101.

sound and video exhibits (e.g., interviews with a recycling company executive for comparison of interviewing skills over time).

Scoring and Evaluating Student Work. Performance-based assessment taps skills not generally measured by traditional assessments, such as synthesis, analysis, and application. Wiggins and McTighe (1998) suggest that we utilize performance-based measures such as exhibitions and demonstrations to evaluate these skills. For example, the public service announcement activity described in Chapter 2 engages students in a demonstration of their knowledge of human rights and applies this to current events. Students must compare and contrast, synthesize information from historical contexts, utilize creative writing skills, and make a case for the importance of the human rights problem they have selected, presenting a strategy to address the problem in a concise and interesting way. Wiggins (1991) suggested that teachers clarify their expectations by presenting models for excellence and by linking standards to real-world performance. For example, Jorgensen (1998) provided a sample rubric to evaluate students' research during an interdisciplinary unit on careers and the use of mathematics, English, and science within specific careers. In addition to the detailed task description, students were provided with the rubric summarized here:

> *Superior:* Written, visual and oral presentations are free of any errors. The description of how concepts are applied is logical and thorough, and the complexity exceeds the level to which they are taught in school.
>
> *Proficient:* Errors are inconsequential; descriptions are logical and understandable to nonexperts. Complexity is not more than a year below grade level.
>
> *Acceptable:* Some major errors present but self-corrected upon questioning. Descriptions confusing to experts but corrected upon questioning. Complexity is not more than two years below grade level.
>
> *Not yet:* Major errors exist. Descriptions are incomplete or illogical, not corrected with questioning. Applications do not go beyond common knowledge (Jorgensen et al., 1998, p. 114).

Jorgensen extends this example with a brief discussion of how a tenth grader with learning problems (poor comprehension, poor writing skills, and retention difficulty with complex, multifaceted tasks or directions) would participate and how his learning could be evaluated. Rob, the student, has an active interest in medicine as a result of the accident that caused his disability. His interviews could be with physical or occupational therapists, and could be audio- or videotaped, with his accompanying oral presentation to the class (Jorgensen, 1998, p. 114). Alternatively, if a student with more severe disabilities were a member of a class team pursuing this assignment, she might dictate questions to a peer or into a taperecorder for later use or type them into a computerized voice synthesizer. If she were unable to design the questions but could operate a switch-activated device in order to increase her control over the environment, she might record others' questions and the interviewer's responses. Templates for and organization of exhibitions are delineated in Jorgensen (1998, pp. 37–40).

But what about the students with the most severe disabilities? Can portfolio assessment be a meaningful, valid, and reliable measure of student growth?

Measuring Growth in Students with the Most Severe Disabilities

Kleinert et al. (1997) demonstrated and described the process of development and use of Kentucky's alternative portfolio, which was the first of its kind to be an integral part of a high-stakes statewide accountability system on which schools' performance indices and future growth rates are calculated. These researchers faced multiple challenges both in the development and analysis processes, one of which was problems with interrater reliability. Although the portfolio system appeared to have both face (relationship to identified outcomes for all) and concurrent (correlation with measures of best practices) validity, the developers were, at last report, employing new procedures in hopes of increasing reliability. This will be essential to the ongoing usefulness of portfolio assessment.

One of the remaining questions posed by Kleinert et al. (1997) and others relates to the impact of this type of assessment on and relevance for students "characterized as having profound and multiple disabilities" (p. 101). The considerable investment of time and resources for training that Kentucky has put into the portfolio have been made because this type of assessment should, in fact, have an impact on how teachers deliver *instruction* and move people toward documented best practices. This is another argument for keeping all students participating in the statewide system. Initial data from Kentucky indicated that instructional practices were lagging behind the assessment. This reminds us of the adage "You can't fatten the pig by weighing it." The portfolio is a prompt or a reminder. Implementation of curricular and instructional changes by teachers may require a greater emphasis on personnel development in *these* areas.

We would, therefore, argue that all students, including those with the "most severe" disabilities should be a part of such alternative systems as Kentucky has developed. However, we would also argue that another level of analysis may be required to assess less obvious but significant levels of growth among students with multiple disabilities. Of course, the IEP is the one measure that contains the personalized expectations for each student, including the conditions under which goals and objectives will occur as well as observable criteria for their achievement. The IEP forms the backbone for the student's instructional program and for the design of portfolio and other individualized evaluations that inform quarterly progress reports, report cards, and portfolio components.

Perceptions of Achievement. The IEP teams convene a minimum of once a year to review progress and set out new objectives. In a traditional multidisciplinary team, individual members report on the student's progress in "their" area—e.g., speech, occupational or physical therapy, academics, functional skills—submitting data collected over time, tests, and narrative reports. In Chapters 3 and 4, we have described a very different transdisciplinary process which requires that members engage both in role release and consistent sharing of information on student progress. An assessment tool for use by teams reviewing IEP progress is the *Perceptions of Achievement* scale (POA) developed by Halvorsen, Neary, and Hunt (1994) and depicted in Figures 7.1 through 7.4.

Team members are asked to come to consensus on whether specific objectives have been met and on the level of assistance required by the student to complete these tasks or behaviors. They are also asked to respond to a sequence of questions as to whether the student initiates the behavior and whether the behavior has been generalized in terms of settings, people, and materials.

We recommend that IEP teams engage in this type of consensus-based discussion for IEP annual reporting as well as during progress reporting periods as is now required under IDEA. The consensus must be an informed one that results from ongoing functional assessment such as described in Chapters 3 and 4. Samples of the type of outcome data on one objective, a measure such as the POA would yield, are presented for Amanda, Joey, Raymond, and Melissa in Figures 7.1 through 7.4.

We recognize that "outputs" will only be as meaningful as the "inputs" allow. Obviously, student outcome data are inextricably linked to program quality. IEPs themselves should be periodically evaluated in terms of best practice criteria. One valid reliable instrument that has been utilized in multiple studies to examine IEP quality for students with severe disabilities in integrated and inclusive settings was developed by Hunt, Goetz, and Anderson (1986) and has been described in detail elsewhere (cf. Hunt & Farron-Davis, 1992; and Hunt, Farron-Davis, Beckstead, Curtis, & Goetz, 1994). Briefly, the instrument rates objectives across seven indicators: age-appropriate materials, age-appropriate tasks,

FIGURE 7.1 POA Objective Data for Amanda

OBJECTIVES

Objective #3 Domain/Curricular Area: Communication

```
Respond to adapted curriculum questions using augmentative
communication system.
```

A. What is the level of the student's progress on this objective?

1	*2*	*3*	*4*
No Progress	Some Progress	Good Progress	Completed
___	___	<u>X</u>	___

B. *If Completed:*

1. Does student initiate this?

Yes ____ No ____

2. Is this skill generalized

Across activities?	Yes ____	No ____
Across people?	Yes ____	No ____
Across materials?	Yes ____	No ____
Across settings?	Yes ____	No ____
Across related responses/behaviors?	Yes ____	No ____

C. *If Checked 2 (some progress) or 3 (good progress):*

1. Does student initiate this task/skill activity?

Yes <u>X</u> No ____   ```Amanda responds more consistently using her
                         Macaw with peers than adults.```

2. Does student demonstrate consistency in performance level on this objective? (e.g., same level of assistance needed across people)

Yes ____ No <u>X</u>   ```As noted, Amanda appears more motivated to
                         communicate with her friends and needs less
                         support to do so when they are present to
                         encourage her. Her range of motion is
                         better at these times than when she is being
                         assisted by an adult without peers being
                         present.```

---

basic skill, critical activity, interaction activity, skill taught across materials and settings, and skill taught in settings in which its use would naturally occur. This instrument can be used proactively to guide IEP quality and retroactively to evaluate it. Coupled with measures of student outcomes in relationship to the IEP, it presents a powerful combination for student teams, including parents, students, educators, and support personnel. This type of evaluation parallels the key standards selected by Kentucky through an intensive research

FIGURE 7.2   POA Objective Data for Joey

OBJECTIVES

Objective #8   Domain/Curricular Area: Language Arts

> Joey will develop a sight word vocabulary of frequently used words taken from his classroom experiences and academics, adding five new words weekly to be utilized in individual stories and put into his personal dictionary.

A. What is the level of the student's progress on this objective?

1	*2*	*3*	*4*
No Progress	Some Progress	Good Progress	Completed
___	___	X	___

> Joey is learning an average of three new words weekly. His dictionary now has sixty words!

B. *If Completed:*

   1. Does student initiate this?

   Yes _____   No _____   NA

   2. Is this skill generalized

   Across activities?   Yes _____   No _____

   Across people?   Yes _____   No _____

   Across materials?   Yes _____   No _____

   Across settings?   Yes _____   No _____

   Across related responses/behaviors?   Yes _____   No _____

C. *If Checked 2 (some progress) or 3 (good progress):*

   1. Does student initiate this task/skill activity?

   Yes _X_   No _____   Joey asks peers and adults if the word can be added to his dictionary, points to words he wants to select, shows his words to others.

   2. Does student demonstrate consistency in performance level on this objective? (e.g., same level of assistance needed across people)

   Yes _X_   No _____

---

review process in its design for the alternative portfolios. The dimensions included *performance* (target skills, plan and initiate, monitor and evaluate); *settings* (instruction in natural, multiple settings for generalization; *classroom instruction* tied to real-life performance) and *interactions* (frequent interactions with typical peers, initiate and sustain interactions, develop friendships) (Kleinert et al., 1997, p. 3).

FIGURE 7.3   POA Objective Data for Raymond

OBJECTIVES

Objective #2, 3   Domain/Curricular Area: Social-behavioral

> 2—Requests a break when needed using speech and break card and
> 3—Maintains appropriate behavior across settings.

A. What is the level of the student's progress on this objective?

1	*2*	*3*	*4*
No Progress	Some Progress	Good Progress	Completed
___	___	X	___

B. *If Completed:* (#2)

1. Does student initiate this?

Yes _X_ No ____   Raymond consistently initiates use of his
break card, and this helps him to maintain
appropriate behavior.

2. Is this skill generalized

Across activities?   Yes _X_   No ____

Across people?   Yes _X_   No ____

Across materials?   Yes _X_   No ____

Across settings?   Yes _X_   No ____

Across related responses/behaviors?   Yes ____   No _X_

C. *If Checked 2 (some progress) or 3 (good progress):* (#3)

1. Does student initiate this task/skill activity?

Yes _X_   No ____

2. Does student demonstrate consistency in performance level on this objective? (e.g.,
same level of assistance needed across people)

Yes ____   No _X_   Not always, but he is improving in this
area. He appears better able to maintain
appropriate behavior when his _active_
participation in the lesson or activity _is_
required.

SUMMARY

In this chapter we provide an overview of system and student-level accountability and
evaluation strategies, including the purposes of each and the relationship of system and
student evaluation to each other. District and school level planning and evaluation measures are described, including best-practice tools and a cost analysis strategy.

FIGURE 7.4 POA Objective Data for Melissa

OBJECTIVES

Objective #4   Domain/Curricular Area: Learning Strategies

Will demonstrate independent use of CAPS reading strategy.

A. What is the level of the student's progress on this objective?

1	*2*	*3*	*4*
No Progress	Some Progress	Good Progress	Completed
___	___	X	___

B. *If Completed:*

   1. Does student initiate this?

   Yes _____   No _____

   2. Is this skill generalized

Across activities?	Yes _____	No _____
Across people?	Yes _____	No _____
Across materials?	Yes _____	No _____
Across settings?	Yes _____	No _____
Across related responses/behaviors?	Yes _____	No _____

C. *If Checked 2 (some progress) or 3 (good progress):*

   1. Does student initiate this task/skill activity?

   Yes _X_   No _____   Remembers she needs to use it. Omits one
                        step occasionally.

   2. Does student demonstrate consistency in performance level on this objective? (e.g., same level of assistance needed across people)

   Yes _X_   No _____   When staff rehearse strategy with Melissa
                        prior to starting assignment, she is very
                        consistent.

Student outcomes are examined in relationship to statewide assessment practices, with specific emphasis on performance-based strategies. Portfolio development and assessment are highlighted with specific examples. Suggested measures to augment portfolio assessment for students with multiple, severe disabilities are presented.

Let's think back to Chapter 1. As educators it is critically important that we examine both the integrity of our interventions and educational programs as well as the impact of these on our students' learning. We strongly encourage you to adapt tools and strategies discussed here and to explore others which will assist you in examining essential questions related to your school's effectiveness. When someone asks, "Does that inclusion idea really work for kids?" you will be able to provide answers based on data, not merely anecdotes.

CHECKING FOR UNDERSTANDING

1. How would you go about designing an evaluation plan for the district inclusion plan in Appendix A? What would you want to include? How would you obtain these data?

2. Think about a topic area or unit that you have taught in the past two years. How did you assess student knowledge? If you did not use a performance-based demonstration, how could you alter the task to require this?

3. Read the middle-school interdisciplinary cooperative learning-lesson outline regarding postal service rates in the box below. Brainstorm (with a partner) an outline for an exhibition or demonstration that you would require of the groups to demonstrate their understanding.

4. Write a rubric for assessing products developed for item 3.

5. Discuss how you would adapt this outline for students with mild disabilities and students with severe disabilities.

COOPERATIVE GROUP TASK LESSON PLAN DEVELOPMENT

You are designing a cooperative lesson for middle-school students that incorporates multiple disciplines. The lesson revolves around predicting the cost of first-class postage in the year 2010. You are expecting that students will use information regarding the history of the postal service, trends in economics, numerical prediction strategies, changes in technology, and any other contributing factors. Your goals are that students will be able to

1. identify at least 5 factors that may contribute to changes in postal rates;
2. describe the history of postal services in the United States since 1800;
3. develop a clear position with supporting factual information about likely first-class postage in 2010;
4. provide at least two predictive strategies, such as graphing, to support predictions;
5. participate as a contributing member of a team in research, product development, and presentation;
6. actively participate in presenting the information to the class and answer the questions from others;
7. ask thoughtful questions of other presenters.

You are free to add other, more extensive learning goals to this lesson, and you may allow creative strategies for presenting the information to the class.

CHAPTER EIGHT

INCLUSION IN THE CONTEXT OF SCHOOL RESTRUCTURING: HOW WE CHANGE AND WHERE WE'RE GOING

Upon completion of this chapter you will be able to

1. Define multiple aspects and stages of educational change processes
2. Identify change strategies that address participants' levels of concern
3. Identify ways in which you as an individual might work to accomplish school change
4. State the relationship between inclusion and school reform
5. Define components of effective restructuring
6. Describe effective personnel development efforts to support reform
7. Identify stakeholders' roles in the change process

As you have read these stories of how students and teachers have worked to make schools effective for all learners, you may have been thinking, "How can I bring this about in my classroom, school, or district? I am a lone parent, teacher, or principal. My school doesn't have the *energy* to make the kinds of changes that are necessary. My school doesn't even recognize the *need* for change."

A good friend of ours, Alycia Chu, likes to remind us that "No one likes change except a wet baby" (Personal communication, May 21, 1998). We might add that even babies often dislike the *process* of change. Roemer (1991) points out that too often, past educational reforms produced "change without difference" (p. 447). Change for the sake of novelty is not what we propose, because we recognize the intensive effort that is involved in designing schools that work for all of their students. So, what can be achieved by a lone voice or a small group working together? In this chapter we outline some steps and processes involved in generating and sustaining integrated reforms that can move your schools to achieve more personalized education for all students. We also discuss restructuring in relationship to inclusive education and provide strategies to support the change process.

STEPS TOWARD CHANGE

Michael Fullan, one of our country's foremost authorities on educational reform, assured us that *neither* top-down nor bottom-up strategies result in effective change; rather, a complex mix of *both* must occur if we are to ensure the success of school reforms (1993). As individuals—whether teachers, parents, or administrators—we can initiate the change process in our schools with activities such as the following.

1. *Initiate a reflective practice group.* Look for colleagues (parents, teachers, administrators) who share your interest in exploring new ideas for your school's structure, curriculum, and instruction. You might approach those teachers whose classrooms and instruction you have admired, those who ask questions in meetings, who contribute ideas, who offer materials to others. Invite parents you often see at PTA meetings, at school personnel development activities, or at training and information sessions in the community. You are trying to identify other "seekers," people who are committed to their students but who always seem to be looking for more. Invite this small group to coffee, lunch, whatever, and share some of your questions. Invite others to share their questions, concerns, ideas. Suggest that the group begin by selecting an article, book, or book chapters on educational reform and operate like a book club at first (see Table 8.1). Set future meetings, dates, frequency, times, and begin discussion of how the group wants to function.

2. *Visit restructured, inclusive schools* in your community or nearby districts. If there are no such schools in your immediate area, contact your state department of education or key professional and advocacy groups for assistance in finding these schools regionally or statewide. Look for schools that would be a good match for yours in terms of demographics such as size, diversity, socioeconomic status, or type of community (suburban, urban, or rural). (See Table 8.2 for a list of groups or organizations involved in school change which might be able to assist in this process.) Prepare lists of questions you want to pursue on these visits. Consider visiting in pairs, and ask principals if it will be possible to meet with them and any other staff or parents after your visit. Prepare to present your findings to your group.

3. *Visit schools on-line* by utilizing the many reform networks and resources that list or *link* to participating schools (also see Table 8.2). Take advantage of virtual school tours and of chat rooms associated with these. Many sites also have list servs of members to which you can subscribe and can submit questions.

TABLE 8.1   Suggested Initial Reading List

Armstrong, T. (1984). *Multiple intelligences in the classroom.* Alexandria, VA: Association for Supervision and Curriculum Development.

Armstrong, T. (1987). *In their own way.* Los Angeles: Tarcher.

Fullan, M. (1993). *Change forces: Probing the depth of educational reform.* London: Falmer Press.

Gardner, H. (1983). *Frames of mind: The theory of multiple intelligences.* New York: Basic Books.

Goldman, J., & Gardner, H. (1997). Multiple paths to educational effectiveness. In D. Lipsky and A. Gartner (Eds.), *Inclusion and school reform.* Baltimore: Paul H. Brookes.

Jorgensen, C. M. (Ed.), (1998). *Restructuring high schools for all students.* Baltimore: Paul H. Brookes.

Lipsky, D., & Gartner, A. (1997). *Inclusion and school reform.* Baltimore: Paul H. Brookes.

Meier, D. (1995). *The power of their ideas: Lessons for America from a small school in Harlem.* Boston: Beacon Press.

Paul, J., Rosseli, H., & Evans, D. (1995). *Integrating school restructuring and special education reform.* New York: Harcourt-Brace.

Sage, D. (Ed.) (1997). *Inclusion in secondary schools.* Port Chester, NY: National Professional Resources.

Sailor, W. (1991). Special education in the restructured school. *Remedial and Special Education, 12*(6), 8–22.

Sizer, T. (1992). *Horace's school: Redesigning the American high school.* Boston: Houghton Mifflin.

Villa, R. A., Thousand, J. S., Stainback, W., & Stainback, S. (Eds.) (1992). *Restructuring for caring and effective education: An administrative guide to creating heterogeneous schools.* Baltimore: Paul H. Brookes.

Wiggins, G. (1989). The futility of trying to teach everything of importance. *Educational Leadership, 47*(3), 44–59.

TABLE 8.2   Selected Organizations Involved with Inclusive Educational Reform

NAME	ADDRESS AND WEB ADDRESS
Academy for Educational Development (AED)	1875 Connecticut Avenue, N.W. Washington, DC 20009 (202) 884-8000 FAX–8400 www.aed.org/us/ed
American Federation of Teachers (AFT)	555 New Jersey Avenue, N.W. Washington, DC 20001 www.aft.org
AskEric (through CEC)	Educational Research & Information Center ericec.net/intbodc.htm#reform
The Association for Persons with Severe Disabilities (TASH)	29 Susquehanna Ave. Suite 210 Baltimore, MD 21204 (410) 828-8274 FAX–6706 www.tash.org
Association for Supervision and Curriculum Development	1703 No. Beauregard St. Alexandria, VA 22311-1714 (800) 933-ASCD (2723) (703) 578-9600 www.ascd.org
Coalition of Essential Schools (high schools)	CES National Office 1814 Franklin Street Suite 700 Oakland, CA 94612 (510) 433-1451 FAX–1455 Amy Gerstein, Exec. Dir. www.essentialschools.org
Council for Exceptional Children (CEC)	1920 Association Drive Reston, VA 20191-1589 (707) 620-3660–voice phone (703) 264-9494–FAX (703) 264-9446–TTY www.cec.sped.org
Institute on Community Integration, University of Minnesota	109 Pattee Hall 150 Pillsbury Dr. S.E. Minneapolis, MN 55455 (612) 624-4512 FAX–9344 www.ici.coled.umn.edu/ici
Institute on Disability University of New Hampshire	University Affiliated Program UNH, 7 Leavitt Lane Suite 101 Durham, NH 03824-3522 (603) 862-4320 (603) 862-0555 (FAX) www.iod.unh.edu/projects/
National Association of State Boards of Education (NASBE)	1012 Cameron Street Alexandria, VA 22314 (800) 368-5023 (703) 684-4000 (700) 836-2313 (FAX) www.nasbe.org

TABLE 8.2 CONTINUED

NAME	ADDRESS AND WEB ADDRESS
National Association of State Directors of Special Education	1800 Diagonal Road #320 Alexandria, VA 22314 703 519-3800, -7008 703 519-3808 FAX www.lrp.com
National Center on Educational Outcomes (NCEO)	University of Minnesota 350 Elliott Hall 75 East River Road Minneapolis, MN 55401 (612) 624-8561 FAX–0879 www.coled.umn.edu/nceo
National Education Association (NEA)	1201 Sixteenth Street NW Washington, DC 20036 (202) 833-4000 www.nea.org
National Parent Network on Disabilities	1220 G Street, N.W. Suite 800 Washington, DC 20005 (202) 434-8686 (202) 638-0509 FAX www.npnd.org
Parent Advocacy Coalition for Educational Rights (PACER)	4826 Chicago Avenue So. Minneapolis, MN 55417 (612) 827-2966 (612) 827-7770 (TDD)

4. *Identify and attend local, regional, state, or national conferences* on inclusive educational reform in your area (or beyond as finances permit!). Ask your principal and faculty for an opportunity to share information obtained at a future faculty meeting or in staff development events. Prepare a presentation or workshop to highlight key content.

5. *Contact your district's curricular and personnel development unit or office.* Find out the year's training agenda and how it is formulated. Inquire about the process for input, and consider having volunteers from your group work with the district committee. If the year's committee is already formed, volunteer for related tasks, such as collecting needs assessment data at your school. Find out whether training will be site based and whether faculty, staff, and parents (i.e., general *and* special education) are included in professional development *together* (cf. McGregor et al., 1998).

6. As your group's work progresses and you identify specific practices which you want to pursue, *suggest topics or speakers* for school forums, meetings, or trainings to your principal and school-site council. Consider inviting teams (e.g., administrator, teachers, parents, others) from schools you have visited to generate interest within a broader audience.

7. *Present to your school faculty, PTA, individual departments, or school-site council* the kinds of innovations you are seeing and reading about. Encourage others to join your group.

8. *Make a brief informational presentation to your board of education,* highlighting the exciting developments you have seen as well as the need for their support in order to expand these innovations to other interested schools. Invite board members to visit these schools as well as your own. Share specific student outcome data that you can obtain from school "report cards." Ask a board member and your principal to meet with your group and begin discussions of replication or adaptation of some of these effective features for your school.

9. Make a similar presentation and follow up with your district's *special education advisory council* (if one exists).

10. *Contact your state department of education* to determine whether state grants or funds exist that would assist schools in planning for and implementing inclusive restructuring. Find out deadlines, requirements, and discuss application with your principal and with key staff beyond your reflective group.

11. *Contact local libraries and conduct on-line searches* for information on private foundations that fund education projects. Frequently, county offices of education, district media centers, or development offices will have much of this information on hand. Local university libraries are another source as well, and public universities usually provide for community access. Some larger communities may also have foundation libraries that focus on securing private funding and grants for nonprofit agencies and schools.

12. *Establish a relationship with university(ies) in your vicinity.* Contact education departments or schools as well as departments such as psychology, social work, etc. Inquire as to their interest in partnerships with local schools and their ability to support your efforts in some way. You might suggest that faculty

- Facilitate a teacher action research group
- Participate on a school reform team by attending meetings, providing resource materials, or linking the school with other schools
- Co-author grant proposals to support collaborative reform efforts
- Provide student teachers and interns who can support instructional innovations, and work with master teachers on site
- Conduct staff development activities collaboratively with the school community

When grass-roots strategies such as these begin to align with the district or school's agenda, the effect is powerful. A decade ago, in the Davis Joint Unified School District in California, parents interested in developing inclusive options pursued a series of activities that led the way for their development, bringing educators on board as they moved ahead. They took ironing boards or cardtables to local shopping centers and passed out information on inclusive education. They held a videofest, during which they showed commercially available tapes about inclusive schools and invited their district director of special education as well as parents in their neighborhoods and local teachers. They made presentations to the board of education. They accomplished all of these activities in a positive climate, keeping communication lines open. The district had plans to open a special class for their sons and daughters, but when space was unavailable, the district was able to consider the inclusive option because they had *information* at hand and a group that was ready and willing to plan with them. This was the beginning of the *first* systematic effort to include students with moderate to severe disabilities in northern California.

In southern California, Whittier High School initiated a site-level change process that began several years ago and continues as a work in progress (Falvey et al., 1997). Whittier High School lagged well behind the "high school on the hill" in test scores and graduation rates. Faculty embarked on an exploration process to determine how to improve their school's performance, particularly in terms of student outcomes, as their superintendent desired.

In 1985, Whittier initiated the first service-delivery change with the return of students with mild learning disabilities to general education for the majority of their instruction, utilizing a collaborative consultation model (Nevin et al., 1990). Classes for students with severe disabilities were centrally located for maximum integration during nonacademic periods and campus-wide activities, and in 1989, all Whittier segregated sites were closed, and their students returned to regular district schools. The school special education staff members were engaged in best practices for integration (cf. Halvorsen & Sailor, 1990), organizing peer support systems and teaching within general education to maximize students' involvement in the life of the school (Falvey et al., 1997). However, much of the success of these efforts and access to general education was dependent upon the good will of general educators and the communication skills of their special education staff.

In the early 1990s, Whittier High School faculty began to analyze the school's mission and practices in relationship to its postschool outcome data. With only 10 percent to 15 percent of each senior class going to college and a 30 percent dropout rate, Whittier High School faculty and the district recognized the need for significant change. The Whittier High School community established a new mission, which stated a commitment to valuing and recognition of all students "...to maximize students' potential, emphasize high expectations and standards, and develop pride in appreciation for education and achievement" (Falvey et al., 1997, p. 49). This was followed by a set of specific outcomes expected of all students.

With these in hand and after much exploration through reading and reflection, Whittier High School decided to pursue restructuring efforts patterned after the Coalition of Essential Schools (Sizer, 1992), and in 1994 the school became one of the Coalition's recognized high schools. As an integral part of this ongoing process, Whittier High School developed a school-site plan that, for the first time, included all special education services within a restructured, collaborative model. In 1993, when the ninth grade was organized into smaller teams, two support (special education) teachers were assigned with eight to ten core faculty, an administrator, and counselor. (For a detailed description of school organization and instruction, see Falvey et al., 1997). The staff assignments reflect the instructional and curricular changes: personalized instruction for each student; integrated curriculum (e.g., Humanities block combining English and Social Studies); block scheduling to facilitate integration and common planning time, and heterogeneous groupings of students, with inclusion of all students with IEPS across the teams.

Each support teacher works with a cross-categorical caseload of about seventeen students, whose needs range from mild to substantial. These teachers now work with their respective Math, Science, Social Studies, and English faculty to write curricula, plan, and deliver instruction. All special educators co-teach with their general education partners, thus increasing the adult-to-student ratios and supporting students without IEPS, who may be at risk for school failure.

The data on the outcomes of this ongoing restructuring process have begun to emerge. Whittier High School has now cut its dropout rate nearly in half and has a higher proportion of students who meet the eligibility criteria for admission to the California state university system than does the "high school on the hill" (Falvey, personal communication, January 21, 1999). This brief vignette provides one example of a school that has engineered significant change in the education of all of its students, with inclusive education as one cornerstone of that restructuring.

WHAT DO WE MEAN BY RESTRUCTURING?

Sailor (1991), Skrtic (1990), and others (cf. McGregor & Vogelsberg, 1998) have argued that the term "educational reform" is inadequate to describe the governance and organizational changes required to make a supportive framework for curricular and instructional innovation. For this reason, many authors have endorsed the term "restructuring," which emphasizes the notion that change cannot be accomplished by simply a top-down set of policy recommendations or interventions nor by ground-up grass roots efforts in isolated schools (cf. Darling-Hammond & Berry, 1988). Restructuring is systemic in nature and, therefore, requires simultaneous efforts, with both ends moving toward an encounter in the middle (Sailor, 1991). Lewis (1989) described restructuring as those actions that allow and encourage higher expectations of both teachers and students.

Why do we propose a relationship between inclusive education and overall restructuring? In Hargreaves's 1997 analysis of the reasons that many educational changes do not succeed, he noted nine major barriers to change or reasons for its failure. One of these was the *lack of relationship of the change to other reform initiatives.* Inclusive education has too often occurred on a parallel or *entirely separate track from general education reform,* sometimes being ahead of those changes, which thwarts its becoming a pervasive ethic and practice within the school.

A case in point: In some states there is no special education funding mechanism to support included students. As a result of such antiquated systems, districts and schools include as few students as possible, because they will not receive special education dollars for them. In another instance of this, a school system does not allow included students' names to appear on general education teachers' rosters. The outcome of this was a lack of ownership of students with disabilities by their classroom teachers, in part because the students were "extra," above and beyond the typical class size. The *structures* did not support the innovation. An example of separate reforms would be a school that has made a conscious decision to seek grants to obtain on-site school-linked services such as mental health, a parent center, an afterschool homework program. Students with disabilities are included at the school, but their staff and parents are unaware of the proposals, and general educators don't think to invite them to participate. The obvious opportunities inherent in coordinating inclusive education and school-linked services are lost. We have witnessed many such lost opportunities that seem to result from the lack of a shared history of general and special educators.

Many authors have noted the separation of general and special education reform, citing the failure of the so-called "regular education initiative" (REI) (Will, 1986) of the 1980s (Sailor, 1991). Even the label "REI" was a misnomer, because the initiative sprang from special, not general, education (Singer, 1988). Over the past decade, increasing numbers of parents and educators with inclusive experiences have recognized that the policy and program changes required for effective inclusion *are* quite congruent with the goals of general education reform: to change our schools to address the needs of an increasingly diverse population through strategies that are informed by research on pedagogy as well as service and curricular innovations (Bauwens & Hourcade, 1995; Lipsky & Gartner, 1997; McGregor & Vogelsberg, 1998; Sailor, 1991; Semmel & Gerber, 1990). In short, inclusive education cannot be built separately from general education reform. Inclusion is a fundamental change for all system levels. As Lipsky and Gartner (1997) noted, "Given that the root issue in the failure of the special education system is its separateness; the reform of special education necessarily requires its integration with broader educational restructuring" (p. 221).

Restructuring is the appropriate term for fundamental changes depicted within this book. This is not mere incremental change or "tinkering around the edges." Inclusive school reform is restructuring of governance, of resources, service delivery and coordination, adult and student roles, instructional practices, curriculum, school climate, and community participation. Outstanding schools, says *U.S. News & World Report* writer Thomas Toch (1999), are "...schools where students progress steadily toward higher academic standards and where every student matters" (pp. 48–49). These are the inclusive schools we all are trying to build, and as the adage goes, getting there is half the battle. So, let's talk about change.

Ingredients of Sustainable Change

"Systems change is not for the conceptually or interpersonally faint-hearted" (Sarason, 1990). Because effective, enduring change must be both top-down and bottom-up, it requires multiple components as listed here.

Leadership. Six years ago a large urban district offered no inclusive general education classroom assignment for students with severe disabilities and few such opportunities for students with mild to moderate disabilities. The district was in a state of transition at both the superintendent and director levels, with the new superintendent looking for appropriate special education leadership. Parents desiring inclusive classrooms approached the superintendent directly to advise him of this and present their advocacy plans. Four preschoolers were included during the superintendent's first year, and a director was recruited who had had significant experience developing inclusive placements in another urban center. At this point the joint leadership role became clear, as the two formed a districtwide *inclusion task force* to develop plans and recommendations for the inclusion process; provided workshops for interested schools, established a timeline to begin elementary inclusion across several schools by September, and changed one program consultant support position to focus solely on facilitating the inclusion process.

Within two years, this district was offering inclusive student assignments within fifteen elementary, one middle, and one high school, with plans to expand further in upcoming years, building capacity until each school in the district could offer an inclusive option to its students. Along the way, this leadership resulted in several corollary accomplishments: passage of new board of education policy on inclusive education, semiannual personnel development offerings for involved and targeted schools, specific training for groups such as paraprofessionals, attendance by school teams at annual state-sponsored summer institutes on inclusive education, alignment of placement procedures with general education, and development of a district *Handbook on Inclusive Education* as well as teacher contract language on inclusion.

Today, forty—nearly half—of that district's schools provide inclusive options. An important development in the past year has been the superintendent's granting of financial support for a detailed plan drafted by the inclusion task force. The plan was aligned with the district mission and goals and involved the development and use of model schools, mentor systems, personnel development, and expansion of parental access to information and training on inclusion. This superintendent has since created a special education management team of special and general educators to design a new structure and plans to address special education and other categorical programs in an integrated approach that will enable and require *all* schools to be responsible for and to effectively educate all of their students. This leader has a vision of where the district needs to go and the ability to articulate that vision to a wide variety of stakeholders. He also has the ability to assess where the district is in relationship to that vision, and can, therefore, help people to keep it in sight as they move through change.

Commitment. Ownership needs commitment at both grass-roots and upper administrative levels as well as at every level between. This can be fostered by strong leadership at the superintendent, director, or board level. For example, consider a recent case in the high-growth suburban district of Emerson Middle School. Most students with moderate to severe disabilities had attended programs operated by the county office of education, the majority of which were not inclusive and were situated outside the district. Two events occurred during the same year to initiate the change process: an active parent was elected to the district's board of education, and the county placed a team-taught kindergarten, designed and developed by a general and a special educator, in one of the district's schools. The board began to question the costs of the county-operated program. At the same time, they heard more about inclusive options from everyone involved with the kindergarten. Real grass-roots support at the school level began to stimulate inclusion of those kindergartners in first grade and beyond. The board approved the formation of a district level *inclusive education planning team* of key players to make recommendations to the Board and Administration. A year later, other students were being included in their home elementary, middle, and high schools; the district team developed short- and long-term plans to return all the students to home schools; the director retired and was replaced by a new proactive administrator; and coordination among these special education activities and district restructuring efforts began to emerge.

Recognition of the Problem.   In order to initiate change, we must first see the need for it. "I've been teaching the same way for 27 years, and I'm not going to change for this student" (inservice teacher, somewhere in California, 1998); "If you have always done it that way it is probably wrong" (Charles Kettering, inventor, cited in Bridges, 1991). Change usually means we move from a place of competence and comfort to a place of incompetence and discomfort (Neary, 1996). So what motivates us to go there? We, the system, our leadership, someone or some group within the system has to *recognize that a problem exists.* Is the problem "merely" one of access? Are we simply trying to obtain choices for students and families that correspond with school choices available to their peers in general education? Although access in itself is no simple matter, the answer is *no;* that is necessary but insufficient. Multiple problems within our separate special education system have reinforced the separateness of the students. At the same time, problems for general education classrooms and students reached enough of a critical mass in the 1980s that they were *recognized,* written about, and translated into a force for change (e.g., Goodlad, 1984; Holmes Group, 1986; Lewis, 1989; Lilly, 1987; Lipsky & Gartner, 1989; Perrone, 1989; Sailor, 1991).

What were and are some of the problems from a special education perspective? Disproportionate overrepresentation of students of color in certain labeled categories and in separate special education programs has been one recognized problem (cf. Shapiro, Loeb, Bowermaster, Wright, Headden, & Toch, 1993; and Lipsky & Gartner, 1997, for a comprehensive discussion), as well as overrepresentation of male students in some categories and service models (e.g., more than two thirds of secondary students receiving special education services are male according to Lichtenstein, 1996). Here is a problem that has been recognized, reported on, litigated, written about, and incorporated within consent decrees as well as site or district goals. Yet it has not been resolved. One might hypothesize that we have gotten stuck in a "problem-admiration" mode instead of finding solutions (Neary, 1996). We talk about it; we advance theories; scholars write books; lawyers bring appropriate suits—yet it continues.

Inclusive education—a blueprint for an outcomes-driven, unified general and special education system—can be a response to this critical problem of overidentification of some groups of students. If we are crafting systems that utilize resources collaboratively to address any student's need, we will (a) be better armed to support students without labelling them and to address the issue before it becomes necessary to label them, (b) be able to *support* identified students with specialized instruction without removal from general and special education, and, thus, (c) be *visible* within our schools as a reminder to everyone that all of these students are members of the community, that there is no "someplace else."

In recognizing our problems as forces for change, we need to also look at general education's reflection of ourselves. If we take the ethnic and gender problems just reviewed, we see that we have helped to create them by our focus on the expert nature of special education, by our assertion that "we know" what to do with the student who "doesn't fit." The message is "We design programs to fit the student, so send him to us." As Neary (1996) quipped, special education has presented itself as the Statue of Liberty of education: "Send us your tired, your acting-out, your student who learns differently, your...." In other words, we have helped to create problems of overidentification by communicating a false message that students should fit a general mold and that teachers with students who do not "fit" the mold should refer them to "us." We send two powerful concommitant messages with this approach: that general education teachers are unable to teach students who learn differently and, indeed, are not responsible for them and that students have to earn and prove their right to belong—in other words, all students are at risk for removal to another place (Kunc, 1992).

Educators have begun to recognize the "co-dependence" of special and general education's failure to teach our diverse student populations. This is a first step and can be a significant catalyst for inclusive education.

Stakeholder Participation in the Change Process

From President Johnson's 1960s initiative known as the War on Poverty to the work of change agents in the world of business (cf. Bridges, 1991; Covey, 1989) and, finally, to the seminal work of early and current education reformers (cf. Fullan, 1993), a cardinal principle of effective change is the involvement of the "changees," the constituents, in the design of the process. In this way, top-down and grass-roots efforts unite to ensure a workable plan in relationship to the desired vision. Only those "on the ground"—teachers, principals, parents, paraprofessionals, support personnel, and students—can truly understand the day-to-day implications and effects of these changes, and only they can provide the grist for their successful implementation.

An old adage states that the camel is a horse designed by committee (cited in Friend & Bursuck, 1999). The first step in designing a horse that can survive in the desert is having the key players represented at the table. Karasoff, Alwell, and Halvorsen (1992) described a blueprint for district-level inclusive systems change involving key stakeholders; Davern, Schnorr, Erwin, Ford, & Rogan (1997) have laid out a site-level process. In both of these works, the authors emphasize identifying representative constituents who can serve as liaisons to the groups they represent and who are committed to the end goals.

Let's examine the district case illustrated under "Leadership." This urban superintendent brought stakeholders into the process from the outset and gave the inclusion task force a broad charge as well as recognized *status* in the district as an agent for change. The task force included administrators, teachers, parents, paraprofessionals, related services, organizations such as parent advisories and the teachers' association and began its work by formulating a mission and goals congruent with the district's overall vision. They then worked within a process that has been labelled "backward mapping," identifying the barriers within the structures, procedures, and processes which will need to be overcome in order to achieve those goals (Pumpian & Fisher, 1997).

Here then is an instance in which the components of leadership, commitment, and recognition of the problem came together in *action*. A cross-constituent group engaged in the following multiple activities.

1. Assessing their district and sites in relation to the vision
2. Setting goals and recommending activities to meet them
3. Crafting a plan and overseeing its implementation
4. Evaluating the activities and their impact in terms of student and school outcomes

Appendix A contains a sample first-year plan designed by a district to initiate the change process.

Groups such as these generally meet one to two times per month, using a combination of afterschool (voluntary) meeting times and some longer time periods using released time, and summer stipends for smaller groups working on specific tasks. For example, the *curriculum* activities noted in Appendix A might involve teacher writing teams who meet for two consecutive days in each of three months. The *personnel development* or "training" subgroup would use a similar schedule and work with district personnel development staff to select, refine and develop introductory and advanced level training materials for future training sessions. A third group on *procedural issues* would work in tandem with administration to revise procedures for enrollment, school assignments, and staffing for inclusive schools. And the fourth group in this plan would develop a district "*starter kit*" or handbook on inclusive education that would incorporate portions of each of the above as well as the additional components listed in Figure 8.1.

FIGURE 8.1   Sample District Handbook Contents

I. Introduction
- What is inclusive education?
- District history and current status of inclusive education
- Frequently asked questions
- Rationale
- Benefits for students, families, staff

II. Procedures
- District guidelines on inclusive education, board policy, teachers association guidelines
- Roles and responsibilities
- Service delivery and support model
- Student assignment process
- Miscellaneous: IEPs, grading, report cards, field trips, testing, photo permissions, parent–teacher conferences, etc.
- Collaborative problem solving

III. Curricular adaptation and instruction
- Overview
- Types of adaptation examples keyed to core curriculum and district standards
- Classroom strategies
- Student-level planning process
- Individualized student participation plan
- Peer participation
- Positive behavioral support strategies

IV. Resources
- District planning team membership list and meeting schedule
- Site and student planning teams
- Training opportunities calendar
- Print and media resources available in the district and on-line
- Mentoring systems: teachers, parents, schools

These task forces are problem solvers. They collaborate to provide the blueprint for change. They, and all of the stakeholders they represent, will need *support* for the change process, the next ingredient for sustainable innovation.

Supporting People through Change

Too often we fail to accomplish effective change because we fail to recognize that change is loss; that change exposes dysfunction within the existing system; that change is complex, messy; and that it is a *process,* not an event.

The bell curve, the curve of natural distribution, can be used to describe participants in change, because individuals naturally respond to change in a variety of ways. (See Figure 8.2.) There are, first of all, the innovators or trailblazers as described by Schlecty (1993). These are the people who lead the effort and are happiest when they are doing so.

There is no right or wrong about our individual relationship to a particular innovation; we are part of the normal distribution. It is the way things are, and we put ourselves at risk if we ignore this fact. Schlecty (1993) suggests that we view this change process—our move to inclusive, restructured schools—as a journey to uncharted territory. There will be those trailblazers who are constantly on the prowl. They go to places where no one has gone before, where there are no maps, no empirically based models. They are motivated by novelty and excited by risks. They need a clear vision, and they are sometimes maniacal about their vision and mission. They know where they're going but not necessarily how they'll get there. Obstacles are viewed in personal terms. Trailblazers need to be with other trailblazers. They need to share their experiences with others and be excited by analogous experiences. They need to be reminded that the quest is a community quest, not a personal one. Think of the people you know who could be described this way.

The second role is that of the *pioneer.* Pioneers are also adventurous people who are willing to take considerable risks. They also need to hear about the vision and link their personal quest to the larger agenda. They need to know that the quest is worthwhile. They need demonstrations of the concept but not necessarily skill development. If you look at some of the staff developers and speakers about inclusion, you'll see a lot of pioneers. They need the stories of the trailblazers and are great at getting people to start something. They are usually less maniacal than the trailblazers, and are, thus, better at working with others to support change. If you are intrigued by a new, radical idea and stick your neck out, you're a pioneer. You are grounded but willing to take a risk if it strikes a chord with your personal values.

The next role is the *settler.* Think about the bell curve. Now we're talking about larger numbers of people, the solid core of our teaching staff. In terms of the people who settled our frontiers, these folks came after the maps were made and some of the area already made safe. They need assurances that the venture was worthwhile. They need to know why we should do business differently than we have. They are bold, but they're not as adventurous as the pioneers. They ask us to assure them that this can be accomplished, show them how it works, teach them the skills to do this, tell them what to expect. Settlers will usually not move on until they believe they have the required skills. They will institutionalize the process, refine it. Settlers need training, but they also need strong leadership to assure them they will not be left out there alone. They need to know the "fort" is nearby.

The *stay-at-homes* require a lot more to motivate their changing. Their present condition must be so intolerable to their interests and values that the only alternative is to do something. Or the new vision must be so compelling that it inspires the hope of a new day, a better life, and overrides the risks they see in changing. Stay-at-homes are just not easily motivated to change. Even less-than-adequate situations are tolerable.

Saboteurs are in some ways similar to trailblazers. They are not afraid of risk or of operating alone. Whereas trailblazers are likely to go where none has gone before, saboteurs are likely to stay where none dares to stay. To be persecuted is to be appreciated. An interesting point is that saboteurs might once have been trailblazers or pioneers who became cynical, who were not adequately acknowledged or supported through previous changes.

Why is it important to categorize our colleagues in this way? It is essential. The people are the innovators, and, no matter how inspiring the vision and how elegant the plan, if we cannot bring along the people, we are not going anywhere. We need to treat our colleagues with the same respect and support that we treat our students. How can we do that?

Hall and Hord (1987) have characterized participants in a change process according to *levels of concern* and recommend that the educational system respond to the concern at the expressed level, because it is only by matching the concern with appropriate information and action that we can begin to make settlers out of "stay-at-homes" and pioneers out of settlers. Hall and Hord (1987) described seven levels of concern starting with (awareness, informational, personal), (management), (consequences, collaboration, and finally, refocusing). Figure 8.3 provides a listing of these stages and an expression of each level

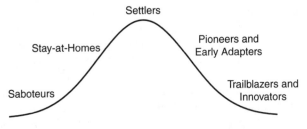

FIGURE 8.2   A Normal Distribution of People Experiencing Change

FIGURE 8.3   Stages of Concern

THE CONCERNS-BASED ADOPTION MODEL (CBAM)

STAGE OF CONCERN	EXPRESSION OF CONCERN
6. Refocusing	"I can think of some ways we can make our inclusive program even better than it is."
5. Collaboration	"I am concerned about relating what we're doing to include more students with disabilities to what other teachers are doing."
4. Consequence	"How will this inclusive education effort affect the rest of my class?"
3. Management	"I don't know how to organize or manage such a diverse classroom. I have only so much time and energy."
2. Personal	"How will inclusion affect me and my workload?"
1. Informational	"I would like more information about inclusive education and what it means."
0. Awareness	"What are you talking about?"

Adapted from *Schools Are for All Kids: Training Module for School Teams,* by J. Servatius, M. Fellows, and D. Kelly, 1990, San Francisco: San Francisco State University, California Research Institute; and *Change in Schools: Facilitating the Process* by G. E. Hall and S. M. Hord, 1987, Albany, NY: SUNY UP.

of concern and is adapted from the work of Hall and Hord (1987) and Servatius, Fellows, and Kelly (1990).

Halvorsen et al. (1997) designed a personnel development activity to assist educators in recognizing their own and their colleagues' stages of concern and so begin to address these real issues with appropriate action. Let's examine a faculty meeting at Monroe High School at which this activity is taking place in the spring prior to the initial phase of inclusive education.

Monroe High School: Initiating the Change Process

Introduction.   Ms. Bryant, the Monroe High School principal, has engaged the faculty in a series of exploratory activities to stimulate discussions about whether and how the school can restructure its educational programs to increase positive outcomes for all of its diverse student population. Faculty members, in conjunction with the larger community of parents, support staff, and students, have crafted a new mission statement for Monroe.

> The Monroe High School Community embraces its responsibility to ensure that all students are challenged to learn to their highest potential, to obtain the knowledge, skills, and citizenship necessary to become productive members of their families, communities, and society. We believe in the following underlying assumptions of this mission: (1) All students can learn; (2) All students are of equal worth and full members of our educational community; (3) Academic and social expectations are legitimate goals of the educational experience; (4) All learners should have access to instruction and curriculum, including necessary modifications, that will enable them to master essential skills and demonstrate competence in required areas of knowledge; and (5) Faculty members recognize diversity in learning strengths and styles and are equipped to provide instruction personalized to the individuals they teach.

The development of the mission has occurred over a series of meetings. The next phase of work will be planning for its implementation. Ms. Bryant and the faculty recognize that they are entering uncharted territory. Although the mission was formulated through a consensus-based process, many varied concerns are brewing regarding its implementation, specifically in terms of the inclusion of students from special education programs in the school. Ms. Bryant worked with the school to determine what they need for the next step. They have requested time and a structure to examine the change process and the supports they will need. A facilitator from the district personnel development office, Mr. Watkins, is here for that purpose.

The Activity.   Mr. Watkins begins by asking participants to think and then to write for three minutes about their concerns regarding inclusive education:

> When you think about your school, including students with disabilities into general classrooms, what are you concerned about? (Do not discuss what you think others are concerned about, but only what concerns you have now.) Please be frank and respond in complete sentences.

Immediately after this "quick-write" opportunity, Mr. Watkins and three volunteer teachers enact two short role plays, wearing signs that label their "stage" of concern in the change process, one of which is portrayed in Figure 8.4.

After each role play in which different stages of concern are represented and responded to, Mr. Watkins asks participants if they recognize their own concerns in that role play. As volunteers respond, he explains the meaning of each label in the model (awareness, informational, personal, management, consequences, collaboration, and refocusing). He points out the variety in participants' concerns and emphasizes that anyone may have any or all of these concerns at a particular time, that people often reflect different levels of concern, which can make for a better change process for all, because we can assist each other with these issues.

Mr. Watkins then moves to the overhead or chart of *stages of concern* and provides some background on the concerns-based adoption model developed by Hall and Hord (1987). He notes that we are all experiencing continual societal changes, and, as educators, we are often at the heart of these changes in terms of economics, diversity of our population, etc. We have the greatest need for flexibility. Inclusive education is just one small area of change, and it is part of our role as educators to assist families and students to deal with these changes in a positive way. For these reasons, it's critical that we spend

FIGURE 8.4   Role Play

1. PLAYERS	PLACE
Principal, elementary school Special education administrator Two general education teachers	Weekly faculty meeting

Principal: (wears label—AWARENESS)   So in summary, our special education administrator is telling us that we will have new students with severe disabilities as well as other mildly disabled students in our grades next year. I for one need some background on where this is coming from and what the purpose is in bringing these kids here.

Administrator: Inclusion isn't new to the district, but I understand that it is new to your school. I would like to discuss the best way to share more information beyond this meeting—perhaps visits to other schools?

Teacher #1:   (wears label—INFORMATIONAL)   That would be great. I just need to know what it looks like. What do the kids think? How do they feel? What do parents feel about it? I have a lot of questions.

Teacher #2:   (wears label—PERSONAL)   Those aren't the only things as far as I'm concerned. I want to know just how this will affect me and all the teachers who receive included kids. How will this increase my workload? I'm sure it will, so how much?

time addressing legitimate concerns in our schools on an on-going basis and that we acquire tools that will assist us in doing so. He points out that often our concerns about inclusion have resulted from our own beliefs, misinformation, or stereotypes about people with disabilities, which are a direct result of the past isolation or segregation of people, much as was the case prior to the racial desegregation of our schools or to equal rights for women in the United States.

To illustrate this point, Mr. Watkins uses the following quotes (on overhead) from selected periods in history to demonstrate the dramatic difference in our values and changes since these times:

> To escape intolerable persecution and contempt, Negroes are glad to be herded together by themselves. (Bullock, 1967)

> All the reflections of women ought to be directed to the study of men...for as regarding works of genius, they are out of the reach of women. (Rousseau, p. 386)

Mr. Watkins notes that he is using these statements to demonstrate changes in our values and that schools have been the first harbingers and "do-ers" in these societal changes. Including students with disabilities, he notes, is a logical step in expanding our celebration of diversity. He acknowledges that this inclusion brings with it its own set of real hurdles. He reminds participants that their concerns, those of their colleagues, or of parents and students are all legitimate. These concerns must be responded to with strategies that speak to the specific concern. He then directs participants to work in table groups to characterize their own concerns in terms of these stages and to brainstorm potential activities, responses, information that would speak to the issue presented. He provides them with a resource handout of strategies (Table 8.3) that may be useful for the twenty-minute activity.

Following the individual group work, reporters from each table debrief the activity. Mr. Watkins works with the large group to prioritize the suggested activities into an action plan.

Personnel Development Supports.   As we can see from the Monroe example, people in changing schools need new information as well as new skills or opportunities to refine existing skills. Professional or personnel development, often described as "inservice training," is an essential ingredient to support schools in the restructuring process. We can't make it happen if we don't know what "it" is or how to do it.

In a recent issue brief on this subject, McGregor et al. (1998) noted that school reform and personnel development must occur in tandem, and development activities must reinforce the new forms of teacher involvement that have been identified in restructured schools. Berends and King (1994) described some of these roles and responsibilities:

- Staff participate in training design, which is based on their local needs.
- Teachers function in differentiated roles, including mentoring, peer supervision, collegial planning, curriculum development, and policy making.

To address these needs, McGregor et al. (1998) suggested that we use our knowledge about adult learning as well as the empirical base on staff development to design training that is

- Based on research, best practices, and needs assessment
- School focused, with emphasis on both individual and organizational development
- Directed by a cohesive school-site plan
- Embedded as much as possible within the job of teaching, through participatory learning such as coaching, study groups, and peer observation

TABLE 8.3   Resource Handout

STRATEGIES FOR ADDRESSING CONCERNS IN FACILITATING CHANGE

A first step in change is to know what concerns the individuals have, especially their most intense concerns. The second step is to respond to those concerns. Unfortunately, there is no absolute set of universal prescriptions, but the following suggestions offer examples of interventions that might be useful.

STAGE 0—AWARENESS CONCERNS

a. Involve all stakeholders in discussions and decisions about inclusive education.

b. Share enough information to arouse interest, but not so much that it overwhelms.

c. Acknowledge that a lack of awareness is expected and reasonable and that no questions about inclusive education are foolish.

d. Encourage unaware persons to talk with colleagues who know about inclusive education.

e. Take steps to minimize gossip and inaccuracies about inclusive programs.

STAGE 1—INFORMATIONAL CONCERNS

a. Provide clear and accurate information about inclusion.

b. Use a variety of ways to share information—verbally, in writing, and through any available media. Communicate with individuals and with small and large groups.

c. Invite persons who have successfully included students in other schools to visit with your school. Visits to those schools could also be arranged.

d. Help teachers see how their current practices are related to the inclusive education effort.

e. Be enthusiastic and enhance the visibility of others who are excited.

STAGE 2—PERSONAL CONCERNS

a. Legitimize the existence and expression of personal concerns. Knowing these concerns are common can be comforting.

b. Use personal notes and conversations to provide encouragement and reinforce personal adequacy.

c. Connect these individuals with others whose personal concerns have diminished and who will be supportive.

d. Show how inclusive education can be implemented systematically. It is important to establish expectations that are attainable, with specific goals and timelines.

STAGE 3—MANAGEMENT CONCERNS

a. Clarify the steps toward and components of an inclusive classroom.

b. Provide answers that address the small specific "how-to" issues that are so often the cause of management concerns.

c. Demonstrate exact and practical solutions to the logistical problems.

d. Help teachers sequence specific activities and set timelines for their accomplishments.

e. Attend to the immediate demands of the inclusive effort, not what will be or could be in the future.

STAGE 4—CONSEQUENCE CONCERNS

a. Provide these individuals with opportunities to visit other settings that are inclusive and to attend conferences on the topic.

b. Don't overlook these individuals. Give them positive feedback and support.

c. Find opportunities for these persons to share their skills with others.

d. Share information about the results of inclusive programs.

STAGE 5—COLLABORATION CONCERNS

a. Provide these individuals with opportunities to develop skills necessary for working collaboratively.

b. Bring together those persons, both within and outside the school, who are interested in collaborating to help inclusive education develop.

(continued)

TABLE 8.3 CONTINUED

STRATEGIES FOR ADDRESSING CONCERNS IN FACILITATING CHANGE

STAGE 5—COLLABORATION CONCERNS

c. Help the collaborators establish reasonable expectations and guidelines.

d. Use the collaborators to provide technical assistance to others.

e. Encourage the collaborators, but don't attempt to force collaboration on those who are not interested.

STAGE 6—REFOCUSING CONCERNS

a. Respect and encourage the interest these persons have in finding a better way.

b. Help these individuals channel their ideas and energies in ways that will be productive rather than counterproductive.

c. Encourage these individuals to act on their concerns for program improvement.

d. Help people access the resources they may need to refine their ideas and put them into practice.

e. Be aware of and willing to accept the fact that some people may wish to significantly modify existing inclusion.

Adapted from *Taking Charge of Change,* by S. M. Hord, W. Rutherford, L. Huling-Austin, and G. Hall, 1987, Alexandria, VA: ASCD and from *Schools Are for All Kids: Training Module for School Teams,* by J. Servatius, M. Fellows, and D. Kelly, 1990, San Francisco: San Francisco State University, California Research Institute.

- Focused on desired *student* outcomes as the reference point for identifying teachers' skill needs
- Planned and facilitated by the school community
- Inclusive of parents and all school staff, from principals to paraprofessionals, office staff, and other support personnel

Personnel Development is one essential support for the change process, and its use implies two additional necessary supports: *time,* and the *financial resources* for time and training as well as for materials and related activities such as mentoring, classroom observation, attendance at relevant conferences, or work on curriculum-design teams. In Chapter 6 we discussed several creative ways that schools find common planning time, such as block scheduling or "banking" minutes toward one short day. In an interesting report in a 1998 *Education Week,* we learned that teachers in both Japan and Germany teach far *less* of the instructional day than do their U.S. counterparts, and their remaining time is given over to collaborative curricular planning, individual planning, and subject area work. The rigor and reputations of these countries' educational systems are maintained in part by recognizing that teaching is a multidimensional job. We require people to work together collaboratively. This cannot occur unless they plan together for significant parts of their contracted time as well as contribute some of their own time as is the case with any effective professional.

Resources for Managing Change.   As we have already said, some financial support for the activities that facilitate change will be essential. Can we change *without* new dollars? Yes, if budgets and resources themselves are restructured to move money or personnel where required, such as in the Whittier High School example or in our examples of Emerson, Vineyard, and Monroe. However, we must be careful not to expect a free ride. Start-up costs always exist in the marketing of a new product; why should education differ?

When we do not provide the necessary financial supports to accomplish change strategies such as those discussed earlier, we further endanger progress. Bridges (1991) described transitions as having a beginning, a neutral zone, and an ending. We tend to focus most of our energy and resources on the beginning of the process and too little on the neutral zone, the time when we are not yet established. The honeymoon is over, and Bridges (1991) compares the neutral zone to a period of "wandering in the desert." We are especially vulnerable at this time; we are anxious, full of self-doubt. If we do not find ways to support people as they face the real problems of implementation, we can expect that there will be a strong tendency to return to what was or for the whole process to be "hijacked" by new alternatives that promise the necessary support *and* positive outcomes.

Think about weight loss programs. Imagine that the new one you have subscribed to requires changing almost all of your current eating habits—when, where, what, and how much you eat. You begin with great enthusiasm and a specific goal of losing twenty pounds in six months. You attend orientation sessions, group meetings, and food preparation classes. You lose half the weight in the first two months, and then your weight loss starts to slow down. There are no meetings going on for the people like yourself. Weigh-ins occur only monthly, with brief staff intervention. You don't want to go back to meetings with people who just started; they don't have the problems you have. Nothing in the information or material you received tells you how long to expect that this slump might last. You think maybe you're alone in this problem. Along comes a friend who tells you about her herbal remedy and all the weight she's lost. You switch over to her plan, delighted to have some peer support. The herbal concoctions promise much.... A year later you have regained most of the initial weight loss.

Recidivism is a risk in all "weighty" changes but is most likely to occur during the neutral period as new problems arise and anticipated support does not materialize. The change process must build in these supports from the outset, so that participants have a place to turn, to problem solve, to try out ideas, and to voice concerns. This support may take a variety of forms, and examples are listed in Table 8.4.

How Will We Know When We Get There?

In their discussion of postmodern schools, Sailor and Skrtic (1995) described such schools as places where meaningful change means a *cultural* change driven by the collective voices of "consumers" (children and families) and the "workers" (teachers and staff) of the school.

TABLE 8.4 Support Strategies for the Neutral Zone

SCHOOL SITE
- Collaborative teaching or planning teams with dedicated, consistent common planning time
- Reflective practice group facilitated by mentor
- Released time to visit other classrooms on site or in other schools and to attend their collaborative meetings
- Site- or grade-level monthly planning meetings to monitor change process
- List servs to facilitate teacher communication within and across schools
- Summer retreat or institutes for teams of school faculty, parents, others from the school community

DISTRICT
- Allotment of special grants or funds to schools engaged in restructuring (through competitive proposal requests)
- Provision of ongoing teacher discussion groups with open access through district teacher center
- Ongoing needs assessment and responsive personnel development
- Provision of funds to school sites to design their own personnel development plans
- On-line e-mail teacher networks with chat room access and recommended electronic resources and links
- Leadership academies and ongoing support connecting principals and other school leaders
- Role-alike sessions for various personnel and parents facilitated by their role peers

Subsystems within and outside the school that have been "…formerly fragmented, isolated, categorical…are brought together and reorganized in a manner that benefits all the children in a school" (p. 424). They argued that this change from *within* the school is actually a re-contextualization: people change the way they view the teaching and learning process and, ultimately, the way they act in these contexts (Sailor & Skrtic, 1995, p. 421).

In postmodern schools, special and general education as well as other categorical programs are unified for students' inclusion and for adult collaboration and sharing of expertise. In addition, the community is linked with the postmodern school to meet local needs. This "service integration" may take a variety of forms, from subsidized after-school care, a family resource center, "one-stop shopping" for social service and health needs, to interaction with local colleges or universities for internships, student teachers, and other program supports (cf. Sailor, Gerry, & Wilson, 1993).

The schools we have described in this volume are on the road to postmodernism. They are each in different places along the road, and they themselves are the only ones who can determine when they are "there" and where they are going next.

SUMMARY

In this chapter we focus on change, and the process, nature, and goals of restructuring for inclusive education. Initial sections emphasize grass-roots strategies for change agents and resources to inform and support. Specific school examples are provided. The next section on restructuring defines the relationship between inclusion and school reform and delineates necessary components of restructuring from district and site perspectives, including leadership, commitment, problem recognition, stakeholder involvement, action planning, personnel development, and resource supports.

CHECKING FOR UNDERSTANDING

Read the scenario that follows. If possible, join with a group of your peers (fellow teachers, parents, university students) to complete the Think Outside the Box activity on the next page.

■ ■ ■ ■ ■ ■ ■ ■

ELEMENTARY SCHOOL SCENARIO

THE SCHOOL AND STUDENTS

Redding Elementary School has an enrollment of 570 K–5 students. The school has had three special education classes for several years, but this year all students with IEPs are returning to their home schools in the district. Redding will now have eleven students who experience moderate to severe disabilities across the six grades, as shown at the bottom of the grid.

There will be one special education inclusion support teacher and three instructional assistants to support students' instruction in general education as called for in their IEPs.

There are twenty K–5 students with mild disabilities who were already attending Redding, which is their home school. These students have learning and/or speech and language disabilities. In the past, they have received primarily pull-out services for up to 50 percent of the day.

There will be a full time special education resource specialist and instructional assistant.

Redding has five classes per grade for K–3 with twenty students in each as a result of class size reduction. There are three classes per grade for fourth and fifth, with thirty-three to thirty-four students per class, with a wide range of economic and cultural family backgrounds.

THE STAFF AND RESOURCES

26   General education classroom teachers

1   Principal

1	Speech and language specialist
1	P.E. teacher
1 each P/T (.50 FTE)	Music, Art, Science consultants hired through PTA and school improvement program funds
5 P/T	Reading assistance program (RAP) volunteer adult tutors
25	Peer tutors, cross-grade tutors, peer conflict managers (fourth–fifth graders)
8	High school or community service tutors, one hr per day each
1	ESL teacher

THINK OUTSIDE THE BOX!

1. Read.
2. Discuss the resources available.
3. Analyze the resources in relationship to the students and classes on the grid.
   - How would you distribute students and resources in the ways that would be most effective for the students? What else do you need?
   - Consider the following key questions and make your plans with the group.
   - The recorder should put your group's major points for each question on the overhead to share later with the group.

KEY QUESTIONS

1. How can the students with disabilities be supported by special education staff in a non- or crosscategorical manner within general education?
2. How can special education teachers divide grade assignments to facilitate cross-categorical support and to assist them in becoming curricular specialists at specific grade levels?
3. What kinds of personnel development (training or technical assistance) for school staff, students, and parents will be needed to introduce the school community to inclusive education, and what kinds of resources will be needed for this?
4. How will the roles of instructional assistants and general and special education teachers look different than they have in the past?

GRID FOR ELEMENTARY SCHOOL SCENARIO

CLASS/ GRADE	K	GRADE 1	GRADE 2	GRADE 3	GRADE 4	GRADE 5
Class 1						
Class 2						
Class 3						
Class 4					(n/a)	(n/a)
Class 5					(n/a)	(n/a)
Students	■ 3 students with moderate–severe disabilities ■ 3 students with mild–moderate disabilities	■ 2 students with moderate–severe disabilities ■ 2 students with mild–moderate disabilities	■ 1 student with moderate–severe disabilities ■ 3 students with mild–moderate disabilities	■ 3 students with moderate–severe disabilities ■ 5 students with mild–moderate disabilities	■ 1 student with moderate–severe disabilities ■ 5 students with mild–moderate disabilities	■ 1 student with moderate–severe disabilities ■ 7 students with mild–moderate disabilities
Staffing	26 general education faculty, 2 special education teachers, 1 speech and language teacher, 4 special education paraprofessionals, 1 principal, 1 ESL teacher, P/T Music, Art, Science, 1 F/T P.E. teacher, peer tutors, and conflict managers					

AFTERWORD

In this volume we have introduced you to best practices for inclusive schools by first defining inclusive education and providing the legal, research, and best-practices bases for the term. We moved quickly into implementation or, as we teachers like to say, the "nuts and bolts." Our work has focused on best practices for *all* students, including students with disabilities. As teachers, you have had the opportunity to explore effective instructional practices at the classroom *and* student level as well as the collaborative peer and adult practices that enable these to flourish. We have followed four students throughout the book to illustrate specific steps, practices, and outcomes. We have emphasized consideration of essential evaluation questions and techniques for examining the impact of your efforts. Finally, we have provided a glimpse of the school change process and strategies to assist pioneers with their efforts to build schools like Vineyard, Emerson, and Monroe.

Building Inclusive Schools: Tools and Strategies for Success is a book for schools—for teachers, parents, and administrators in practice and for the preservice candidates who will populate and generate our inclusive schools of the future.

DISTRICT INCLUSION PLAN

BEST PRACTICE— DISTRICT MODEL	STRATEGIES AND ACTIVITIES TO REACH GOAL	EXPECTED OUTCOMES	EVALUATION— HOW TO MEASURE
1. Inclusive education as an option in every school by 2001	■ Enrollment procedures ■ Increase accessibility of buildings ■ Increased training and ongoing information opportunities for all staff and students ■ Increased information available to families; new vehicles for information and training to them ■ Work two years ahead of time with prospective schools; identify mainstreaming teachers who want to move into inclusion ■ Increased access of Special Education to principals' meetings and ongoing principals' inclusion meetings	■ Any IEP team can access inclusive support at child's home school ■ Students do not have to leave school to obtain special education services ■ Increased school ownership of students and staff involved with special education ■ School-level adaptations on model to fit site	■ Presence of inclusive education noted in all school report cards ■ Inclusive option and related information are available through LEA web site ■ Staff development calendars ■ Staff evaluations of trainings on inclusive education
2. Inclusive transition programs (post-high school—22) are in place	■ Task force plan now for high school students graduating who want inclusive option (students completing IEP but not high school diploma)	■ Range of inclusive options: continuing education, work experience for graduates	■ Transition follow-up data on included students post-high school ■ Individual Transition Plans
3. Inclusive preschool options (3–5) available throughout the city	■ Task force work with preschool program consultant, etc., to assist in defining, designing, and implementation of new and future inclusive options (See #1)	■ Variety of inclusive preschool options available ■ Increasing number of kindergarteners coming from inclusive preschools ■ Increase in number of IEPs requesting inclusion as students enter prekindergarten and kindergarten	■ Numbers of preschool students in inclusive preschools from year to year; IEP face sheets as documentation
4. Inclusive summer programs available	■ Develop secondary work and recreation programs ■ Continue inclusive summer school support across age levels	■ Students have inclusive summer experiences extending their school year; learning and social relationships enhanced	■ Sample of IEPs ■ Surveys of parents and teachers

BEST PRACTICE—DISTRICT MODEL	STRATEGIES AND ACTIVITIES TO REACH GOAL	EXPECTED OUTCOMES	EVALUATION—HOW TO MEASURE
5. Site level groups—planning teams in each school	■ Utilize existing or develop new group for forward and transition planning; have representative from this group be liaison to district task force	■ Cohesive planning and oversight of inclusive education implementation at the school level; staff and families feel supported; increased staff ownership and knowledge	■ School team meeting minutes; school action plans; sample of schools surveyed; inclusion appears in school-site report card each year
6. Transportation matches school calendar, start and end times	■ Task force and special education administrative work with transportation department; hold working meeting on this	■ Reduced transportation costs when using general education buses ■ Students able to participate in *full* school day	■ Bus schedules ■ IEPs (transportation category)
7. Student level planning teams are functioning for each pupil	■ Work toward obtaining elementary prep time ■ Set annual calendar of meetings ■ Use portion of common planning time at secondary level ■ Obtain comp time for para-professionals attending outside hours ■ Utilize portion of grade level or subject matter and conference days	■ Student's participation, support, and expectations are clearly laid out and understood by all ■ Adaptations are timely ■ Grading decisions are clarified ■ Roles of each staff person clarified ■ Access to advance planning information for curriculum adaptations to be in place on schedule	■ Sample of IEP objectives to survey achievement ■ Student participation plans, report cards ■ Team minutes ■ Lesson plans ■ Student IEP matrices
8. Information and training are available to all ■ Prior to inclusion (grade to grade, school to school) ■ For transitions ■ Ongoing	■ See matrix of training needs, content, resources developed by task force ■ Add to matrix: teacher, mentor, parent mentors, paramentor systems, resource teams development ■ New handbook ■ Future web pages ■ Annual calendar of staff development offerings, e.g., full day for future schools in fall; series after school during year	■ Increased awareness, knowledge base of staff, students ■ Increased ownership by schools ■ Ongoing support ■ More in-depth planning process available ■ Staffs and parents feel better prepared; sites can begin own planning early	■ Staff surveys ■ Mentorship evaluations ■ Training evaluations ■ Aggregate training evaluation data
9. Infusion of content within district inservice (e.g., Mathlands) on new curricula	■ District-sponsored summer workgroups (general and special education to put together adaptation information and strategies across content areas and grade levels ■ Coordination with staff development unit	■ District curricular inservices are inclusive of relevant information and new strategies, adaptations ■ Curricula more relevant to special needs of individual students	■ Inservice evaluation data ■ Inservice materials and activities ■ Sample of teacher lesson plans in those areas ■ Individual student participation plans
10. Transition planning across schools and grades	■ Design, adopt, and implement specific timelines and activities for advance planning (visits, observations, team meetings., etc.) ■ Investigate vehicles for released time for transition IEPs, visits, etc. ■ Student circles participate in planning	■ Smoother transitions ■ Information available to teachers in advance ■ Long-range calendar of activities and timelines for each year ■ Higher satisfaction of students, staff, and families	■ Transition plans in IEPs ■ Survey samples in each category annually

(continued)

CONTINUED

BEST PRACTICE—DISTRICT MODEL	STRATEGIES AND ACTIVITIES TO REACH GOAL	EXPECTED OUTCOMES	EVALUATION—HOW TO MEASURE
11. Student support networks	■ Individualized systems are set up by student planning teams, e.g., ■ Circles, MAPS, tutors, buddies, "pit crew"	■ Nondisabled students participate with included students in curricular planning, adaptation design, ways to support each other's learning ■ Friendship development	*Samples of:* ■ Student schedules ■ Surveys of students ■ IEPs ■ Student meeting minutes
12. Staff members share responsibility for all students	■ Special education staff (teachers, paraprofessionals, support-related services) collaborate with general education and provide classroom support to all students in conjunction with support to included student ■ Co-teaching units, lessons, subjects ■ Cross-categorical service delivery ■ General education teachers support and instruct students with special needs as part of class	■ Collaborative classrooms with adults working together ■ Increased ownership for all students ■ Greater parity between special education and general education ■ More support to at-risk students ■ Increased team effectiveness	■ Lesson plans, schedules ■ Surveys to teachers ■ Compare referral rates to student study team and special education from inclusive classrooms with other classes ■ Team self-survey ■ IEP quality

DISTRICT- AND SITE-LEVEL NEEDS ASSESSMENT TOOLS

CALIFORNIA CONFEDERATION ON INCLUSIVE EDUCATION
INCLUSIVE EDUCATION NEEDS ASSESSMENT: DISTRICT LEVEL

Completed by: _____ Date: _____

District/LEA: _____

Address: _____ Phone: _____

FAX: _____

Administrator: _____ Phone: _____

Demographical/categorical information for the district:

❏ Rural   Number of students who qualify for: Chapter 1 _____

❏ Urban   LEP _____

❏ Suburban   Bilingual _____

                                                     Free or reduced lunch _____

Population demographics	Number	Percent
African American		
Native American or Alaskan Native		
Asian American or Pacific Islander		
Hispanic		
White		

Grade levels included in district: _____

Total number of students enrolled in district: _____

Number of students with IEPs in district: _____

Number of students receiving RSP services: _____   SDC services: _____

DIS services: (duplicated) _____   (unduplicated) _____

Number of students served in other districts: _____   Included: _____

In SDC: _____   RSP services: _____   Segregated school: _____

Adapted from *Implementation Site Criteria for Inclusive Programs,* by A. T. Halvorsen and T. Neary, 1994; formatting from *Inclusion Practices Survey,* 1995, Boston: University of Massachusetts, Graduate College of Education, Institute for Community Inclusion (UAP).

OVERVIEW

The purpose of this needs assessment is to assist school districts and school sites in assessing the current status of inclusive education in order to develop a unified educational system that offers the option of inclusion for each student, and in particular, for students with the most challenging disabilities. The assessment is designed to identify areas of strength in current inclusive educational practices and also to identify areas where further development is necessary to ensure that inclusive education has the best opportunity for success.

The information gathered in this process will enable the agency to generate goals and objectives for a strategic plan for inclusive education. It is important to note that the use of this survey is for internal program development purposes only.

The plan developed by the agency builds on strengths and addresses the areas of need identified through this process. Specific actions delineated should include responsible individuals and timelines for ensuring goals and objectives are met.

The *district-level* inclusive education needs assessment is divided into the following areas

1. Policy
2. Resources
3. Accessibility
4. Personnel
5. Preparation
6. Students
7. Parents
8. Transportation

INSTRUCTIONS

1. Complete the general information sheet.
2. Place an "X" in the box that best describes the implementation of a particular practice in your school or district.
3. Place an "X" in the box that best describes the need for training and technical assistance for that particular practice in your school or district.

   It is intended that inclusive education support teams involved in completing this needs assessment will reach consensus on each item. Only when this is not possible after gathering additional information to reach agreement, the team will vote, with the majority vote being acceptable to the team.

4. Note actions necessary to move forward at the end of each area.

GENERAL INFORMATION

---

1. School District: _____   **2.** Date: _____

3. Please indicate your position or role:

❏ Parent or guardian

❏ General educator

❏ Special or inclusion educator

❏ Vocational educator

❏ Instructional support staff (paraprofessional, job coach)

❏ Related services staff

❏ Central or administrative staff

❏ Student

❏ Other: _____

4. Please indicate the type of school or program you work in or, if you are a parent, the type of program your child attends: (check all that apply)

❏ Early intervention program

❏ Preschool program

❏ Elementary program

❏ Middle school or junior high school

❏ High school

❏ Vocational program

❏ Other (please specify)

CURRENT PLACEMENTS

Total LEA enrollment: _____   Grades served: _____

COMMENTS

1. How many students receive special education services in the district?		
2. How many students are served in special centers?		
3. How many students are served in special day classes (SDC) in regular school sites?		
4. How many schools are involved in inclusive education for students with severe disabilities?		
5. How many students are served in inclusive education? (Full membership in general education classroom)		
a. How many of these students are served in the school of parent choice?		
b. How many of these students are served in a "magnet inclusive school"?		

(continued)

CONTINUED

    c. How many of these students are served in another school?

6. How many students are served outside the district?

7. The following numbers of students are served in:

    a. County programs

    b. SELPA programs

    c. Nonpublic schools (NPS)

    d. Other districts outside the SELPA

(Attach relevant placement policies)

Please rate the implementation of the following practices:

Please rate each of the following in relation to the need for assistance:

DISTRICT LEVEL

excellent	satisfactory	unsatisfactory	not at all	POLICY / Inclusion indicator	extensive	moderate	somewhat	not at all
❏	❏	❏	❏	**1.** There is a current board of education policy on inclusion.	❏	❏	❏	❏
❏	❏	❏	❏	**2.** There is an existing long-range LEA plan for inclusion.	❏	❏	❏	❏
❏	❏	❏	❏	**3.** There is an *inclusion task force* and *LRE Committee* in the LEA that is cross-constituency and assists in planning for inclusive education.	❏	❏	❏	❏
❏	❏	❏	❏	**4.** Policies exist that have been negotiated between the teachers' association and the school district in regard to the implementation of inclusion.	❏	❏	❏	❏
❏	❏	❏	❏	**5.** The LEA has a working definition of inclusive education.	❏	❏	❏	❏
❏	❏	❏	❏	**6.** This definition of inclusive education has been disseminated to parents and staff throughout the LEA.	❏	❏	❏	❏
				RESOURCES / *Inclusion indicator*				
❏	❏	❏	❏	**7.** Procedures guides or handbooks on inclusive education have been developed and disseminated.	❏	❏	❏	❏
❏	❏	❏	❏	**8.** Training opportunities and resources are available for the planned transition to inclusive education for:	❏	❏	❏	❏
❏	❏	❏	❏	**a.** Teaching staff	❏	❏	❏	❏
❏	❏	❏	❏	**b.** Administrators	❏	❏	❏	❏
❏	❏	❏	❏	**c.** Support personnel	❏	❏	❏	❏
❏	❏	❏	❏	**d.** Parents	❏	❏	❏	❏
❏	❏	❏	❏	**9.** Resources exist for site modifications in schools and in outside areas of the campus.	❏	❏	❏	❏
❏	❏	❏	❏	**10.** Resources exist for materials and equipment for curricular participation including communication and mobility.	❏	❏	❏	❏

excellent	satisfactory	unsatisfactory	not at all	**RESOURCES** *Inclusion indicator*	extensive	moderate	somewhat	not at all
❏	❏	❏	❏	11. Resources exist for released time for teachers to visit prospective classrooms and to meet with other teachers, related service providers, and parents.	❏	❏	❏	❏
				ACCESSIBILITY *Inclusion indicator*				
❏	❏	❏	❏	12. Targeted or potential school sites in the LEA are accessible.	❏	❏	❏	❏
❏	❏	❏	❏	13. All internal areas at each site are accessible.	❏	❏	❏	❏
❏	❏	❏	❏	14. Plans exist for the site modifications if there are too few or no accessible schools available.	❏	❏	❏	❏
❏	❏	❏	❏	15. There is a plan to keep students within natural proportions in schools.	❏	❏	❏	❏
				PERSONNEL *Inclusion indicator*				
❏	❏	❏	❏	16. Special education teachers have been involved in planning for inclusive education.	❏	❏	❏	❏
❏	❏	❏	❏	17. Plans have been developed for any necessary transfers of staff to support inclusive models.	❏	❏	❏	❏
❏	❏	❏	❏	18. Specific criteria for recruiting and selecting general and special education teachers for teaching in inclusive schools have been developed.	❏	❏	❏	❏
❏	❏	❏	❏	19. Principals are responsible for supervision of inclusive support personnel.	❏	❏	❏	❏
❏	❏	❏	❏	20. There is a plan for technical assistance support for special education staff.	❏	❏	❏	❏
❏	❏	❏	❏	21. There is a plan for technical assistance support for general educators in inclusive schools.	❏	❏	❏	❏
❏	❏	❏	❏	22. Plans are in place for special education support for students in inclusive settings.	❏	❏	❏	❏
❏	❏	❏	❏	23. Student caseloads for inclusion support teachers have been defined as well as the number of schools each teacher will serve.	❏	❏	❏	❏
❏	❏	❏	❏	24. There is a plan for related service delivery on inclusive sites.	❏	❏	❏	❏
❏	❏	❏	❏	25. Related service personnel have been involved in planning for inclusive educational services.	❏	❏	❏	❏
❏	❏	❏	❏	26. Related services will be delivered to students in inclusive classrooms and community sites.	❏	❏	❏	❏
❏	❏	❏	❏	27. Adequate paraprofessional support is provided for inclusive programs.	❏	❏	❏	❏

(continued)

CONTINUED

excellent	satisfactory	unsatisfactory	not at all	**PREPARATION** *Inclusion indicator*	extensive	moderate	somewhat	not at all
❑	❑	❑	❑	**28.** A district training plan has been developed for staff, students, and parents in the district.	❑	❑	❑	❑
❑	❑	❑	❑	**29.** The LEA has defined whether the training is voluntary for all.	❑	❑	❑	❑
❑	❑	❑	❑	**30.** There will be released time available for teachers for ˙ training.	❑	❑	❑	❑
❑	❑	❑	❑	**31.** There will be released time available for paraprofessionals for training.	❑	❑	❑	❑
❑	❑	❑	❑	**32.** Timelines have been developed for training.	❑	❑	❑	❑
❑	❑	❑	❑	**33.** Teachers have had opportunities to visit model inclusive programs in the LEA or elsewhere.	❑	❑	❑	❑
❑	❑	❑	❑	**34.** Released time will be available for collaborative planning.	❑	❑	❑	❑
				STUDENTS *Inclusion indicator*				
❑	❑	❑	❑	**35.** Initial students to be included have been identified.	❑	❑	❑	❑
❑	❑	❑	❑	**36.** IEPs have been held to identify inclusive educational placements.	❑	❑	❑	❑
❑	❑	❑	❑	**37.** Students are slated to attend home schools or schools of parent choice.	❑	❑	❑	❑
❑	❑	❑	❑	**38.** All students in the LEA will have the opportunity for inclusive placement.	❑	❑	❑	❑
❑	❑	❑	❑	**39.** The IEP cover page and forms are altered to delineate membership in general education classes if necessary.	❑	❑	❑	❑
				PARENTS *Inclusion indicator*				
❑	❑	❑	❑	**40.** All parents have been informed about the district's plans for inclusive education.	❑	❑	❑	❑
❑	❑	❑	❑	**41.** Parent concerns have been addressed in the district's plan for inclusive education.	❑	❑	❑	❑
❑	❑	❑	❑	**42.** Parents are participating in planning for inclusive education.	❑	❑	❑	❑
❑	❑	❑	❑	**43.** The Community Advisory Council for special education is involved in planning for inclusive education.	❑	❑	❑	❑
❑	❑	❑	❑	**44.** The PTA is involved in planning for inclusive education.	❑	❑	❑	❑
❑	❑	❑	❑	**45.** Parents have been provided with opportunities to visit model inclusive programs in the LEA or outside it.	❑	❑	❑	❑
❑	❑	❑	❑	**46.** Parents and students will be included in teacher inservices regarding inclusion.	❑	❑	❑	❑
❑	❑	❑	❑	**47.** Parents and students will be involved in the school-site team at inclusive sites.	❑	❑	❑	❑

excellent	satisfactory	unsatisfactory	not at all	TRANSPORTATION *Inclusion indicator*	extensive	moderate	somewhat	not at all
❑	❑	❑	❑	48. Students with special needs are transported with students without disabilities.	❑	❑	❑	❑
❑	❑	❑	❑	49. Transportation representatives have been involved in inclusive education planning.	❑	❑	❑	❑
❑	❑	❑	❑	50. Transportation pick-ups and drop-offs match the school hours for students in general education at schools involved.	❑	❑	❑	❑
❑	❑	❑	❑	51. The public transportation system is accessible.	❑	❑	❑	❑

Adapted from *Integration/Inclusion Needs Assessment,* by A. T. Halvorsen, T. Neary, L. Smithey, and S. Gilbert, 1992, Hayward, CA: California State University, PEERS Project.

SITE-LEVEL NEEDS ASSESSMENT

The *site-level* inclusive education needs assessment is divided into the following areas:

1. Environment
2. School climate
3. Staff integration and collaboration
4. Student integration

INSTRUCTIONS

1. Complete the general information sheet.
2. Place an "X" in the box that best describes the implementation of a particular practice in your school or district.
3. Place an "X" in the box that best describes the need for training and technical assistance for that particular practice in your school or district.

It is intended that inclusive education support teams involved in completing this needs assessment will reach consensus on each item. Only when this is not possible after gathering additional information to reach agreement, the team will vote, with the majority vote being acceptable to the team.

4. Note actions necessary to move forward at the end of each area.

GENERAL INFORMATION

1. School Site: _____   2. Date: _____

3. Please indicate your position or role:

   ❑ Parent or guardian

   ❑ General educator

   ❑ Special or inclusion educator

(continued)

CONTINUED

❏ Vocational educator

❏ Instructional support staff (paraprofessional, job coach)

❏ Related services staff

❏ Central or administrative staff

❏ Student

❏ Other: _____

4. Please indicate the type of school or program you work in or, if you are a parent, the type of program your child attends: (check all that apply)

❏ Early intervention program

❏ Preschool program

❏ Elementary program

❏ Middle school/junior high school

❏ High school

❏ Vocational program

❏ Other (please specify)

Format adapted from *Inclusion Practices Survey,* 1995, Boston: University of Massachusetts, Graduate College of Education, Institute for Community Inclusion (UAP).

Please rate the implementation of the following practices:				SITE LEVEL	Please rate each of the following in relation to the need for assistance:			
excellent	*satisfactory*	*unsatisfactory*	*not at all*	**ENVIRONMENT** *Inclusion indicator*	*extensive*	*moderate*	*somewhat*	*not at all*
❏	❏	❏	❏	1. Students are included in their age-appropriate general education classrooms or classes.	❏	❏	❏	❏
❏	❏	❏	❏	2. The school is the one these students would attend if they were not disabled.	❏	❏	❏	❏
❏	❏	❏	❏	3. Preschool through twelfth grade inclusive programs have been established for students with disabilities, including students with severe disabilities.	❏	❏	❏	❏
❏	❏	❏	❏	4. Students with disabilities have the same calendar and hours as their regular education peers.	❏	❏	❏	❏
❏	❏	❏	❏	5. The number of students with disabilities are within natural proportion guidelines (within 10 percent of student body).	❏	❏	❏	❏

excellent	satisfactory	unsatisfactory	not at all	**ENVIRONMENT** *Inclusion indicator*	extensive	moderate	somewhat	not at all
❑	❑	❑	❑	6. The school is physically accessible to all students.	❑	❑	❑	❑
❑	❑	❑	❑	7. Students travel to and from school with their nondisabled peers.	❑	❑	❑	❑
				SCHOOL CLIMATE *Inclusion indicator*				
❑	❑	❑	❑	8. The principal is ultimately responsible for the program, which includes supervision and evaluation of program staff.	❑	❑	❑	❑
❑	❑	❑	❑	9. There is a defined plan or process for supporting staff in implementation (e.g., time for team planning meetings).	❑	❑	❑	❑
❑	❑	❑	❑	10. The general school community is accepting of students with disabilities.	❑	❑	❑	❑
❑	❑	❑	❑	11. The school mission or vision statement emphasizes a conviction that every child can learn and the program is accountable for all students.	❑	❑	❑	❑
❑	❑	❑	❑	12. The school mission statement emphasizes responsiveness to families and support to meet family needs.	❑	❑	❑	❑
❑	❑	❑	❑	13. The school community is welcoming to families of students with special needs.	❑	❑	❑	❑
❑	❑	❑	❑	14. The school mission statement emphasizes the continued professional growth and development of all.	❑	❑	❑	❑
❑	❑	❑	❑	15. The principal applies the same standards and expectations to special education staff and programs as to general education staff.	❑	❑	❑	❑
❑	❑	❑	❑	16. The principal observes special education programs and staff.	❑	❑	❑	❑
❑	❑	❑	❑	17. General and special education administrative staff work collaboratively to address school-site level issues and planning.	❑	❑	❑	❑
❑	❑	❑	❑	18. Special education programs and the inclusion of students with disabilities are a part of reform and restructuring efforts at the school site.	❑	❑	❑	❑
❑	❑	❑	❑	19. Inservice programs are inclusive of special education staff.	❑	❑	❑	❑
❑	❑	❑	❑	20. Parent participation programs and activities are directed toward parents of students with and without disabilities.	❑	❑	❑	❑
❑	❑	❑	❑	21. Parents and students are offered inclusive educational opportunities as an option at this school.	❑	❑	❑	❑
				STAFF INTEGRATION AND COLLABORATION *Inclusion indicator*				
❑	❑	❑	❑	22. *Special and general educators:*...meet at least once a month for collaborative, student-level planning for students who are included.	❑	❑	❑	❑

(continued)

CONTINUED

excellent	satisfactory	unsatisfactory	not at all	STAFF INTEGRATION AND COLLABORATION *Inclusion indicator*	extensive	moderate	somewhat	not at all
❑	❑	❑	❑	**23.** *Special and general educators:* …collaborate to make material and environmental adaptations for students with disabilities to access the core curriculum within general education classes and facilitate participation throughout the school.	❑	❑	❑	❑
❑	❑	❑	❑	**24.** …collaborate to develop systematic transition plans for students who are moving within schools or to new schools.	❑	❑	❑	❑
❑	❑	❑	❑	**25.** …work to provide safe, orderly, and positive learning environments for all students.	❑	❑	❑	❑
❑	❑	❑	❑	**26.** …establish high expectations for all students.	❑	❑	❑	❑
❑	❑	❑	❑	**27.** …consistently model positive attitudes toward and appropriate interactions with all students.	❑	❑	❑	❑
❑	❑	❑	❑	**28.** …use age-appropriate terminology, tone of voice, praise and reinforcement with all students.	❑	❑	❑	❑
❑	❑	❑	❑	**29.** …employ age-appropriate materials in instruction.	❑	❑	❑	❑
❑	❑	❑	❑	**30.** …individualize activities for students, design, and utilize systematic instructional strategies and monitor progress systematically.	❑	❑	❑	❑
❑	❑	❑	❑	**31.** …encourage and support friendship development for all students and develop systems to promote natural peer supports.	❑	❑	❑	❑
❑	❑	❑	❑	**32.** *Special educators:* …attend faculty meetings and parent conferences with general education staff.	❑	❑	❑	❑
❑	❑	❑	❑	**33.** …participate in regular supervisory duties (e.g., lunch, bus, yard duty).	❑	❑	❑	❑
❑	❑	❑	❑	**34.** …participate in extracurricular responsibilities (e.g., chaperone dances, work with students clubs, serve on school committees).	❑	❑	❑	❑
❑	❑	❑	❑	**35.** …follow school protocol: keep principal or appropriate administrator (e.g., head teacher, department head) informed on an ongoing basis.	❑	❑	❑	❑
❑	❑	❑	❑	**36.** …demonstrate positive public relations skills with general education staff.	❑	❑	❑	❑
❑	❑	❑	❑	**37.** …take lunch breaks and prep periods in the same areas as general education staff at least once per week.	❑	❑	❑	❑
❑	❑	❑	❑	**38.** …are adequately prepared to support students with disabilities in inclusive educational settings.	❑	❑	❑	❑
❑	❑	❑	❑	**39.** …have a caseload and job description that allows them to adequately support students in inclusive settings.	❑	❑	❑	❑
❑	❑	❑	❑	**40.** *General educators:* …participate as IEP team members for included students.	❑	❑	❑	❑

excellent	satisfactory	unsatisfactory	not at all		extensive	moderate	somewhat	not at all
				STAFF INTEGRATION AND COLLABORATION *Inclusion indicator*				
❑	❑	❑	❑	41. *General educators:* …utilize innovative instructional strategies, such as cooperative learning, active learning strategies, and multiple intelligence strategies.	❑	❑	❑	❑
❑	❑	❑	❑	42. …form instructional groups that allow students to demonstrate common interests and a range of skills.	❑	❑	❑	❑
❑	❑	❑	❑	43. …are adequately prepared and supported to effectively teach students with disabilities in their classes.	❑	❑	❑	❑
				STUDENT INTEGRATION *Inclusion indicator*				
❑	❑	❑	❑	44. *Students' IEPs and instructional programs:* …include behavioral support strategies, if necessary, that are positive and utilize natural consequences and corrections.	❑	❑	❑	❑
❑	❑	❑	❑	45. …reflect interaction with nondisabled peers at students' chronological age and grade levels and across all areas of the curriculum.	❑	❑	❑	❑
❑	❑	❑	❑	46. …demonstrate collaboration with related service personnel in the design and delivery of services.	❑	❑	❑	❑
❑	❑	❑	❑	47. …reflect the use of authentic assessment strategies and techniques.	❑	❑	❑	❑
❑	❑	❑	❑	48. …are based upon individual student needs (e.g., work study, community-based instruction, personal care skills, mobility).	❑	❑	❑	❑
❑	❑	❑	❑	49. …include necessary support services and equipment, including training and support for assistive technology.	❑	❑	❑	❑
❑	❑	❑	❑	50. *General school activities offer students with disabilities:* …access to all school environments for instruction and all other functions.	❑	❑	❑	❑
❑	❑	❑	❑	51. … participation in the same school-related activities as their age and grade peers (e.g., eighth grade dance, sixth grade environmental camp, seniors graduation).	❑	❑	❑	❑
❑	❑	❑	❑	52. …strategies to facilitate interaction and friendships through circles, MAPS, networks, tutoring, etc.	❑	❑	❑	❑
❑	❑	❑	❑	53. *Ongoing provision of information offers:* …general education students positive information about people with disabilities.	❑	❑	❑	❑
❑	❑	❑	❑	54. …students without disabilities information about other languages and communication system needs (e.g., ASL, communication boards).	❑	❑	❑	❑

Adapted from *Implementation Site Criteria for Inclusive Programs,* by A. T. Halvorsen and T. Neary, 1994, Hayward, CA: California State University, Department of Educational Psychology, PEERS Outreach Project.

FIRST STEPS TOWARD INCLUSIVE SCHOOLS:
FLOW CHARTS

District Administration

↓

Establish District Stakeholders Task Force

↓

Conduct District-Level Needs Assessment

↓

Action Plan Development

Initial Steps
- Initial school sites identified and orientation sessions held*
- Professional and parent development training needs identified and plans defined
- Resources and staff identified to support site needs
- Policy and procedures reviewed for any necessary revisions
- Short- and long-range plans submitted for district approval

↓

Next Steps
- District-wide parental and IEP team access to information on inclusion
- Short- and long-range plans initiated
- School sites represented on district task force and linked with each other
- Personnel development for school sites, parents and parent groups, specific staff role groups
- Stakeholder workgroups established in areas, i.e., curriculum, personnel development, evaluation, handbook on inclusion
- Evaluation plans designed and initiated

↓

Continuing Activities
- Policy and procedural changes approved and implemented in, e.g., LRE policy, enrollment and placement, IEP forms, related services delivery
- Additional schools provide inclusive option each year
- Inclusive education unified with other educational reforms in the LEA
- Ongoing data review and feedback used for program improvement and changes in plans

*Go to site-level flow chart for further detail

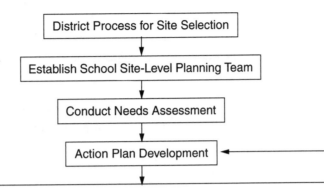

```
District Process for Site Selection
            │
            ▼
Establish School Site-Level Planning Team
            │
            ▼
   Conduct Needs Assessment
            │
            ▼
   Action Plan Development  ◀──────────┐
            │                          │
            ▼                          │
```

Initial Steps

- Student assignment to classes
- Special education staff assigned
- General orientation for school community
- Grade level and subject matter meetings
- Ability awareness for student body
- Partner and mentor school(s) identified
- Professional and parent development and training needs identified and plans made
- Students are members of their age-appropriate general education class(es)

Next Steps

- Professional and parent development and training occur:
  - PTA-SSC participation
  - Mentor school and district assistance
- Team planning meetings structure established for proactive vehicle to address roles and responsibilities, scheduling, support approaches, curricular and instructional needs
- Students' IEPs addressed in general education curricular context with support
- Collaborative teaching and support relationships initiated among general and special educators
- Evaluation process defined and data collection initiated

Continuing Activities

- School-site council and SST's roles defined
- School links with other inclusive sites
- School represented on LEA-level task force
- Ongoing support from partner and mentor schools
- Inclusion unified with other school reforms
- Service delivery and support model structured to meet site needs
- Peer support networks
- Parent and community participation in school
- Evaluation data reviewed by site teams and utilized for program improvement

CURRICULAR DEVELOPMENT
AND ADAPTATION WORKSHEETS

FAMILY INTERVIEW

Interview date _____

Student _____

Birthdate _____

Address _____

_____

Phone (Home) _____   Phone (Work) _____

Directions to place of interview _____

_____

Parent or care provider's name _____

Other individuals to contact:

   Name _____

   Phone _____

   Relation _____

   Permission granted _____

   Best time and day for contact _____

   Phone _____

   Best time and day(s) available for planning meetings _____

Local environments: _____

_____

Medical considerations: _____

_____

Equipment considerations: _____

_____

Additional service providers (Regional Center, CCS, etc.): _____

_____

Adapted from *Teaching That Works: The Individualized Critical Skills Model,* by K. T. Holowach, 1989, Sacramento, CA: Resources in Special Education.

WEEKDAY SCHEDULE

Student _____

List information from the time the student gets up and goes to school until the time he or she arrives home from school and goes to bed.

Morning Routine

STUDENT PARTICIPATION	AREA TO TARGET	FAMILY	STUDENT

Adapted from *Teaching That Works: The Individualized Critical Skills Model,* by K. T. Holowach, 1989, Sacramento, CA: Resources in Special Education.

CONTINUED

Afterschool Routine

STUDENT PARTICIPATION	AREA TO TARGET	FAMILY	STUDENT

Adapted from *Teaching That Works: The Individualized Critical Skills Model,* by K. T. Holowach, 1989, Sacramento, CA: Resources in Special Education.

CONTINUED

Evening Routine

STUDENT PARTICIPATION	AREA TO TARGET	FAMILY	STUDENT

Weekend Routine

STUDENT PARTICIPATION	AREA TO TARGET	FAMILY	STUDENT

Adapted from *Teaching That Works: The Individualized Critical Skills Model,* by K. T. Holowach, 1989, Sacramento, CA: Resources in Special Education.

BEHAVIORAL AND BASIC SKILLS INFORMATION

Student _____

ACTIVITIES STUDENT LIKES TO DO/DOES NOT LIKE TO DO

HOW DOES S/HE LET YOU KNOW? *(IF PARENT IS PROVIDING INFORMATION)*

INTERACTION STUDENT ENJOYS/DOES NOT ENJOY

HOW DOES S/HE LET YOU KNOW?

TELL ME ABOUT FRIENDSHIPS/RELATIONSHIPS. WHAT ARE SOME OF THE THINGS YOUR CHILD DOES WITH FRIENDS?

WHAT ARE YOUR DREAMS FOR YOUR SON/ DAUGHTER?

IS THERE ANY ADDITIONAL INFORMATION ABOUT YOUR SON/DAUGHTER THAT WE HAVEN'T TALKED ABOUT REGARDING:

Communication (receptive/expressive):

Mobility:

Toileting:

Foods/drinks s/he likes or dislikes:

ARE THERE ANY BEHAVIORS OF CONCERN?

(continued)

Adapted from *Teaching That Works: The Individualized Critical Skills Model,* by K. T. Holowach, 1989, Sacramento, CA: Resources in Special Education.

CONTINUED

BEHAVIORAL AND BASIC SKILLS INFORMATION

HOW DO YOU DEAL WITH PROBLEM BEHAVIORS?

DESCRIBE THE BEST WAY FOR YOUR CHILD TO LEARN A NEW SKILL.

DESCRIBE YOUR CHILD'S OPPORTUNITIES FOR DECISION/CHOICE-MAKING.

LIST SOME OF YOUR CHILD'S STRENGTHS.

HOW DOES YOUR CHILD PROBLEM SOLVE? MAKE DECISIONS?

MEDICAL

Medications used _____

When _____

Physician _____

Allergies _____

Side effects of medication _____

Impact on learning _____

Other _____

What things that we haven't talked about yet are important to you or other family members?

Adapted from *Teaching That Works: The Individualized Critical Skills Model,* by K. T. Holowach, 1989, Sacramento, CA: Resources in Special Education.

CONTINUED

	STUDENT	PARENT
How do you feel about the school program? Types of support you would like? What are your preferences for: Extracurricular activities? Classes/subjects Activities Clubs Jobs		
	PARENT	
How would you like to be involved in the school? What is the best way for us to communicate? What are some of the benefits you see as a result of the school program?		

Adapted from *Teaching That Works: The Individualized Critical Skills Model,* by K. T. Holowach, 1989, Sacramento, CA: Resources in Special Education.

FIGURE 3.2 CONTINUED

FAMILY PREFERENCE FOR ACTIVITIES AND ENVIRONMENTS

Student _____   Date _____

1. List the preferred activities (not basic skills) and environments for one, two, or three years from now in each of the following areas.
   Interviewer: Use your information from community inventory file and student's immediate neighborhood inventory to assist parents and care providers.

2. After completing the list, note whether it is a student or family preference for each activity.

DOMESTIC	S F PREF.	RECREATION/LEISURE	S F PREF.	SCHOOL	S F PREF.	COMMUNITY	S F PREF.	VOCATIONAL	S F PREF.

Adapted from *Teaching That Works: The Individualized Critical Skills Model*, by K. T. Holowach, 1989, Sacramento, CA: Resources in Special Education.

INITIAL SUMMARY OF BASIC SKILLS AND CRITICAL ACTIVITIES

Student _____   Date _____

	PRIORITY 1, 2, 3, 4	HIGH-PREFERENCE ACTIVITIES	BASIC SKILLS									
DOMESTIC												
REC./LEISURE												
SCHOOL												
COMMUNITY												
VOCATIONAL												

Adapted from *Teaching That Works: The Individualized Critical Skills Model*, by K. T. Holowach, 1989, Sacramento, CA: Resources in Special Education.

TEAM MEETING FOR: _____

Student: _____

Date/time: _____

Location: _____

If you are unable to attend, please contact: _____

Team members:

_____

_____

_____

_____

Communication backup:

_____

_____

_____

Agenda for this meeting: Time limit:

 1.

 2.

 3.

 4.

Agenda for the next meeting: Next meeting date/time: _____

 1.

 2.

 3.

 4.

Roles:

For this meeting   For next meeting

Facilitator _____

Recorder _____

Timekeeper _____

CONTINUED

MEETING NOTES	TO DO:	PERSON(S) RESPONSIBLE	DATE TO BE COMPLETED

Student Participation and Skills Matrix

Student _____

Grade/Teacher _____

School _____

Date _____

SCHOOL SUBJECTS AND ACTIVITIES

IEP GOALS					

California Confederation on Inclusive Education, 1996.

CLASSROOM ACTIVITY ANALYSIS WORKSHEET

❏ As Is   ❏ Physical Assistance   ❏ Adapt Materials   ❏ Multilevel   ❏ Curriculum Overlap

Name _____   Date _____

Activity _____

CLASSROOM ACTIVITY STEPS	STUDENT PERFORMANCE	SPECIFIC ADAPTATIONS	SKILLS IN NEED OF INSTRUCTION

Comments/Recommendations:

ROUTINE CHART

SUBJECT/TIME

Student _____   School _____

Grade/Teacher _____   Date _____

CLASS ROUTINE	STUDENT'S ACTIVITIES/ ROUTINE	SUPPORT	IEP GOALS

California Confederation on Inclusive Education, 1996.

ADAPTING LESSONS

STUDENT: _____   SUBJECT AREA: _____

LESSON: _____

EXPECTED LEARNER OUTCOMES: PRODUCTS/DEMONSTRATIONS
(Students will be able to…)   OF COMPETENCE:

1. _____   1. _____

_____   _____

2. _____   2. _____

_____   _____

3. _____   3. _____

_____   _____

4. _____   4. _____

_____   _____

5. _____   5. _____

_____

ACCOMMODATIONS

INPUT MODIFICATIONS	TIME ALLOWED	SUPPORT STRATEGIES

DIFFICULTY/AMOUNT	ALTERNATIVE WAYS TO REPRESENT KNOWLEDGE

TEST ADAPTATIONS	

Adapted from *Best Practices Workshop,* by J. Bauwens, 1998, Santa Rosa, CA: Sonoma County Special Education Planning Area. Used with permission.

Anderson, J. L., Mesaros, R., & Neary, T. (1996). *National inservice training program manual.* Hayward, CA: California State University Hayward, Department of Educational Psychology, Research & Training Center on Community-Referenced Nonaversive Behavior Management.

Armstrong, T. (1994). *Multiple intelligences in the classroom.* Alexandria, VA: ASCD.

Baumgart, D., Brown, L., Pumpian, I., Nisbet, J., Ford, A., Sweet, M., Messina, R., & Schroder, J. (1982). Principle of partial individualized adaptations. *Journal of the Association for the Severely Handicapped, 7,* 17–27.

Bauwens, J., & Hourcade, J. J. (1995). *Cooperative teaching: Rebuilding the schoolhouse for all students.* Austin, TX: Pro-Ed.

Benjamin, S. (1989). An ideascape for education: What futurists recommend. *Educational Leadership, 7*(1), 8–14.

Berends, M., & King, M. (1994). A description of restructuring in nationally nominated schools: Legacy of the iron cage? *Educational Policy, 8*(1), 28–50.

Berman, S. (1990). The real ropes course: The development of social consciousness. *ESR Journal,* 1–18. Cited in Kohn (1996).

Beukelman, D. R., & Mirenda, P. (1992). *Augmentative and alternative communication: Management of severe communication disorders in children and adults.* Baltimore: Paul H. Brookes.

Biklen, D., Bogdan, R., Ferguson, D., Searl, S., & Taylor, S. (1985). *Achieving the complete school: Strategies for effective mainstreaming.* New York: Teachers College Press.

Billingsley, F. F., & Kelley, B. (1994). An examination of the acceptability of instructional practices for students with severe disabilities in general education settings. *Journal of the Association for Persons with Severe Handicaps, 19*(2), 75–83.

Billingsley, F. F., & Romer, L. T. (1983). Response prompting and the transfer of stimulus control: Methods, research, and a conceptual framework. *Journal of the Association for the Severely Handicapped, 8*(2), 3–12.

Blatt, B. (1987). *The conquest of mental retardation.* Austin, TX: Pro-Ed.

Bloom, B. S., Englehart, M. D., Furst, E. J., Hill, W. H., & Krathwohl, D. R. (1956). *Taxonomy of educational objectives, Handbook I: Cognitive domain.* New York: MacKay.

Boggeman, S., Hoerr, T., & Wallach, C. (1996). *Succeeding with multiple intelligences: Teaching through the personal intelligences.* St. Louis, MO: The New City School.

Bridges, W. (1991). *Managing transitions: Making the most of change.* Reading, MA: Addison-Wesley.

Bullock, H. A. (1967). *A History of Negro education in the South from 1619 to the present.* Cambridge, MA: Harvard University Press.

Burton, T. A., & Hirshoren, A. (1979, May). The education of severely and profoundly retarded children: Are we sacrificing the child to the concept? *Exceptional Children,* pp. 598–602.

Calculator, S. N., & Jorgensen, C. M. (1994). *Including students with severe disabilities in schools: Fostering communication, interaction, and participation.* San Diego, CA: Singular.

California Department of Education. (1992). *Fact sheet: Handbook of educational information.* Sacramento, CA: Author.

Checkley, K. (1997). The first seven...and the eighth: A conversation with Howard Gardner. *Educational Leadership, 55*(1), 8–13.

Chu, A. (1998). SFUSD changes for inclusion. Invited address. Hayward, CA: CSU Hayward, Department of Educational Psychology, Ed Psych 5021 class, Spring 1998.

Comforty, J. (Director). (1991). *Choices. The inclusion series* [Videotape]. Evanston, IL: Comforty Media Concepts.

Consortium on Inclusive Schooling Practices. (1996, December). *A framework for evaluating state and local policies for inclusion.* Issue brief. Pittsburgh, PA: Allegheny University of Health Sciences, Child and Family Studies. Author.

Consortium on Inclusive Schooling Practices (1998, April). *Including students with disabilities in accountability systems.* Issue brief. Pittsburgh, PA: Allegheny University of Health Sciences. Author.

Covey, S. (1989). *The seven habits of highly effective people.* New York: Harcourt Brace.

Darling-Hammond, L., & Berry, B. (1988). *The evolution of teacher policy.* Santa Monica, CA: Rand Corporation.

Davern, L., Schnorr, R., Erwin, E., Ford, A., & Rogan, P. (1997). Working toward inclusive secondary schools: Guidelines for developing a building-based process to create change. In D. Sage (Ed.), *Inclusion in secondary schools: Bold Initiatives Challenging Change* (pp. 195–232). Port Chester, NY: National Professional Resources.

Davis Joint Unified School District. (1992). *Multicultural education curriculum: Grades K–12.* Davis, CA: Author.

Dawson, J. (1997). *Witness to evil.* New York: Fawcett Crest.

Demchak, M. A. (1989). A comparison of graduated guidance and increasing assistance in teaching adults with severe handicaps leisure skills. *Education and Training in Mental Retardation, 24,* 45–55.

Donnellan, A. M., La Vigna, G. W., Negri-Shoultz, N., & Fassbender, L. L. (1988). *Progress without punishment.* New York: Teachers College Press.

Duchnowski, A., Dunlap, G., Berg, K. & Adiegbola, M. (1995). Rethinking the partricipation of families in the education of children: Clinical and policy issues. In J. Paul, H. Rosselli, & D. Evans (Eds.), *Integrating school restructuring and special education reform* (pp. 105–118). New York: Harcourt Brace.

Duchnowski, A., Townsend, B., Hocutt, A., & McKinney, D. (1995). Designing studies that are sensitive to the complexity of inclusion: Creating a knowledge base. In J. Paul, H. Rosselli, & D. Evans (Eds.), *Integrating school restructuring and special education reform* (pp. 373–388). New York: Harcourt Brace.

Eby, J. W. (1996). *Reflective planning teaching and evaluation: K–12* (2nd ed.). Upper Saddle River, NJ: Merrill.

Elliott, J. (1997). Invited commentary. *Journal of the Association for Persons with Severe Handicaps, 22*(2), 104–106.

Erickson, R (1997). *Accountabilty standards and assessment.* Washington, DC: The Federal Resource Center for Special Education, Academy for Educational Development.

Eshilian, L. (1997). Public service announcement commercial: "We can make a difference" (Whittier High School presentation). Oakland, CA: California Confederation on Inclusive Education, Summer Institute for School Teams.

Falvey, M. (1995). *Inclusive and heterogeneous schooling: Assessment, curriculum and instruction.* Baltimore: Paul H. Brookes.

Falvey, M., Brown, L., Lyon, S., Baumgart, D., & Schroeder, J. (1980). Strategies for using cues and correction procedures. In W. Sailor, B. Wilcox, & L. Brown (Eds.), *Methods of instruction for severely handicapped students* (pp. 109–133). Baltimore: Paul H. Brookes.

Falvey, M., Eshilian, L., Miller, C., Zimmerman, F., Russell, R., & Rosenberg, R. (1997). Developing a community of learners at Whittier High School. In D. Sage (Ed.), *Inclusion in secondary schools* (pp. 45–74). Port Chester, NY: National Professional Resources.

Falvey, M., Forest, M., Pierpoint, J., & Rosenberg, R. (1994). Building connections: Circles, MAPS, and paths. In J. Thousand, R. Villa & A. Nevin (Eds.), *Creativity and collaborative learning.* (pp. 347–368). Baltimore: Paul H. Brookes.

Fisher, D., Roach, V., & Kearns, J. (1998, March). *Statewide assessment systems: Who's in and who's out?* Pittsburgh, PA: Allegheny University of Health Sciences, Consortium on Inclusive Education.

Fitzgerald, M. A., Staum, M., McGinnity, T., Houghton, L., Toshner, J., & Ford, A. (1997). The Grand Avenue Middle School Story. In D. Sage (Ed.), *Inclusion in secondary schools: Bold initiatives challenging change* (pp. 75–102). Port Chester, NY: Natural Professional Resources.

Ford, A., Davern, L., & Schnorr, R. (1992). Inclusive education: Making sense of the curriculum. In S. Stainback & W. Stainback (Eds.), *Curriculum considerations in inclusive classrooms: Facilitating learning for all students* (pp. 37–64). Baltimore: Paul H. Brookes.

Ford, A., Messenheimer-Young, T. Toshner, J., Fitzgerald, M. A., Dyer, C., Glodoski, J., & Laveck, J. (1995). *A team planning packet for inclusive education.* Milwaukee, WI: Wisconsin Department of Public Instruction, Wisconsin, School Inclusion Project.

Ford, A., & Mirenda, P. (1984). Community instruction: A natural cues and corrections decision model. *Journal of the Association for Persons with Severe Handicaps, 9*(2), 79–88.

Forest, M., & Lusthaus, E. (1989). Promoting educational equality for all students: Circles and MAPS. In S. Stainback, W. Stainback, & M. Forest (Eds.), *Educating all students in the mainstream of regular education* (pp. 43–57). Baltimore: Paul H. Brookes.

Forest, M., & Pierpoint, J. (1992). Putting all kids on the MAP. *Educational Leadership, 50*(2), 26–30.

Friend, M. & Bursuck, W. (1999). *Including students with special needs: A practical guide for classroom teachers* (2nd ed.). Boston: Allyn & Bacon.

Friend, M., & Cook, L. (1996). *Interactions: Collaboration skills for school professionals* (2nd ed.). White Plains, NY: Longman.

Fuchs, D., & Fuchs, L. S. (1994). Inclusive schools movement and the radicalization of special education reform. *Exceptional Children, 60*(4), 294–309.

Fullan, M. (1993). *Change forces: Probing the depth of educational reform.* London: Falmer Press.

Gardner, H. (1983). *Frames of mind: The theory of multiple intelligences.* New York: Basic Books.

Gardner, H. (1995, November). Reflections on multiple intelligences. *Phi Delta Kappan, 77*(3), 200–209.

Gee, K., Alwell, M., Graham, N., & Goetz, L. (1994). *Inclusive instructional design: Facilitating informed and active learning for individuals who are deaf-blind in inclusive schools.* San Francisco: California Research Institute, San Francisco State University.

Giangreco, M. J., Cloninger, C. J., & Iverson, V. S. (1993). *Choosing options and accommodations for children (COACH): A guide to planning inclusive education.* Baltimore: Paul H. Brookes.

Glatthorn, A. (1987). Cooperative professional development: Peer-centered options for teacher growth. *Educational Leadership, 45,* 31–35.

Goetz, L., Haring, T., & Anderson, J. (1990). Educational assessment of social interaction (EASI): Revision 6. Unpublished instrument. San Francisco: San Francisco State University, California Research Institute.

Gold, M. W. (1980) *Did I say that? Articles and commentary on the try another way system.* Champaign, IL: Research Press.

Goodlad, J. (1984). *A place called school.* New York: McGraw-Hill.

Goodlad, J. (1990). *Teachers for our nation's schools.* San Francisco: Jossey-Bass.

Gorevin, R., Kanda, B., Meinders, D., Neary, T., & Perlroth, P. (1992). *Family interview.* Sacramento, CA: California Department of Education.

Grady, E. (1996). What's in a name? In S. Boggeman, T. Hoerr, & C. Wallach (Eds.), *Succeeding with multiple intelligences: Teaching through the personal intelligences* (pp. 217–223). St. Louis, MO: The New City School.

Graham, N. (1992). Adapted lesson plan. Workshop presentation. Napa, CA: PEERS Project, Statewide Institute on Inclusive Education for Collaborative School Teams.

Haas, S., Johnson, R. E., Haas, J. E., Gordon, L., & Hull, M. (1989). Employment of youth with and without handicaps following high school: Outcomes and correlates. *Journal of Special Education, 23,* 243–255.

Hall, G. E., & Hord, S. M. (1987). *Change in schools: Facilitating the process.* Albany, NY: SUNY UP.

Halle, J., Marshall, A., & Spradlin, J. (1979). Time delay: A technique to increase use and facilitate generalization in retarded children. *Journal of Applied Behavior Analysis, 12,* 431–439.

Halle, J. W. (1982, Winter). Teaching functional language to the handicapped: An integrative model of natural environment teaching techniques. *Journal of the Association for Persons with Severe Handicaps, 7,* 29–37.

Halle, J. W. (1987). Teaching language in the natural environment: An analysis of spontaneity. *Journal of the Association for Persons with Severe Handicaps, 12*(1), 28–37.

Halvorsen, A. (1997). Lesson plan. Hayward, CA: CSUH, EPSY 5021.

Halvorsen, A., Anderson, J., Chu, A., Goetz, L., Gorevin, R., Johnson, K., Libby, J., O'Farrell, N., Cho, L., Porter-Beckstead, S., Polit, M., Weissman, J., Triulzi, L., & Alwell, M. (1997). *Valuing diversity in California schools: Introductory sessions on inclusive education.* Hayward, CA: CSU Hayward, California Confederation on Inclusive Education.

Halvorsen, A., & Neary, T. (1996a). *District level needs assessment for inclusive education* (rev. ed.). Hayward, CA: CSU Hayward, California Confederation on Inclusive Education.

Halvorsen, A., & Neary, T. (1996b). *Site level needs assessment for inclusive education* (rev. ed.). Hayward, CA: CSU Hayward, California Confederation on Inclusive Education.

Halvorsen, A., Neary, T., & Hunt, P. (1994). *Perceptions of achievement scale (POA).* Hayward, CA: CSU Hayward, PEERS Project.

Halvorsen, A., Neary, T., Piuma, C., & Hunt, P. (1996). *A model for evaluating the cost effectiveness of inclusive and special classes.* Hayward, CA: CSU Hayward, PEERS Project.

Halvorsen, A. T., & Sailor, W. S. (1990). Integration of students with severe and profound disabilities: A review of research. In R. Galylord-Ross (Ed.), *Issues and research in special education* (vol. 1) (pp. 110–172). New York: Teachers College Press.

Hargreaves, A. (1997). Rethinking educational change: Going deeper and wider in the quest for success. In A. Hargreaves (Ed.), *1997 ASCD yearbook. Rethinking educational change with heart and mind* (pp. 1–26). Alexandria, VA: Association of Supervision and Curriculum Development.

Haring, T. G., Neetz, J. A., Lovinger, L., Peck, C., & Semmel, M. I. (1987). Effects of four modified incidental teaching procedures to create opportunities for communication. *Journal of the Association for Persons with Severe Handicaps, 12*(3), 218–226.

Harris, K. C. (1998). *Collaborative elementary teaching: A casebook for elementary special and general educators.* Austin, TX: Pro-Ed.

Hart, B. M., & Risley, T. R. (1982). *How to use incidental teaching for elaborating language.* Lawrence, KS: H&H Enterprises.

Harvey, J. B. (1988). *The Abilene paradox and other meditations on management.* Lexington, MA: Lexington Books in association with University Associates, San Diego, CA.

Helmstetter, E., Peck, C. A., & Giangreco, M. F. (1995). Outcomes of interactions with peers with moderate or severe disabilities: A statewide survey of high school students. *Journal of the Association for Persons with Severe Handicaps, 19,* 263–276.

Holmes Group. (1986). *Tomorrow's teachers: A report of the Holmes Group.* East Lansing, MI: Authors.

Holmes Group. (1990). *Tomorrow's schools: Principles for the design of professional development schools.* East Lansing, MI: Authors.

Holowach, K. T. (1989). *Teaching that works: The individualized critical skills model.* Sacramento, CA: Resources in Special Education.

Hord, S., Rutherford, W., Huling-Austin, L., & Hall, G. (1987). *Taking charge of change.* Alexandria, VA: Association for Supervision and Curriculum Development.

Horner, R. H., & Billingsley, F. F. (1988). The effect of competing behavior on the generalization and maintenance of adaptive behavior in applied settings. In R. H. Horner, G. Dunlap, & R. L. Koegel (Eds.), *Generalization and maintenance: Life-style changes in applied settings* (pp. 197–220). Baltimore: Paul H. Brookes.

Horner, R. H., Dunlap, G., & Koegel, R. L. (Eds.) (1988). *Generalization and maintenance: Lifestyle changes in applied settings.* Baltimore: Paul H. Brookes.

Hunt, P., Alwell, M., & Goetz, L. (1990). *Teaching conversation skills to individuals with severe disabilities with a communication book adaptation: Instructional handbook.* San Francisco, CA: San Francisco State University, California Research Institute, Conversation & Social Competence Research Project (Grant # G00870083).

Hunt, P., Alwell, M., Farron-Davis, F., Wrenn, M. & Goetz, L. (1996). *Promoting interactive partnerships: Contextual arrangements in inclusive educational settings.* San Francisco, CA: San Francisco State University, California Research Institute.

Hunt, P., Farron-Davis, F., Beckstead, S., Curtis, D., & Goetz, L. (1994). Evaluating the effects of placement of students with severe disabilities in general versus special classes. *Journal of the Association for Persons with Severe Handicaps, 19,* 200–214.

Hunt, P., & Farron Davis, F. (1992). A preliminary investigation of IEP quality and content associated with placement in general education vs. special education classes. *Journal of the Association for Persons with Severe Handicaps, 17*(14), 247–253.

Hunt, P., & Farron-Davis, F. (1992). A preliminary investigation of IEP quality and content associated with placement in general education versus special education classes. *Journal of The Association for Persons with Severe Handicaps, 17*(4), 247–253.

Hunt, P., & Goetz, L. (1997). Research on inclusive educational programs, practices and outcomes for students with severe disabilities. *Journal of Special Education, 31*(1), 3–29.

Hunt, P., Goetz, L. & Anderson, J. (1986). *IEP Quality Indicators Instrument.* San Francisco: San Francisco State University, California Research Institute.

Hunt, P., Goetz, L., Doering, K., & Karasoff, P. (1998b). *Needs assessment for building a school community.* San Francisco: San Francisco State University, California Research Institute.

Hunt, P., Hirose-Hatae, A., Goetz, L., Doering, K., & Karasoff, P. (1998a). Community is what I think everyone is talking about. Manuscript submitted for publication. San Francisco, CA: San Francisco State University, California Research Institute.

Hunt, P., Staub, D., Alwell, M., & Goetz, L. (1994). Achievement by all students within the context of cooperative learning groups. *Journal of the Association for Persons with Severe Handicaps 19*(4), 290–301.

Hunter, M. (1982). *Mastery teaching.* El Segundo, CA: TIP.

Idol, L., Nenn, A., & Paolucci-Whitcomb, P. (1987). *Collaborative consultation* (2nd ed.). Austin, TX: Pro-Ed.

Individuals with Disabilities Education Act of 1997 (IDEA), PL 105-117. Title 20, U.S.C. 1400 et seq. U.S. Statutes at Large.

Johnson, D. W., & Johnson, R. T. (1987). *A meta-analysis of cooperative, competitive and individualistic goal structures.* Hillsdale, NJ: Lawrence Erlbaum.

Johnson, D. W., & Johnson, R. T. (1989). *Cooperation and competition: Theory and research*. Edina, MN: Interaction Books.

Johnson, D. W., & Johnson, R. T. (1992). *Learning together and alone: Cooperative, competitive and individualistic learning* (3rd ed., pp. 1–21). Englewood Cliffs, NJ: Prentice Hall.

Jorgensen, C. (Ed). (1998). *Restructuring high schools for all students: Taking inclusion to the next level*. Baltimore: Paul Brookes.

Jorgensen, C., & Calculator, S. N. (1994). The evolution of best practices in educating with severe disabilities. In S. N. Calculator & C. M. Jorgensen (Eds.), *Including students with severe disabilities in schools* (pp. 1–26). San Diego, CA: Singular.

Karasoff, T., Alwell, M., & Halvorsen A. (1992). *Systems change: A review of effective practices*. San Francisco: San Francisco State University, California Research Institute.

Kettering, C. (1991). Cited in W. Bridges (1991). *Managing transitions: Making the worst of change*. Reading, MA: Addison-Wesley.

Kleinert, H. L., Kearns, J. F., & Kennedy, S. (1997). Accountability for all students: Kentucky's alternate portfolio assessment for students with severe cognitive disabilities. *Journal of the Association for Persons with Severe Handicaps, 22*(2), 88–101.

Knapp, M., Turnbull, B., & Shields, P. (1990). New directions for educating the children of poverty. *Educational Leadership, 48*(2), 4–8.

Kohn, A. (1996). *Beyond discipline: From compliance to community*. Alexandria, VA: Association for Supervision and Curriculum Development.

Kreisman, S., Knoll, M., & Melchior, T. (1995). Toward more authentic assessment. In A. Costa & B. Kalick (Eds.), *Assessment in the learning organization* (pp. 114–138). Alexandria, VA: ASCD.

Krueger, R. A. (1994). *Focus groups: A practical guide for applied research*. Thousand Oaks, CA: Sage.

Kunc, N. (1992). The need to belong: Rediscovering Maslow's hierarchy of needs. In R. Villa, J. Thousand, W. Stainback, & S. Stainback (Eds.), *Restructuring for caring and effective education* (pp. 25–40). Baltimore: Paul H. Brookes.

Latham, A. S. (1997). Technology and LD students: What is best practice? *Educational Leadership 55*(3), 88.

Learning Disabilities Association. (1993, January). *Position paper on full inclusion of all students with learning disabilities in the regular classroom*. Pittsburgh, PA: Author.

Leinhardt, G., & Zigmond, N. (1988). The effects of self-questioning and story structure training on the reading comprehension of poor readers. *Learning Disabilities Research, 4*(1), 41–51.

Lewis, A. (1989). *Restructuring America's schools*. Arlington, VA: American Association of School Administrators.

Lichtenstein, S. (1996). Gender differences in the education and employment of young adults: Implications for special education. *Remedial and Special Education, 17*(1), 4–20.

Lilly, M. S. (1987). Lack of focus on special education in literature on educational reform. *Exceptional Children, 53,* 325–326.

Linder, T. (1993). *Transdisciplinary play-based intervention: Guidelines for a meaningful curriculum for young children*. Baltimore: Paul H. Brookes.

Lipsky, D., & Gartner, A. (1997). *Inclusion and school reform: Transforming America's classrooms*. Baltimore: Paul H. Brookes.

Litwack, L. (1973). Education separate and unequal. In M. B. Katz, (Ed.), *Education in American history: Readings on the social issues*. New York: Praeger.

Martin, J., Jorgensen, C. M., & Klein, J. (1998). The promise of friendship for students with disabilities. In C. Jorgensen (Ed.), *Restructuring high schools for all students: Taking inclusion to the next level* (pp. 145–182). Baltimore: Paul H. Brookes.

McCarney, S. B., McCain, B. R., & Bauer, A. M. (1995). *Adaptive behavior intervention manual: Revised*. Columbia, MO: Hawthorne Educational Services.

McCarney, S. B., Wunderlich, K. C., & Bauer, A. (1988). *The pre-referral intervention manual* (2nd ed.). Columbia, MO: Hawthorne Educational Services.

McDonnell, J. (1987). The effects of time delay and increasing prompt hierarchy strategies on the acquisition of purchasing skills by students with severe handicaps. *Journal of the Association for Persons with Severe Handicaps, 12*(3), 227–236.

McGregor, G., Halvorsen, A., Fisher, D., Pumpian, I., Bhaerman, B., & Salisbury, C. (1998). *Professional development for all personnel in inclusive schools*. Pittsburgh, PA: National Consortium on Inclusive Schooling Practices, Allegheny University of Health Sciences and Alexandria, VA: National Association of State Boards of Education. *Issue Brief,* November, *3*(3), 1–12.

McGregor, G., and Vogelsberg, T. (1998). *Inclusive schooling practices: Pedagogical and research foundations*. Baltimore: Paul H. Brookes.

Meyer, L. H., Eichinger, J., & Park-Lee, S. (1987). A validation of program quality indicators in educational services for students with severe disabilities. *Journal of the Association for Persons with Severe Handicaps, 12*(4), 251–263.

Mount, B., & Zwernick, K. (1988). *It's never too early, it's never too late: A booklet about personal futures planning.* St. Paul, MN: St. Paul Metropolitan Council.

Murray-Seegert, C. (1989). *Nasty girls, thugs, and humans like us: Social relations between severely disabled and nondisabled students in high school.* Baltimore: Paul H. Brookes.

The National Joint Committe on Learning Disabilities. (1993, January). A reaction to "full inclusion": A reaffirmation of the right of students with learning disabilities to a continuum of services. Washington, DC: Author.

Neary, T. (1996). Well I certainly believe in inclusion but I'm concerned about…change. Invited keynote address, Irvine, CA: Integrated Resources Institute Annual Conference.

Neary, T., & Halvorsen, A. T. (1994). *Guidelines for inclusive education.* Hayward, CA: CSU Hayward: Department of Educational Psychology, PEERS Outreach Project.

Neary, T., Halvorsen, A., Kronberg, R., & Kelly, D. (1992). *Curriculum adaptations for inclusive classrooms.* San Francisco: San Francisco State University, California Research Institute, and Hayward, CA: California State University, Hayward, PEERS Project.

Nevin, A., Thousand, J., Paolucci-Whitcomb, P., & Villa, R. (1990). Collaborative consultation: Empowering public school personnel to provide heterogeneous schooling for all or, Who rang that bell? *Journal of Educational and Psychological Consultation, 1*(1), 41–67.

Nisbet, J. (1992). *Natural supports in school, at work, and in the community for people with severe disabilities.* Baltimore: Paul H. Brookes.

Osnosko, J. J., & Jorgensen, C. M. (1998). Unit and lesson planning in the inclusive classroom: Maximizing learning opportunities for all students. In C. Jorgensen (Ed.), *Restructuring high schools for all students: Taking inclusion to the next level* (pp. 71–106). Baltimore: Paul H. Brookes.

Parrish, T. (1994). *Fiscal policies in special education: Removing incentives for restrictive placements.* Palo Alto, CA: American Institute for Research, Center for Special Education Finance, Policy Paper #4.

Parrish, T. (1997). Fiscal issues relating to special education inclusion. In D. Lipsky & A. Gartner (Eds.), *Inclusion and school reform* (pp. 275–298). Baltimore: Paul H. Brookes.

Patton, M. Q. (1986). *Utilization-focused evaluation* (2nd ed.). Thousand Oaks, CA: Sage.

Perrone, V. (1989). Teacher education and progressivism: A historical perspective. In V. Perrone (Ed.), *Working papers: Reflections on teachers, schools, and communities.* New York: Teachers College Press.

Peterson, M., Leroy, B., Field, S., & Wood, P. (1992). Community-referenced learning in inclusive schools: Effective curriculum for all students. In S. Stainback & W. Stainback (Eds.), *Curriculum considerations in inclusive classrooms: Facilitating learning for all students* (pp. 207–228). Baltimore: Paul H. Brookes.

Pilkey, D. (1993). *Dogzilla.* New York: Harcourt Brace.

Piuma, C. (1993). *Inclusion Cost Analysis Scale (INCAS).* Presented by C. Piuma in *Will full inclusion cost more than other programs serving students with severe disabilities?* Paper presented at the annual meeting of the Education Committee, The Association for Persons with Severe Handicaps (TASH), Chicago.

Pressman, H., & Blackstone, S. (1996). *Teacher-led integrated technology project.* Berkeley, CA: Berkeley Unified School District.

Pumpian, I., & Fisher, D. (1997). *Backward mapping as a policy tool.* San Diego, CA: San Diego State University, Interwork Institute, unpublished document.

Rainforth, B., & York-Barr, J. C. (1997). *Collaborative teams for students with severe disabilities: Integrating therapy and educational services* (2nd ed.). Baltimore: Paul H. Brookes.

Rainforth, B., York, J., & Macdonald, C. (1992). *Collaborative teams for students with severe disabilities: Integrating therapy and educational services.* Baltimore: Paul H. Brookes.

Reddy, W. B., & Jamison, K. (1988). *Team building: Blueprints for productivity and satisfaction.* Alexandria, VA: National Institute for Applied Behavioral Science and San Diego, CA: University Associates.

Roach, V. (1992). *Winners all: A call for inclusive schools.* Alexandria, VA: National Association of State Boards of Education.

Roach, V. (1994). *Winning ways: Creating inclusive schools, classrooms and communities.* Alexandria, VA: National Association of State Boards of Education.

Roemer, M. (1991). What we talk about when we talk about school reform. *Harvard Educational Review, 61,* 434–448.

Rosen, P. (Producer) (1989). *How difficult can this be?* Public Broadcasting System videos.

Rousseau, J. J. Cited in A. Bloom (1979) *Emile on education: Introduction, translation and notes.* New York: Basic Books.

Ryba, K., Selby, L., & Nolan, P. (1995). Computers empower students with special needs. *Educational Leadership, 53*(2), 82–84.

Sailor, W. (1997). Invited commentary. *Journal of the Association for Persons with Severe Handicaps, 22*(2), 102–103.

Sailor, W. S. (1991). Special education in the restructured school. *Remedial and Special Education, 12*(6), 8–22.

Sailor, W., Anderson, J., Halvorsen, A. T., Doering, K., Filler J., & Goetz, L. (1989). *The comprehensive local school: Regular education for all students with disabilities.* Baltimore: Paul H. Brookes.

Sailor, W., Gee, K., & Karasoff, P. (1993). Full inclusion and school restructuring. In M. Snell (Ed.), *Instruction of students with severe disabilities* (4th ed., pp. 1–30). New York: Macmillan.

Sailor, W., Gerry, M., & Wilson, W. (1991). Disability and school integration. In T. Husen & T. N. Postlewaite (Eds.), *International encyclopedia of education: Research and studies* (2nd suppl., pp. 158–163). Oxford, England: Pergamon Press.

Sailor, W., Goetz, L., Anderson, J., Hunt, P., & Gee, K. (1988). Research on community intensive instruction as a model for building functional, generalized skills. In Horner, Dunlap, & Koegel (Eds.), *Generalization and maintenance: Lifestyle changes in applied settings* (pp. 67–98). Baltimore: Paul H. Brookes.

Sailor, W., & Skrtic, T. (1995). Modern and postmodern agendas in special education: Implications for teacher education, research and policy development. In J. Paul, H. Rosselli, & D. Evans (Eds.), *Integrating school restructuring and special education reform* (pp. 418–432). New York: Harcourt Brace.

Sapon-Shevin, M. (1990). Student support through cooperative learning. In W. Stainback & S. Stainback (Eds.), *Support networks for inclusive schooling* (65–79). Baltimore: Paul H. Brookes.

Sapon-Shevin, M., Dobblelaere, A., Corrigan, C., Goodman, K., & Mastin, M. (1998). Everyone here can play. *Educational Leadership 56*(1), 42–45.

Sarason, S. (1982). *The culture of the school and the problem of change.* Boston: Allyn & Bacon.

Sarason, S. (1990). *The predictable failure of educational reform.* San Francisco: Jossey-Bass.

Schlecty, W. (1993). On the frontier of school reform with trailblazers, pioneers and settlers. *Journal of Staff Development, 14*(4), 46–51.

Schnorr, R. C. (1990). "Peter? He comes and goes…" First grader's perspectives on a part-time mainstream student. *Journal of the Association of Persons with Severe Handicaps, 15*(4), 231–240.

Schumaker, J. B., Deshler, D. D., & Denton, P. (1984). *The learning strategies curriculum: The paraphrasing strategy.* Lawrence, KS: University of Kansas.

Semmel, M. Y., & Gerber, M. M. (1990). If at first you don't succeed, bye, bye again: A response to general educators' views on the REI. *Remedial and Special Education, 11*(4), 53–59.

Servatius, J. (1992). Foreword. In T. Neary, A. Halvorsen, R. Kronberg & D. Kelly (Eds.) *Curriculum adaptation for inclusive classrooms.* San Francisco: San Francisco State University, California Research Institute, and Hayward, CA: California State University, Hayward, PEERS Project.

Servatius, J. (1995). Effective instruction for all students. Invited address. Napa, CA: PEERS Project, Statewide Institute on Inclusive Education for Collaborative School Site Teams.

Servatius, J., Fellows, M., & Kelly, D. (1990). *Schools are for all kids: Training module for school teams.* San Francisco, CA: San Francisco State University, California Research Institute.

Servatius, J., Fellows, M., & Kelly, D. (1992, February/March). Meeting the needs of all students. *Thrust for Educational Leadership,* 2–3, 36–38.

Servatius, J., Fellows, M., & Kelly, D. (1992). Preparing leaders for inclusive schools. In R. Villa, J. Thousand, W. Stainback & S. Stainback (Eds.), *Restructuring for caring and effective education* (pp. 267–284). Baltimore: Paul H. Brookes.

Shanker, A. (1993a, September 19). Rush to inclusion [Paid advertisement of the American Federation of Teachers]. *The New York Times.*

Shankar, A. (1993b, December 15). Moratorium on inclusion [Paid advertisement of the American Federation of Teachers]. *The New York Times.*

Shapiro, J. P., Loeb, P., Bowermaster, D., Wright, A., Headden, S., & Toch, T. (1993, December 13). Separate and unequal: How special education programs are cheating our children and costing taxpayers billions each year. *U.S. News and World Report.*

Simon, M., Karasoff, P., & Smith A. (1992). *Effective practices for inclusive programs: A technical assistance planning guide.* San Francisco: California Research Institute.

Singer, G. H. (1997). Participatory action research meets the Emic, the Etic and Program Evaluation: A response to Vaughn et al. and Fox et al. *Journal of the Association for Persons with Severe Handicaps, 22*(4), 215–217.

Singer, J. D. (1988). Should special education merge with regular education? *Educational Policy, 2,* 409–424.

Singer, J. D., & Butler, J. A. (1987). The Education for All Handicapped Children Act: Schools as agents of social reform. *Harvard Educational Review, 57,* 125–152.

Sizer, T. (1992). *Horace's school: Redesigning the American high school.* Boston: Houghton Mifflin.

Skrtic, T. (1987). *An organizational analysis of special education reform.* Washington, DC: The National Inquiry into the Future of Education for Students with Special Needs.

Skrtic, T. M. (1990). Social accommodation: toward a dialogical discourse in educational inquiry. In E. Guba (Ed.), *The paradigm dialog* (pp. 125–135). Newbury Park, CA: Sage.

Slavin, R. (1991). Synthesis of research on cooperative learning. *Educational Leadership, 48*(5), 71–82.

Slavin, R. E. (1990). *Cooperative learning: Theory, research, and practice.* Englewood Cliffs, NJ: Prentice Hall.

Smelter, R. W., Rasch, B. W., & Yudewitz, G. J. (1994). Thinking of inclusion for all special needs students? Better think again. *Phi Delta Kappan, 76*(1), 35–38.

Snell, M. E. (1982). Analysis in time delay procedures for teaching daily living skills to retarded adults. *Analysis and Intervention in Developmental Disabilities, 2,* 139–155.

Snell, M. E. (1993). *Instruction of students with severe disabilities* (4th ed.). New York: Macmillan.

Snell, M. E., & Gast, D. L. (1981). Applying time delay procedures to the instruction of the severely handicapped. *Journal of the Association for the Severely Handicapped, 6,* 3–14.

Staub, D. (1998). *Delicate threads: Friendships between children with and without special needs in inclusive settings.* Bethesda, MD: Woodbine.

Stephens, J. (1996). A former traditional teacher speaks out. In S. Boggeman, T. Hoerr & C. Wallach (Eds.), *Succeeding with multiple intelligences* (pp. 223–225). St. Louis, MO: The New City School, Inc.

Stevens, K. A., & Folchman, R. (1998). Using participatory action research to evaluate programs serving people with severe disabilities: Reflections from the field. *Journal of the Association for Persons with Severe Handicaps, 23*(3), 203–210.

Thomas, C. C., Correa, V. I., & Morsink, C. V. (1995). *Interactive teaming* (2nd ed.). Englewood Cliffs, NJ: Merrill.

Toch, T. (1999, January 18). Outstanding high schools. *U.S. News & World Report,* 48–52.

Touchette, P. (1971). Transfer of stimulus control: Measuring the moment of transfer. *Journal of the Experimental Analysis of Behavior, 15,* 347–354.

Turnbull, H. R., & Turnbull, A. (1998). *The law and children with disabilities* (5th ed.). Denver: Love.

Villa, R. A., & Thousand, J. S. (1992). Restructuring public school systems: Strategies for organizational change and progress. In R. Villa, J. Thousand, W. Stainback, & S. Stainback (Eds.), *Restructuring for caring and effective education: An administrative guide to creating heterogeneous schools* (pp. 109–140). Baltimore: Paul H. Brookes.

Villa, R. A., & Thousand, J. S. (1992). Student collaboration. In S. Stainback & W. Stainback (Eds.), *Curriculum considerations in inclusive classrooms* (Chapter 7, pp. 17–141). Baltimore: Paul H. Brookes.

Villa, R. A., Thousand, J. S., Stainback, W., & Stainback, S. (1992). *Restructuring for caring and effective education.* Baltimore: Paul H. Brookes.

Wagner, M., Newman, L., D'Amico, R., Jay, E. D., Butler-Natlin, P., Marder, C., & Cox, R. (1991). *Youth with disabilities: How are they doing?* Menlo Park, CA: Stanford Research Institute (SRI) International.

Wang, M. C. (1992). *Adaptive education strategies: Building on diversity.* Baltimore: Paul H. Brookes.

Wang, M., & Reynolds, M. (1996). Progressive inclusion: Meeting new challenges in special education. *Theory into Practice, 35*(1), 20–25.

Wehmeyer, M., Agran, M., & Hughes, C. (1998). *Teaching self-determination to students with disabilities: Basic skills for successful transition.* Baltimore: Paul H. Brookes.

Whyte, W. F. (Ed.) (1991). *Participatory action research.* Thousand Oaks, CA: Sage.

Wickler, L., Wasow, M., & Hatfield, E. (1983, July/August). Seeking strengths in families of developmentally disabled children. *Social Work,* 313–315.

Wiggins, G. (1989). The futility of trying to teach everything of importance. *Educational Leadership, 47,* 44–48.

Wiggins, G. (1991). Standards, not standardization: Evoking quality student work. *Educational Leadership 48*(5), 18–25.

Wiggins, G., & McTighe, J. (1998). *Understanding by design.* Alexandria, VA: ASCD.

Will, M. (1986). Educating children with learning problems: A shared responsibility. *Exceptional Children, 52*(5), 411–415.

Wilson, P. G., Schepis, M. M., & Mason-Main, M. (1987). In vivo use of picture prompt training to increase independent work at a restaurant. *Journal of the Association for Persons with Severe Handicaps, 12,* 145–150.

Wolery, M., Ault, M. J., M., & Doyle, P. M. (1992). *Teaching students with moderate to severe disabilities: Use of response prompting strategies.* White Plains, NY: Longman.

York-Barr, J. C. (1996). (Ed.). *Creating inclusive school communities: A staff development series for general and special educators: Manual 3b.* Baltimore: Paul H. Brookes.